CREATION
and
HISTORY

THEOLOGY AND LIBERATION SERIES

Pedro Trigo

CREATION
and
HISTORY

Translated from the Spanish by
Robert R. Barr

ORBIS BOOKS

Maryknoll, New York 10545

First published in 1991 in the United States of America by Orbis Books, Maryknoll, NY 10545, and in Great Britain by Burns & Oates Ltd, Wellwood, North Farm Road, Tunbridge Wells, Kent TN2 3DR

Published in Spain by Ediciones Paulinas, Madrid, under the title *Creación e historia en el proceso de liberación* (1988). Published in Brazil by Editora Vozes Ltda., Petrópolis, under the title *Criação e história* (1988)

Original edition © CESEP—São Paulo and Ediciones Paulinas, 1988

English translation © Orbis Books, 1991

Library of Congress Cataloging-in-Publication Data

Trigo, Pedro.
    [Creación e historia en el proceso de liberación. English]
    Creation and history / Pedro Trigo; translated from the Spanish by Robert R. Barr.
       p. cm. — (Theology and liberation series)
    Translation of: Creación e historia en el proceso de liberación.
    Includes bibliographical references and index.
    ISBN 0-88344-737-1 — ISBN 0-88344-736-3 (pbk.)
    1. Liberation theology. 2. Creation. 3. History (Theology)
    I. Title. II. Series.
    BT83.57.T7513   1991
    231.7'6—dc20   91-290
                                   CIP

Theology and Liberation Series

In the years since its emergence in Latin America, liberation theology has challenged the church to a renewal of faith lived in solidarity with the poor and oppressed. The effects of this theology have spread throughout the world, inspiring in many Christians a deeper life of faith and commitment, but for others arousing fears and concerns.

Its proponents have insisted that liberation theology is not a subtopic of theology but really a new way of doing theology. The Theology and Liberation Series is an effort to test that claim by addressing the full spectrum of Christian faith from the perspective of the poor.

Thus, volumes in the Series are devoted to such topics as God, Christ, the church, revelation, Mary, the sacraments, and so forth. But the Series will also explore topics seldom addressed by traditional theology, though vital to Christian life — aspects of politics, culture, the role of women, the status of ethnic minorities. All these are examined in the light of faith lived in a context of oppression and liberation.

The work of over one hundred theologians, pastoral agents, and social scientists from Latin America, and supported by some one hundred and forty bishops, the Theology and Liberation Series is the most ambitious and creative theological project in the history of the Americas.

Addressed to the universal church, these volumes will be essential reading for all those interested in the challenge of faith in the modern world. They will be especially welcomed by all who are committed to the cause of the poor, by those engaged in the struggle for a new society, by all those seeking to establish a more solid link between faith and politics, prayer and action.

Contents

Abbreviations and Short Forms

Medellín   Second General Conference of Latin American Bishops, held in Medellín, Colombia, in 1968. Translations of the final documents are in vol. 2 of *The Church in the Present-day Transformation of Latin America*. Washington, D.C.: USCC, 1970

Peace   Medellín's document on peace

Puebla   Third General Conference of Latin American Bishops, held in Puebla, Mexico, in 1979. A translation of the "Final Document" can be found in J. Eagleson and P. Scharper, eds., *Puebla and Beyond*. Maryknoll, N.Y.: Orbis, 1980; also in *Puebla*. Slough: St Paul; London: CIIR, 1980

Introduction

1. PROFESSION OF FAITH OR IDEOLOGY?

The Bible opens with the solemn assertion: "In the beginning God created the heavens and the earth" (Gen. 1:1). The Niceno-Constantinopolitan Creed begins: "We believe in God, the Father almighty, creator of heaven and earth." St. Thomas' *Summa Theologiae* first establishes the existence of God as creator, citing the otherwise inexplicable existence of the world. And a familiar catechetical jingle inculcates the same basic tenet of our Christian faith:

> A watchmaker made this watch,
> And God made the world.
> No watch without a watchmaker;
> No world without a creator.

Here we have four examples of an expression of our Christian faith, from four different ages, in four different literary forms. They would seem to constitute an adequate representation of the Christian approach to the concept of creation. They proclaim creation as, respectively, the first truth of revelation, the first article of faith, the first thesis in a properly theological methodology, and the first teaching of the Christian kerygma.

In my view, however, this priority entails the serious risk of rendering the doctrine of creation as irrelevant as unquestioned. After all, it is possible to profess this truth as an ideology. That is, the doctrine of creation can be a comprehensive worldview simply handed down through the process of inculturation, and hence possessed in all serenity without ever being questioned — and without being individually and personally assimilated.

xiii

Indeed, this perfectly logical way of seeing the world as created by God may easily gloss over our actual experience of reality, thereby discouraging us from any deeper questioning. And once we suppress questions, our profession of God as the creator and the world as created will constitute not a response, but a doctrine and nothing more. Such a doctrine, thus "naturalized" as a mere humanism, can place enormous obstacles in our path as we journey toward an adult profession of faith. The fact of having been baptized as children, and having received instruction in Christian doctrine, does not automatically guarantee our response to the gift of faith with an act of personal acceptance. The danger is a serious one: we risk replacing a personal encounter, always a challenging, trying experience, with acceptance of a series of doctrinal, moral, ritual, and disciplinary codes.

2. FAITH IN CREATION AS POINT OF ARRIVAL

We shall dispel this danger only by embarking on a journey that *ends* with a profession of faith in God as creator. Not that we need live in the meantime as if we did not believe this doctrine. I am not proposing a methodological doubt, nor a scientific or philosophical investigation. On the contrary, I accept the challenge of Habakkuk: to dare to live by this faith (Hab. 2:4; cf. Rom. 1:17) — that is, to have the courage not to relegate these propositions to the realm of a mere declaration of principle, or again, to employ them as simple hypotheses awaiting convalidation before the tribunal of rational demonstration, but to deal with them as constituting a complete, finished expression of reality — as the very light of life, a light that illumines everything it encounters in this world in all its reality. I am not proposing a faith that believes out of sheer reverence for authority, bereft of any attempt to penetrate the meaning of what it believes. On the contrary, the Word of God has come into the world as the Light of that world. He asks not blind obedience, then, but acknowledgment, and an acknowledgment such as will enable us to walk in his light. In this way, trying to live with God the creator in a world that is God's creation, and seeing ourselves as creatures of God, we shall come to grasp the connection of this mystery with the other Christian mysteries. As the Greek Fathers put it, we shall pass from initial, naked reliance on God (*pistis*) to an experiential knowledge, a *gnōsis*. That is, we shall arrive at the contemplation of a God creating, and creating us, and a contemplation of ourselves emerging along with the world from the loving hands of that God. In a logical construction (such as we find in the Bible, the creed, the treatises of systematic theology, or a catechism) faith in creation comes first. But in the order of historical genesis (the genesis of the faith of Israel and of the infant church alike), just as in the individual personal process, faith in creation constitutes the point of arrival.

Christian faith in creation, however, is *our* starting point in even more radical a fashion. After all, the one we profess as creator is the Father of Jesus, and, in Jesus, our divine Parent as well. It is one thing to proclaim as creator some unknown god, and something else again to profess that the one who has created us is *our* Lord God. The former is not necessarily a salvific truth. It need not be faith. It can be a sheer philosophical conclusion, or religious truth. To know a truth, to maintain a reasonable opinion, to profess a religious dogma, is not, as such, Christian faith. Christian faith is salvific, and this not only in virtue of having come to us from God, but in virtue, as well, of having the Father of our Lord Jesus Christ as the object that qualifies it and endows it with content.

Otherwise faith would be an unknown quantity, and would engulf our lives in uncertainty. We should be beset with all manner of doubt. What sort of maker have we? To what purpose did this creator bring us into existence—to make sport of us? Or to make use of us as slaves to answer a need in the creator? Perhaps our maker is an indifferent god, or even one who may have simply forgotten having brought us forth from nothing. Perhaps indeed we were not brought forth from nothing: Are we perhaps only God's shadows and dreams—or nightmares? Or perhaps the one who flung the universe into space has died in the interim, passed from existence, casting us adrift and leaving us to meet our fate alone.

When we Christians profess the world, and ourselves within it, to be a creation, we are not simply saying that what exists does so neither by chance nor of itself. We are saying that it is God who has brought it forth here out of nothing. Our profession of faith in the world as God's creation says, very precisely, that all that exists, inasmuch as it comes from the creative love of God, has its proper "density" — that it composes a dynamic, differentiated unity (or irreducible, mutually referred variety). And above all, we are saying that it is good.

If this is what our faith in creation means, then clearly our faith is a point of arrival, not a point of departure.

It is a point of arrival because it is faith in the strict sense of the word and the concept. While I may be able to arrive at the acknowledgment of a first cause, or necessary being, by the sole power of my reason, simply by experiencing the world, it will be only by a faith of which I am already in possession that I shall be able to identify this being with our God. This is how St. Thomas saw it in his *Viae,* which do not lead to God, but to an unmoved mover, a first cause, a necessary being, a supreme being, a universal end, "which all call God," or more explicitly, whom *we* call *our* God. We, of course, are Christians, who have, in the concrete, actually followed other paths to this utterly concrete God who is evidently not the conclusion of any human reasoning.

But our faith is faith primarily because it is not by way of creatures that we come to qualify God as creator or, accordingly, creation as creation. On the contrary, it is by way of experience (in faith) of God that we come to know God. And only in identifying that antecedently known God as creator can we affirm the goodness, density, and differentiated oneness of all that exists.

The only absolute "proof" we have that the Father of Jesus is Lord of life and, accordingly, creator of all, is Jesus' resurrection. Only from a point of departure in Jesus' resurrection can we assert that the God of solidarity is the almighty, and therefore that all creation is good. It is the God revealed as our Parent in the death of Jesus who is revealed as the creator of all in Jesus' resurrection. In the paschal mystery, we learn that creation springs from love — that the creator of all is a God-with-us. But the Easter event does not admit of any scientific proof.

It rests purely on faith in testimony, and on a consequent embrace of Jesus' way in the hope of sharing in his resurrection.

3. FAITH IN CREATION AS VICTORY OVER THIS WORLD

The notion of the goodness of creation, then, is neither a metaphysical doctrine nor an evident experience. It is "an anticipation of things hoped for, proof of realities unseen" (Heb. 11:1). Doubtless there are signs, and these signs nourish our faith. But there is something besides goodness in the shape of this passing world. Present creation finds itself "subjected," "enslaved." We hear its "universal groan," and we too "groan inwardly, awaiting the rescue of our being" (Rom. 8:20–23).

To profess that our God is the creator of heaven and earth, then, means denying a sacred foundation to that which enslaves and subjects the world today; and it means proclaiming as real what has all the appearances of the contemptible, the nameless, or the impossible. To call God our creator is to proclaim that the poor shall behold their liberation, that the dispossessed shall inherit the earth, and that a world where justice dwells is destined to become reality.

Christian faith in God as creator of all, then, has as its privileged subject the believing and oppressed people who are in solidarity with God. For when life unjustly denied is converted into a cry of life, and this cry overflows into perseverance and patience, then this is living by faith. Faith in this world as God's creation is more than a mere positive proposition; it is a dialectical one. Faith defeats both the worship of this world and the discouragement and frustration accompanying any attempt to improve it. This is why this faith is a victory (1 John 5:4).

4. THE MEANING OF FAITH IN CREATION IN TERMS OF THE QUESTION OF HOPE

This, then, is the relevancy of our point of departure. If there are no questions, there will be no answers, but only ideology. If the question is uncommitted, the response will also be irrelevant. If what is at stake is a mere interpretation of reality, then the response will consist simply in renaming the data. But if the

question involves my whole being, then the answer will determine everything about me.

My theological approach to the notion of creation arises from
two basic, interconnected questions. I address the problem of
hope from "this vale of tears," and from the depths of our "old
heart."

To profess our God as creator from this vale of tears is precisely to protest the wretched condition of this earth. For God
is not the creator of this vale of tears. The current state of our
world is the negation of reality: it fails to express the truth of
things. If I believe, then I cannot assign the name of reality to
what my faith tells me is a distortion of reality. Nor may I accept
it or resign myself to it.

It will not be enough to adjudge this situation a situation of
sin, and say that its condition as vale of tears is condign retribution for sin. In the first place, there are too many innocent
victims. It is not true that suffering is always deserved. Many
sufferers are victims, not culprits. But even if we were all culprits, this would not "justify" God: It would not constitute an
adequate theodicy. Our God is defined not as the one who
reveals the truth of hearts—perhaps a hidden truth—and
requites creatures according to their works. Our God is defined
as the one who saves what has been lost. If our God is not a
judge but a justifier—in a word, if our God is creator—then this
divinity will bestow life. Nothing, then, not even sin, can justify
our vale of tears. Our world is "uncreation," and we cry out:
Where is our God?

Thus our belief in a God who is creator, while we mourn and
weep in this vale of tears, moves us to call out to God: "Come
to yourself! Exercise the divine sovereignty!" After all, we are
only praying, "Hallowed be thy name." Our faith is automatically transformed into supplication: "Thy kingdom come!"

But faith in creation is not only protest and petition; it is
prophecy, as well. "When the Lord turns to the supplications of
the defenseless . . . the people to be created will praise the Lord"
(Ps. 102:17, 19). We know neither when nor how, but the world
will one day be wrapped in the splendors of the glorious daughters and sons of God. God's creative design will not be frustrated. The creative word will not have been pronounced in vain.

Our protest, our cry, and our hope are transformed into new hands to serve our God in the implementation of the divine plan of creation. Those who live by faith in the goodness of the God who creates are therefore those who can say with Jesus: "My Father continues working until now, and I work, too" (John 5:17).

But faith in God as creator is without its full efficacy until it expressly touches a creature's inmost heart. When I desire that this world blossom forth as God's creation indeed, and set myself the task that this should come about, I quickly discover that I am part of the problem I am trying to solve. Then it is that, over and above my toil and deprivation, the prayer wells up within me: "Create a pure heart in me, O God!" (Ps. 51:12).

PART ONE

CREATION IN HISTORY

CHAPTER I

Experience and Faith

1. POINT OF DEPARTURE

Can these bones live again? (Ezek. 37:3)

(a) In This Vale of Tears

For the Greeks, the beginning of philosophy was wonder. In our own times, Heidegger opened his *What Is Metaphysics?* in much the same way, by asking why there is more being than nothing. But is being so wonderful? In Latin America, we experience more horror than wonder in our contemplation of reality. We ask ourselves not, "Why being?" but "Why nothingness?" Why the nothingness of our people? Why this abundance of nothingness, this lack, and even more, this unjust privation in the presence of the being of the privileged—being as monopoly of goods and power? There is a growing consensus among us that the answer to these questions lies not only in underdevelopment, but also in oppression. The scant development of our productive forces, and the fact that these forces are not used to enhance the lives of the majorities, are due not to natural causes (a scarcity of resources), or ethnicity (poor work habits, lack of technical skills), and still less to supernatural causes (God's will or permission), but primarily to historical causes: the concerted action of certain social groups that have created, and continue to maintain, our situation of nothingness.

3

And so we de-ontologize the apparent; we refuse to confuse the established order with "reality."

But if the question of the being of what appears is the ultimate one, the response can only be the consecration of appearances: Either they will be praised as sacred order laden with meaning, or blasphemed as a fetish that sucks the blood of life. In any event the present will be absolutized. The first response will materialize among the privileged, those who exploit the "kingdom of this world." The second will issue from the deprived, who, while refusing to accept the dominant ideology, are nonetheless incapable of altering the context of the given. But both responses have this in common, that they are hopeless — bereft of hope — inasmuch as they are limited to an interpretation of the phenomenal, the apparent.

For me, then, the problem of prevailing "reality" in Latin America today cannot constitute the ultimate question. Simply qualifying this situation as one of sin cannot be enough; we also have to ask what we are to do in order that being rather than nothingness may come to prevail in Latin America. And then we have to ask who will do, who can do, and who are doing what needs to be done for the nothingness of the deprived to be transformed into being, and for the rapine of the privileged to become voluntary stripping and shared gift. This question — how to move from nothingness to being, and who are to be the agents of this action — is the question of historical creation today in Latin America:

> Theologically speaking, both subjectively and objectively, poverty in Latin America means that God's creation is genuinely threatened. It means not only that God's original plan for humanity is being imperfectly fulfilled, or that it is being fulfilled with certain limitations, but that it is being perverted, since there are vast masses of the people for whom created being itself is at stake.[1]

How can we believe in a creating God on a continent on which so many millions of persons live a life that is non-life, and where so many millions die before their time, sacrificed to the idols of wealth and power? If God is the giver of life, shall we not have to conclude that God has taken leave of Latin America? Or else that there exist other powers, powers of death, that are at least as powerful as God? From the midst of this vale of tears, how can we speak of a creative God? How can we believe in the God of life in a situation signed by death?

> Shall the shadows rise up to give you thanks?
> Is your loyalty proclaimed in the tomb,
> or your faithfulness in the kingdom of death?
> Are your marvels known in darkness,
> or your justice in the land of oblivion?
> [Ps. 88:10–12]

From among the throngs of the radically excluded, who die of hunger, or who are only half alive, who are ill with the diseases of the poor, or who barely manage their survival; from the midst of those excluded both from the labor market and from access to modern services; from the midst of those denied the lion's share of the fruit of their toil, or any part in decision-making or control when it comes to the direction of public life; from the midst of those the privileged despise as poor, as uncouth, as failures in the struggle for life; from the midst of those who are suspect because they are poor, and hence are harassed and abused by the police and the army; from the midst of those humiliated by the persons who hire them for their labor, by their political leaders, by public functionaries; from the midst of the people of Latin America, who live so badly because they live in subjection and defeat; from the midst of this afflicted people — how can we believe in an almighty God-with-us? How can we believe in a creator of life who remains faithful to us despite all of our sins?

(b) Theological Locus

It is impossible for faith in the God of Jesus as creator to brook the "reality" of this situation.

The daily misery that deals a slow, sure death to thousands, to millions of human beings is tantamount to a hecatomb.

It is the voiding, the cancellation of God's creation. This is why we in the Third World are accustomed to call poverty an expression and product of sin. Poverty is the absolute negation of the primordial will of God. For the same reason, we call this sin "literally mortal," since this cancellation of the will of God is manifested in the fact of death, and in this objective death sin reveals its deepest essence.[2]

A faith that prescinds from this situation, or that attempts to maintain a peaceful coexistence with it, is not faith in the Father of Jesus. But it is not enough to leave the city, "bearing the insult which [Jesus] bore" (Heb. 13:13). God (and we) must build another city, a city in which justice shall dwell. So we have to raise the question of creation in Latin America today.

Indeed, only some manner of personal experience of creation (of a new humanity and a new society) renders Christian language about creation intelligible or endows it with any meaning. Creation here and now (creation in history), then, is the hermeneutic locus of the profession of faith, and of the Christian discourse on creation.

Of course an objection might be raised. Is it not answer enough that we have the inescapable experience of being alive — that we live on earth, in the universe? Neither we nor our universe was ever meant to be eternal. Are we not satisfied with the experience of our fragility and instability — the thousand daily signs of our contingency? The answer to this question is the one already given: No, this is not enough. Even supposing that the cosmological arguments could withstand the criticisms of Kant, even so they lead us only to a first cause, a self-existent being, a necessary being.[3] But how do we know that this being is good and has produced a creation that is good? How do we know that it is involved with its creation? How do we know that it is one, and almighty, and that its plan will triumph? How do we know that it will not abandon rebellious humanity to its fate, if not destroy it itself? How do we know that we have been created by it — and not to serve as its slaves, but to accept its proffered dialogue of everlasting love? Our experience of contingency scarcely shows us the world as an *explicatio caritatis Dei.*[4]

And yet this is precisely the meaning of our Christian faith in the world as a thing created.

In this vale of tears, is not faith in the world as an explanation of God's love a paradoxical faith—Tertullian's *Credo quia absurdum?* But if Christian faith in creation is absolutely indemonstrable, indeed contrary to all experience, and yet not the sacred projection of the self-perception of the satisfied of this world—if indeed the only absolute basis of Christian faith in creation is the resurrection of a Jesus crucified by his oppressors (see Rom. 4:17–25)—then it will be only in this vale of tears, in the form of a defeat and transcendence of the same, that this faith will be possible. Such a faith is possible only for the crucified, and only in the form of the defeat and transcending of their cross.[5] So—again—we have to raise the question of creation in Latin America today.

(c) A New Beginning

The question of creation has forced itself upon our consciousness in the context of our struggles for development and liberation. Since the end of World War II especially, enormous efforts have been expended upon the modernization of our continent. At first we hoped that this process of modernization—which we regarded as inevitable in any case—would wipe out endemic diseases, unsanitary living conditions, malnutrition, and illiteracy; that it would endow our society with productive labor and effective services; that it would succeed in appreciably broadening our horizon of life by creating a society of political and social participation on the part of our entire citizenry; and so on, to the point that, where humanly possible, Latin America would no longer be this vale of tears. And a great deal of progress has been made. But contradictions have appeared, braking and distorting the process: problems among the peoples themselves, internal colonialism, and the international imperialism of money. With their hopes frustrated, the peoples have mobilized in countless ways. To contain them, the national security regimes have appeared, in large part the product of imperialistic oppression.[6] The collapse of the modernization enterprise has been manifested in the Latin American foreign debt, a debt so enormous that it sucks up all of the productive effort that ought to be expended in fostering integral development. And yet, even though the greater share of the blame for our woes must be laid at the imperialist doorstep, the fact remains that these woes would not have befallen us had it not been for our own internal deficiencies. Here, certain sectors are clearly more to blame than others for the crisis that weighs upon us. But no organized group is altogether free of responsibility.

At all events, the most important thing for Latin America today is not a determination of the respective responsibility of each and all, but the discovery of a way out of our prostrate situation. And this will be impossible in a framework of simple continuity. "Liberation" in terms of mere political, and even military, takeovers has demonstrated its inadequacy. What is required is a new beginning. And this is what is occurring in many places, however confusedly.[7] The hallmark of the current moment in Latin America is an awareness of this need, together with efforts actually being exerted to respond to it.

2. CREATION IN LATIN AMERICA TODAY

Be glad for what I am about to create (Isa. 65:18)

(a) "The Lord Creates Anew in the Land" (Jer. 31:22)

We Christians see these times as a *kairos,* as an hour of God. We are convinced that Latin America stands in need of a new beginning, a real creation. And we address those who deem insufficient the salvation proposed to us by our society. For our society proposes: Move elsewhere, climb the social ladder, come down from the hills, move to the city, keep your hands clean (no more manual labor, be a doctor).

We are proposing a wager, issuing a historical challenge: that this defeated, plundered, manipulated continent of ours is not sick unto death, that we are not yet a lost cause. Our longings for an independent, shared development are not deception and illusion. We have not yet shown the half of what we are. And we make this wager, against five centuries of failure, because we read, in this history of ours, not only the superior strength of our enemies (thus far), but our capacity for resistance, as well, and our latent potential.

The kernel of hope that we bring to our situation is our faith in God, who calls into existence that which is not, and bestows life on the dead. Amidst this Latin American history of ours, we profess that God has created us to be creators. And for us, this profession is a concrete hope. Unless creation is a historical experience—in part possessed, in part hoped for—it is nothing; it degrades into a philosophy—an "idea" in the Kantian sense. We have concrete hope for our actual, concrete situation of captivity, our situation as a non-people. We hold out a concrete hope for our colonial, disjointed, powerless, diasporan existence. To save, here, in Latin America, means more than healing wounds, forgiving sins, and aiding development. In Latin America, salvation is re-creation or it is nothing at all.

In the framework of this vision, we can do no other than to reject the immobilism in which we were reared: the belief that God's activity ended the very moment it began; that God founded an immovable world; that the social order is the very reflection of God. Adulation of the established order is worship of God. We Catholics are an orderly folk; we were born that way. Our enemies, those partisans of novelty, strive only for universal anarchy, we tell ourselves. Who are our enemies? The revolutionaries.

And so we have sat, thinking these thoughts. Then suddenly— we receive good news from our God. A gospel is addressed to us, today. We can read it in the words of an unknown prophet of long ago addressing the remnant of the Jewish people held captive in Babylon. The Jews had been defeated and suffered from a defeatist complex; they had been disarmed, ideologically and materially. Then the prophet spoke:

> Remember not the events of the past,
>   the things of long ago consider not;
> See, I am doing something new!
> Now it springs forth, do you perceive it not?
>   [Isa. 43:18–19]

We respond, then. We respond with our lives, and still more with our hope. Yes, there is historical creation in Latin America today. In fact, we dare to proclaim that this creation is not only an incipient experience, and a great yearning, but the very gospel of God in Jesus. We proclaim that God is creating something new among us today. God is creating a new humanity and a new society. Do we not perceive it? For us, to have faith is to know how to discover a new America—an America in the process of gestation. To make that faith come true is to participate with those who are building that America.

Were there no historical creation—were it to be true that, as Qoheleth says, "there is nothing new under the sun" (Eccl. 1:9)—faith in creation would be the consecration of the condemnation in which our Latin American peoples are living: the consecration of what Archbishop Romero called the "empire of hell." Unless there is historical re-creation, God cannot say: "I shall pour out my spirit upon you, that you may live again" (Ezek. 37:14). And the people would be right to complain: "Our bones are brittled, our hope has wafted away; we are lost" (Ezek. 37:11). God would not be the Lord, the holy one of Israel.[8] God would not be the creator, at any rate not in the biblical conception.[9]

(b) Faith in Creation as a Question

God is creating today in Latin America, then. And this thesis is inscribed not only on the nothingness of underdevelopment, but against the lethal backdrop of the acts of economic, political, and military aggression perpetrated on our countries and their peoples by imperialist nations, especially the United States, at the behest of our dominant classes and with their participation. And these agents exacerbate their acts to the point of paroxysm, lest our peoples actually liberate themselves from their dominion.

In these utterly painful, unjust conditions, faith in creation comes to expression as a question. At times it is the question of those of little faith, who, disheartened and perplexed, ask with Zechariah: "What guarantee do I have?" (Luke 1:18); or who, terrified with the apostles, cry out in reproach: "Is it nothing to you that we are foundering?" (Mark 4:38). But there is another faith—the faith of Mary, who, in acceptance and endorsement of the act of God, merely asks: "How shall this be?" (Luke 1:34). And finally—and this is the faith of so many others—there is Jesus' tremendous lamentation: "My God, my God, why have you forsaken me?" (Mark 15:34). This question varies with the situation. Let us attempt to characterize the situations of different peoples:

(i) Those who see the actions of the oligarchies and the empire, which in turn produce communal violence, leading to so many of their near ones and dear ones either dying before their time, or being physically, mentally, or morally annihilated. They see themselves, as well, in daily, mortal danger. How can these people do other than wonder whether human life is sacred, or worth less than a dog's? How can they help wondering whether human beings indeed come from God, and whether God is at all concerned with them?[10]

(ii) Those who feel threatened in their existence as worthwhile persons and as peoples. They come to an awareness of their conditions, would like to rise up against them, and then wonder whether such a gargantuan task is possible.[11]

(iii) Those who, marginalized by the ruling classes, or rising up against them, or even, at times, with their support, have already waged a silent revolution, however incomplete. They wonder whether their gains can be consolidated, to afford a footing for the establishment of a new order that would represent and embody these gains. Experiencing the creative powers of the people, they wonder whether these can last.[12]

(iv) Those who, victorious in their first efforts against the enemy, have tasted the beginning of a new life—and now see their triumph threatened. They wonder whether new life is possible in a historical context of such oppressive aggression.[13]

This is the question of historical creation in Latin America today. It is a question we ask from the midst of a life lived in the presence of death; from the midst of a life that resists death; from the midst of new, inchoate life that, threatened on all sides, struggles for consolidation. It is a question that springs from the heart of a historical creation to some degree experienced and in process. It is not, then, a question of whether there is creation in history, but of how soon it is coming, and its capacity to overcome the forces of backwardness, oppression, repression, and suppression. In Latin America we ask whether those deprived of life can prevail over the privileged by a historical act not of vindictive, but of creative justice. The being (the humanity) of human beings hangs in the balance: Can this historical creation actually transpire? The being that is at stake — being-human, or authentic humanness — is currently possessed neither by those deprived of wholeness, nor by the privileged, who cling to it like booty. Likewise at stake is the being (the sovereignty) of a God committed to those deprived of wholeness, and to the re-creation of the whole of humanity, starting with the former.

But the actualization of historical creation means more than doing away with the privation of the people and the privilege of the oppressors, and arriving at a shared entity through a historical act of re-creative justice. This redistribution of entity will be not only insufficient, but impossible, unless accompanied by a profound process of re-creation of our own humanity. The question of historical creation in Latin America today is thus the question of a new way of being human. Can these wounded hearts of ours receive healing? Can we be genuinely reconciled with ourselves — accept ourselves as we are and hope that we can be better? Can we channel our impulses, and cast out selfishness, vanity, and envy? Can a certain harmony be struck between our quest and our impulses? Can we direct our desire toward beauty and joy, in compassion and the spirit of toil? Shall we find it possible to take up our collective history as a burden and a charge, manage to forgive one another and be reconciled, and embark on a shared life?

I have no hesitation in saying that, while proposing life in the presence of death contains an immense act of faith, affirming new life in the presence of the established order *internalized* represents a greater one still. Here the forces of death reside in a person's heart and soul, and the temptation to cooperate in the maintenance of the situation of privation and privilege is powerful. Only those who have seriously and persistently striven to become worthy builders and citizens of the new society have experienced how the old inclinations can crop up once more, and how internal contradictions bring us time and again to the point of abandoning the whole project. Without any masochism or undue breast-beating, one must nevertheless acknowledge that the failure and difficulties of not a few revolutionary attempts are not to be laid at the doorstep of the superior forces of enemies and involuntary errors. They are also due to our working superficial changes in personnel and the rules of the game, while keeping the old spirit and failings.

It is a mistake to think of the new human being as a more or less automatic by-product of new game rules. We have already had enough experience to be able to deny that this is the case. Propaganda campaigns, and even more, social pressures, are insufficient, indeed counterproductive, when they attempt to substitute for this specific (arduous, subtle, free, and shared) activity of personal re-creation. Granted, neither can this task be understood as incidental or antecedent to the struggle for a new society; on the contrary, it is possible only in the context of this struggle. Just as only in the throes of a struggle for liberation is it possible to live a life of justice, so only a deep love of life will enable us to wage the struggle for liberation. Life holds the primacy—not a life merely professed, preached, dreamed of, and put off till later, but a life daily lived, come what may, be it death itself. Only from out of this experience of life can a liberative struggle ripen and mature.

If the so-called struggles for liberation entail no newness, then, in the strict sense of the term *creation* (i.e., creation both in the process and in the outcome), they will be degraded to a mere struggle for established power, and their propositions will be reduced to ideology—that is, to other ways of conceiving and feeling the same things. But these struggles will indeed entail no newness unless those engaged in them pursue that newness, without and within, until they attain it. There is no faith in creation, then, without conversion. The long experience of the liberation struggles in Latin America has shown us the insufficiency of our Promethean urges. In a context of these tenacious efforts of ours, humility is anything but an empty word. It has been a requirement for the flexibility, self-criticism, convergence, and constancy needed precisely to maintain the struggle. And humility, in Christian terms, is the ability to set oneself aside, to give God and others their rightful places, all occupying theirs with the simplicity of those who only do their duty (Luke

17:10). Humility, when all is said and done, is the attitude of those who have learned from hard experience that "unless the Lord builds the house, in vain do the masons toil" (Ps. 127:1), and who, because they know that God alone is the creator, erect their lives on the steady rock of the implementation of the Lord's word (Matt. 7:24–5). In other words, humility is the attribute of those who live to follow the creative will of God.

(c) It Is Night

If we ask what time it is in Latin America, in this, our hour of need—the need of a new beginning, and of effective efforts to create it—we should have to say that it is night (see John 13:30). We are passing through the "dark night of injustice."[14] The presence of such tremendous forces bent on stifling the bright seed sown among our people is an indication that the midnight hour has struck, and that henceforth we shall ever be nearer the dawn of tomorrow and further from the dusk of yesterday. We do not see the light of that tomorrow. But our refusal to resign ourselves to the civil death that is life under the established order, our stubborn pursuit of what, in the light of the system, seems so impossible, our obsession with life, our tenacious defense of the fortress of our dignity and respect in this hour of the powers of this world, our sense of opportunity, whereby we seize the occasion where we can and move forward ever so little, our capacity for joy amidst such troubles and disappointments, the bonds we secure in the midst of death, our little victories, our ability to get back up on our feet after being felled so many times, and somehow stagger on—all these are signs that we have not long to wait before the dawn. Above all, they are the sacraments of the sacred flame of the God of life, still burning. The fact that all of this is experienced in a faith that is not only food for our souls but a shining light that gives us to see life in this particular way, is the earmark of our faith in God as creator, and in creation in history. This is the faith of the crucified—who yet have their sure hope, and who, with the Spirit who raised Jesus, go in quest of resurrection.

This hour of Latin American time, then, requires of faith two complementary attitudes. The first is that of "hope against hope" (Rom. 4:18). By our faith we live in the future, "although it be night" (St. John of the Cross). We simply will not conform ourselves to the shape of this world (Rom. 12:2). And a faith that lives in the future will one day be our victory over the established order. We are called, like Abraham, to live in a foreign land, and to maintain ourselves in Jesus' word, "I have taken you out of the world" (John 15:19). The second attitude, complementary to the first, as we have suggested, is a sense of the possible—a "nose" for opportunity. This is the approach we take in our practice—little accumulations, gradual advances, small successes; it is a veritable sacrament of hope, investing as it does the horizon of liberation with plausibility. Puebla was able to put its finger on the intersection of these two attitudes, and offers the following description of our people in their cry for true liberation:

> The people create or utilize space for the practice of broth-erhood in the more intimate areas of their lives together. ... Rather than giving way to despair, they confidently and shrewdly wait for the right opportunities to move forward toward the liberation they so ardently desire [Puebla, 452].

(d) Creation Today and the Holiness of God

Even a faith that posits a finished creation, completed from the start, can of course deduce a human obligation to rebuild the world according to the plan of its creator. But what is at stake in Christianity is not only the human will and ability to support God's plan, but the very truth of God. After all, the appellation "creator" does not attach to God as an adventitious quality, or denote some minor, secondary attribute of God, but is an essential divine attribute. We profess the Father as creator of all, the Son as the one through whom all was made, and the Spirit as the giver of life. This profession of faith makes a pred-ication upon the divine Persons themselves. Accordingly, if death seems to have more power than life today, then where is the divinity of God?

Is it legitimate to translate from space to time, and from today to tomorrow, the question of the manifestation of God? If so, the question will be not where God is, but when God will be manifested. As we know, in the Old Testament the question asked by the faithful, and the question their enemies asked of them, as to the whereabouts of Yahweh was often combined with the question of how long the face of Yahweh would continue to be hidden (e.g., Ps. 89:47, 50). Indeed, as the time of catastrophe and prostration continued to make it difficult to recognize the face of God and to await God in history, some Israelites began to think that "a profound breach loomed in history, and began to order everything with a view to this ultimate resolution."[15] In other words, the present was the time to decipher revelation, and thus enter into the last act of history. The possession of this secret permitted these persons to "emerge from the time of the covenant," the time characterized by a dramatic dialectic and by continuity despite all.[16] As we know, Jesus refused to accept this unilateral apocalypticism, and restored the tension between hope for the Kingdom, that object of hope and prayer alone (Luke 21:28; 11:2), and manifestation of the active presence of God (Luke 11:20; 7:16). The signs of the historical times show the presence of the face of God (Luke 12:56), and the way into God's dynamic of life headed for the Kingdom (Luke 17:20–21).

Postwar European theology interpreted this tension with the formula "Already, but not yet," which had the advantage over earlier theology of recovering, in some sort, the eschatological tension that had been sundered by the reduction of eschatology to the "last things," but which was in tremendous danger of sacralizing postwar euphoria and expansion.

We accept that we are raised in Christ, and in him are therefore already a new creation (2 Cor. 5:17). But we still await the redemption of our being. And what we experience within ourselves, with such interior anguish, we also feel as citizens of our Latin American world. We sense that world to be "subject to frustration" (Rom. 8:20). We feel, with Medellín, that there is a "rejection of the Lord himself" (see Matt. 25:31–46) in our world (Peace, no. 14). Hence what we say is not, "Yes, but not yet," but, "No, although. . . ." That is to say: God is not here (in this established order that has rejected God) although God *is* here (in those who, as the historical body of the Lamb of God, bear the weight of the sin of the world). But if, on the one hand, the God of the poor is the God of life, and if, on the other, God wills not the death of sinners but rather that they be converted and live, then we cannot elude the question: Where is the God of life? Where is our almighty partner? Where is God being faithful? This is the question of historical creation in Latin America today.

(e) Ambiguity, Hallmark of History

We cannot foresee the culmination of historical creation in Latin America. Why? Because we do not absolutely know what shape the sovereignty of God in the world will assume. It is not for us "to know the times and dates that the Father has reserved to his authority" (Acts 1:7). No one knows them, "not even the Son, but only the Father" (Mark 13:32). What is asked of us, since it is for this that we have received grace, is that we become daughters and sons of the Kingdom. As long as we live, however, we shall always "await the full condition of sons" (Rom. 8:23), for "strength is made perfect in weakness" (2 Cor. 12:9).

This means that, whatever level creation may achieve in Latin America, there will never be more than barely enough to foster our faith in creation. That is, creation will never be more than a sign of hope: "But hope is not hope if its object is seen; how is it possible for one to hope for what he sees? And hoping for what we cannot see means awaiting it with patient endurance" (Rom. 8:24–5).

In other words, even should we reach a considerable degree of social justice, political and social participation, and shared abundance, we shall still have to say, unless we would reduce our faith in the creator to the standards of this world: "No, although...." This is not the Reign of Life—although the ambiguity of this precarious history does make room for prefigurations of that Reign, that life. There will always be tears in this vale, but there will be joy, as well, and fruitful toil, though sin will not have disappeared. And there will always be the grave danger of sacralizing the prevailing situation.

These precautions will have to be taken against the time when victories are gained, be they little or great. Despite the cost and the solace, these victories will never be more than ambiguous (and will always need great faith and hope in the greater divinity that has created us for its own sake), so that we do not become set in our attainments.

(f) Content of Creation in Latin America Today

On the other hand, must we in our Latin American countries relegate to eschatology what in other countries is a fact of ordinary daily experience? As the prophet says:

> They shall live in the houses they build,
>   and eat the fruit of the vineyards they plant;
> They shall not build houses for others to live in,
>   or plant for others to eat. . . .
> They shall not toil in vain,
>   nor beget children for sudden destruction.
>   [Isa. 65:21–3]

We do not ask not to have to toil or grow weary, or to achieve immortality in this life. In life one must build, plant, and procreate, and all of this involves an expenditure in the currency of care and energy. We ask only that not all be in vain—that the few not be allowed to walk off with all we have produced, that life not end in a catastrophe. We are asking only for the simplest thing, and the most sacred—life.[17] This is the only goal of historical creation in Latin America today. After all, it is no less than life that, in a thousand different ways, is denied our people. How can a Christian consideration of creation omit this question? And how could one think that the Father of Jesus is not committed to this? How could we have imagined that God could leave this for tomorrow? Tomorrow many of the children of this God will be dead. But our God is a God of life; obviously, then, God will defeat death itself. But how could we ever have thought that the creator of this world has made it a purgatory that we are merely to suffer through in order to gain heaven as a reward? Can this life, the "Great Theater of the World," be no more than a place of test and trial?

This is the rigorous theological thesis of Calderón's play,

which sums up an age-old Christian sense. It is not one's social role, not even with the vital circumstances accompanying it, that defines one's person. The player on the stage is not really royalty, not really that beggar we see. He or she only acts as such. Once their roles have been played, and the actors have been stripped of the attributes that have characterized them as personages, they will appear as they are, and receive the reward or punishment appropriate to the manner in which they have discharged their acting assignments. The role that has fallen to each is irrelevant. The important thing is to play it well. This theological representation has the advantage of emphasizing the irreducible, sovereign, and sacred character of the person, and consequently of desacralizing, relativizing, and even subverting social class and rank. It also de-eschatologizes history in the sense of any apocalypticized, realized eschatology. And best of all, it sends us forth to live history in the light of eternity—to live undeceived, then, to live in truth. From the standpoint of a Calderonian spirituality, with its thirst for the definitive encounter with God (Phil. 1:23), life appears indeed as an exile ("Salve Regina"), or, in St. Teresa's expression, "a bad night in poor lodgings."

Calderón's play contains genuinely Christian elements, then. And yet it is unacceptable on the whole. Why? Because of its radical devaluation of the present life. Relative as it is, this life is loved by God for its own sake. Indeed, this life occurs within God (Acts 17:28), and so is sacred. God, therefore, cannot be portrayed as director of the piece. God did not create many of the roles, but rejects them, along with much of the action of the play. God is the God of life. God neither creates nor "wills" nor "permits" murder, although, being the creator, God can draw good from evil. And God has taken this divine creation utterly seriously. God is absolutely committed to this creation, sending Jesus to our history and through him bestowing upon us the divine, lifegiving Spirit (John 19:30). This life of ours *actually affects God,* then. Thus we can say, with the psalmist, "The death of his faithful ones is costly to the Lord" (Ps. 116:15). And from out of our awareness of this commitment to solidarity with us on the part of the almighty, this trusting prayer springs to our lips: "I shall walk in the presence of the Lord in the land of the living" (Ps. 116:9). For the psalmist, the "land of the living" was this earth. Do we not have the right to pray in the same way in Latin America today? Must the land of the living, the community where people are really alive, be just an object of eschatological hope for us? Surely not. Hence the urgency of the theme of historical creation in Latin America today.

3. GOD AND HUMANITY: A THREE-ACT PLAY?

From their birth to their old age shall I sustain them (Isa. 46:3–4).

(a) Synopsis

On the basis of the foregoing premises, I shall now examine a schema which holds itself out as Christian, but which is actually a perfect expression of the eighteenth-century Enlightenment, popularized and accepted, paradoxically, as traditional teaching.

This philosophico-religious schema sees human life in the world in terms of a sequence of three phases, a drama in three acts, each on its own level of reality, and each featuring its own actors, all of whom play definite roles and produce definite actions.

In the first act, the actor is God as creator. The result of God's action is the world, and in the world, humanity. God decrees that humanity is to be free.

In the second act, the player is humanity. As the basic determinant of humanity is freedom, it is in freedom that humanity works good or evil.

The third act will feature both characters: God and humanity. God, now appearing as judge, will reward the good with heaven and punish the evil with hell.

The first act, then, is the beginning of all. Here are laid down the rules by which the deadly serious game of life is to be played. This is the act of creation. Then, having set the whole drama in motion, God moves off stage, leaving humanity to play out the action alone. Now it is our turn: History begins. In history, we and nature fill all space. But over history hangs the future judgment. The fact is a warning—a threat, in fact—and of course a basic principle of reality, however obscured by the passions or the battle for life.

(b) Analysis

In this schema, humanity is the sole actor in history. And yet there is no atheism here, for it is understood that our position in the world stems from a creative act and is referred to a final judgment. In other words, the a-theistic present moves from a divine origin to a divine consummation. Nor, for that matter, is God's presence limited to the origin it founds and the end it defines and consummates. In history too, while we cannot actually behold the presence and activity of God, at least we can detect their traces. Hence religion in spirit and truth is not only possible in history, but reasonable there. This religion consists in acknowledging God, and giving thanks for the gift of freedom and the moral law—the internal, autonomous norm of human freedom. But we not only feel the presence of God within us, we also contemplate it, in wonder, in the book of nature: God's grandeur and regularity not only invite us to understanding, so that we may know the divine laws, but draw our heart to a knowledge above knowledge, and to thanksgiving, or religious emotion.

This schema would be rounded out in our civilization by the activity of Christianity, which, through its sensible symbols, would help the people live as moral beings and creatures of God. People would not easily be persuaded to lead such a life by the use of their reason alone. But at least they can be steeped in the aesthetic emotion of the devotions that communicate truths in the clothing of representation, pacifying the spirit to an acceptance of the discipline the people would reject as a mere imperative of reason.

Furthermore, Christianity brings all human beings, ignorant and learned alike, though in different ways, the figure of Jesus as the absolute example of life in the presence of God, and in this sense Teacher, Way, and Truth.

This scenario seeks to move beyond an animistic conception of nature and a magical sense of history, and to strip religion of its superstition and fanaticism. The secular, worldly status of the universe and its substantiality are given their full due, and the human being is exalted in the universe, the stage of the drama, through the appropriate ascription of human dignity and responsibility. At the same time, the image of the divinity is relieved of all its grotesque, petty representations. No longer tinsel, it gleams discreetly yet starkly in its place: in the moral conscience and in the universe, that is, in the noblest emotions, transcending all representation. God is not a worldly entity. God is truly found only at the origin and end of time, in eternity.

Our schema stakes out roles and responsibilities. God's part has been accomplished. Through a wise creation, fair game rules, the divine traces in nature and conscience, and a period of time allotted for the transpiring of a genuine history, with a place for everything and everything in its place, the divine plan cannot be thwarted. Now it is our turn to take the stage. History is humanity's hour. Let us become aware of our place in the world, and live our lives responsibly. We cannot expect God to do for us what we are to do for ourselves. Nor, consequently, can we cast on God responsibility for our destiny. Humanity carves out its own felicity or ruin, and, in each and every one of us, can and must select and build its various paths to eternity. Whatever we do, at the end God will have the last word.

This religious schema is solid and secure. God is the creator of nature and the moral law. Those who live in conformity with nature are happy. Those who live in conformity with the moral law are faithful. Fidelity and felicity will definitively coincide only on the day of judgment; but they have a tendency to do so in our own history, provided we understand that to live in conformity with nature is the material content of the moral life if the latter is to be realized in principle as universal.

(c) Evaluation

What we should retain, from this schema, is humanity's responsibility in the world, and the worldliness of the universe. Accordingly, if we speak of creation in history, we shall have to explain it in such a way that we do not slip back into a providentialistic occasionalism, which regards God as using human actions merely as strokes of a cosmic pen, in a script which human beings cannot decipher, to write the book of history, whose plot God alone knows.[18] Nor may we understand creation in history in such a way that the legality of the material world is capriciously contravened by its maker. In the language of the gospel, we must resist the first two temptations of Christ, based as they are on a secularization of God, a failure to appreciate the solid reality of the world, and the infantilization of human beings who run to daddy to solve their problems and to reassure them of their status as children of God on the basis of miracles. Against this conception, Bonhoeffer rose up with his adult faith—a respectful faith, and committed to the end.

But we cannot accept a God confined to past and future. We cannot accept a God who is nothing but almighty creator, wise architect and legislator, and just judge. For us, God is above all a Thou—not because this is the conclusion we have come to, but because this is what has been revealed to us. And it has been revealed to us here, in this world, in this history.[19] History, then, is not only the history of humanity, but the history of a humanity with God, and the history of a God who is with us human beings.

This history begins in creation. Accordingly, creation is interior to history, and history is creative; and this historical creation will be consummated in a judgment that will therefore be not a declaration of goodness or evil, but a justification, a renewal, of all things.

God, then, is our God, and not someone we make to our image and likeness. God is revealed in history—a history that has had a beginning and that will have a close. This history is God's, because God has created it from the beginning and judges it without respite—that is, justifies it, saves it. This history is our history. We are created creators who respond in history to the action of God, although we also close ourselves to it (judge ourselves) and can close ourselves to it definitively (judge ourselves in the sense of condemning ourselves—John 3:16–21).

There is only a single act, then. It has had a beginning, but it has not yet been concluded. This single act functions on various levels: on a transcendent level, on which God establishes and saves creation; on another level, on which we human beings respond to God or at least try so to respond. The levels remain distinct, therefore we may say that God does all and we do all. Hence the possibility of establishing a scientific system and an a-theistic culture alongside a theological and religious discourse. But these distinct levels are not divorced from one another: hence the inadequacy of any view that would pretend to universality and yet would regard only the activity of God or that of humanity. Finally, the inseparability of the two levels not only expresses the structure of reality, but also, and especially, underscores the dialogic structure of the same, in a life with God in a personal relationship. Not only does this personal relationship develop at the interindividual level, but God posits it also at the level of peoples—"I shall be your God and you shall be my people"—and of all humanity. Not that this relationship is presented as completely symmetrical and respective. God's word comes first, and is absolutely sovereign. Our word comes second, and consists basically in obedience.

But God's word is not capricious or variable. Our God is a faithful God. In fact, in the Easter mystery God has revealed the divine plan in its totality: On the cross we have been preferred to the Son of God himself (revealing a solidarity with us at all costs); and in the resurrection God has proved the irresistible power of this love/solidarity—a creative love in that it triumphs even over death. Our Father is almighty, then; and our creator is in solidarity with us.

In presenting "this vale of tears" to God our Lord, then, in protest and question, we see the inadequacy of any "explanation." To appeal to the human condition and human sinfulness is poor theodicy—not because these are not real, verifiable factors, but because if they are the last word, God is not an almighty creator in solidarity with us.

From "this vale of tears," then, faith in our creator is a question, and a question that cannot be answered by any discourse. It can have its response only in the creative activity of God in the present and in the future.

4. LIVING AS CREATURES

The language of creation is not protology, then.[20] It is not a discourse on beginnings as such, as some particularly pregnant, archetypal time divided from all other times. The language of creation is historical. It refers to yesterday, today, and tomorrow. Our beginnings have no special privilege, no special revelatory power. To understand them, we need not undertake some ritualistic or mystical journey. They are within our reach today, if we dare to live by faith.[21] But living by faith does not mean offering our adherence to a mysterious fact that we neither see nor perceive but that we somehow know to exist. Nor does it mean an intellectual assent to an act of God in the past that is no longer evident because human actions have neutralized it. If creation was not some mere accident that happened to God, but an act of the divine freedom revealing and characterizing God (as God of life, the Friend of human beings, faithful Love), then to live by faith is to rely on the power of solidarity on which our very being is founded (see Isa. 7:9).

(a) Before God without God

It is not my intent to rehabilitate a providentialistic animism. God does not act through intramundane causality. On this point we must submit to the intuition of the Enlightenment. We shall never be able to see God acting. God is not an object of cognition, in the sense in which the Enlightenment employed the word: as experimental, scientific cognition. Hence if history is defined as the dialectic of human beings and nature, and human beings with one another, a dialectic realized against the background of science through a toil mediated by technology, then surely this history is only the history of human beings, and will have to be defined as the humanization of human beings and the world in whatever both initially have by way of nature. *Humanization* here will mean constitution as a scientific object, and technological manipulation for the empirical construction of the human being and the world. This level is certainly atheistic.

What I am saying is that this level defines neither the human being nor the world. For that matter, this level acquires its authentic dimension, which is responsibility, only when one lives "before God," in an awareness of God. That would be the sense of Bonhoeffer's formula: to live before God without God.[22] This "before God" qualifies our autonomy; it converts it into a determinate response, then, by virtue of the question, however internally self-subsistent that response may be. This was the point that Jesus made to those who asked him whether politics is theocratic or neutral, that is, a-theistic (Mark 12:13–17).[23] Jesus answers that political autonomy is legitimate as long as its concrete exercise is compatible with the sovereign rights of God — that is, as long as politics actually attains to the status of the properly political, which is relative service and relative requital, and does not pretend to be the source of salvation and life, requiring of the citizen a loyalty tantamount to faith. In the latter case Jesus' response is: "You shall render homage only to the Lord your God alone and serve him alone" (Matt. 4:10).

A history (in the particular sense in which we are considering history) which would attain its status of autonomy-before-God would cease to be a salvation history, just as the Enlightenment claims. It would abide in its relative dimension. Instead of being a history of salvation, it would have been transformed into an ideology of progress (or development), promising security and happiness, and demanding our soul as our part of the bargain.

But this relativization is possible only if existence conceived as "before God without God" is limited to constituting a level of existence, and is not permitted to accede to the status of determination of existence. "Before God without God," legitimate as it is, and surely necessary, can be realized only on another, more profound level: We also live with God, and at the ultimate level, actually in God. It is the combination of all three levels and all three vital attitudes that composes, in all its articulated richness, faith in our God as our creator and in ourselves as creatures in a world created by God.

(b) With God

In this context, to live with God means accepting the proposed dialogue in which God's creative act consists. To be created does not mean to be the effect of an impersonal cause. It means to be a personal word, pronounced freely by another personal word. The creative word is a word of life. To live as a creature with God means to respond to a God pronouncing upon the divine creation the divine word of life that we are: "The condition of creature is thus discovered in the human being to be a divine call, in such wise that all reality comes forth to meet this creature as a word of God that both asks that the creature respond with all its being and enables it to do so."[24] We are asked to pronounce *with God* God's *own* word of life. Jesus says the same thing: "My Father works until now, and I, too, work" (John 5:17). I work with him: "with the finger of God" (Luke 11:20).

In this vale of tears, to do "what the Father does" (John 5:19) is to make a people live and be filled with life (John 10:10). In this situation of a non-people—this situation of a colonial, dismembered, powerless, diasporan existence—the eyes of faith see that God is doing the same thing as God did with Jesus: giving life to the dead. And this is what the Son of God is doing in obedience to the word of the Father: "Just as the Father raises the dead and gives them life, the Son, too, gives life to whom he will" (John 5:21). This is the divine deed in which we have been called to cooperate, not out of our strength, but out of our weakness, that it may be clear that all things are God's (2 Cor. 4:7): "By faith the poor have understood that God is directly for them; but by that same faith they have grasped that they are not for themselves. To the hope that responds to God's good news for them, *charity* is joined, as a way of responding, and corresponding, to the very reality of God."[25]

Historical creation, then, is more than our necessary, but relative and always ambiguous, deed. In history, too, God gives life to the dead—and by our ministry. We perform with God the ministry of the giving of life, if we live *with* God.

(c) In God

This personal activity, which becomes obedience in the vicarious performance of the activity of God, is crowned when one lives *in* God. To live in God is to fulfill our highest and deepest potential, for "in him we live, move, and have our being" (Acts 17:28).

The believer speaks of man in terms of creation, in an attempt to express the fact that, at bottom, man *receives* his whole existence and activity from a creative God. Man is, so to speak, God's "first," and only in virtue of this is man what he is. His existence and life are "founded" on God. ... In other words, these creatures, these human beings, do not coincide with their own deepest reality. There is something more in them: an internal reality (which is themselves) referring to a transcendent creative God present in them by immanence. Therefore the reality in which we live and which we are is an unfathomable mystery: the mystery of a God who overflows into creatures.[26]

This is the attitude inculcated by Jesus in the Sermon on the Mount, as the culmination of his interpretation of the Law. To love our enemies is to be the child of our Father in heaven (that is, to do the same thing as our Father—John 5:19), "who makes his sun to rise on the evil and the good and sends his rain upon the just and unjust" (Matt. 5:45).

From a certain metaphysical point of departure (for example, that of *bonum diffusivum sui,* good as tending to spread itself out), as light can only shine, God "by essence" would only be able to give life—would be forced or condemned to do so. As sun and rain make no account of persons, in the biblical image, so would God be constrained to give life indiscriminately, without being able ever to define how that life was going to be employed.

But the personalistic conception adopted here dictates a comprehension of the Father's deed as a personalized one.[27] The gospel text emphasizes the possessive—"his" sun—and the anthropomorphisms "makes to rise" and "sends." Listing persons as good and evil is not meant to emphasize the totality of human beings, but their specification; sun and rain are personal gifts to each of the two types. Ultimately it expresses the personal, sovereign will to do good, to defeat evil by the force of good (Rom. 12:21).

Those in God are able to see God at work in all things as a personalized gift—not, to be sure, as a being of this world, but by the transcendence with which God is so interior to each of us that we are really and genuinely hosts of God.

From the marrow of this faith in the creator and in humanity, a faith in the world as creature of the creator, we discover the most intimate name of God's *philanthrōpia*: fidelity, or patience. This is how the latest writing of the New Testament sees the situation (2 Pet. 3:9). The writer sums up Paul's message in these words: "Consider that the Lord's patience is directed toward salvation. Paul, our beloved brother, wrote you this in the spirit of wisdom that is his, dealing with these matters as he does in all his letters" (2 Pet. 3:15–16).

(d) Violence of Life, Yes; Violence of Death, No

From the standpoint of the vale of tears that is our everyday life in our Latin America, this seems the most current and most hopeful message — not only for our internal situation, but for the global maelstrom in which we are awash. "Let those who suffer as God's will requires continue in good deeds, and entrust their lives to a faithful creator" (1 Pet. 4:19).

If God is not a causality giving, generically, the existence and power that human beings then channel in their own way, but a God who gives, as a personal gift, sun and rain to the just to support them on their way and to evildoers to overcome their evil by dint of patient, respectful, and personalized good, and if it is in this that being a creator consists — then to live by this faith, to be in God, will consist, correspondingly, in operating in the same fashion. This is what Jesus proposes to us in the Sermon on the Mount. In Latin America today, this entails a historical proposition that simply defies all logic, but which, far from being set before us as a mere utopia, is called to make history.[28] Faced with aggression on all levels of existence, we are called to make an integral option for life — as well as, of necessity, for the forces of life, but for those of life only, not those of death. Ultimately our task is gradually and radically to sweep from our horizon of life the violence that culminates in the death of human beings.

The violence of abnegation will always be necessary; so will that of self-giving; so will the violence that love entails, sexual love as well as pedagogical and political; so will the violence of cultivating the soil, the violence of culture, the violence of emulation. This is the violence necessary for entering the Reign: the violence that Jesus, as fire and sword, has come to bring on the earth (Matt. 10:34). This is the violence of testimony to the truth in a society of collaborators in evil, the violence of solidarity in a society of want, the violence the people need to organize and to stay organized in an order that dismembers and represses, the violence indispensable for resisting intimidation and repression, and even the violence required in order to study sciences and technology, to learn to direct and to occupy with discipline one's place within the whole. Resistance and the struggle to liberate oneself require a hefty dose of violence.

But perhaps the newness of our Latin American hour is asking us to curtail another kind of violence: the violence that leads to death. This will not be by virtue of some abstract principle or doctrinaire fundamentalism—the Christian "is not simply a pacifist: he can fight but prefers peace to war" (Medellín, 2, 15). This kind of violence has perhaps been celebrated during these years of institutionalized violence, revolutionary violence, counterinsurgency, and a repressive "dirty war." The "spiral of violence" is not an empty phrase, but a terrible experience. Perhaps in the midst of this measureless torrent of irreparable suffering (see Matt. 2:17–18) the face of our creator has appeared somewhat more clearly in history. We are learning that if God is creator, God cannot uncreate, cannot perform a self-contradiction (2 Tim. 2:13). And the radical way to uncreate is to kill. God does not have this power, since it is not a power that engenders life. The inflicting of death, then, is not susceptible of sacralization. It is always an evil, even in the legitimate case of the defense of an innocent person or entire people. It could be a necessary evil, if in our atavistic instincts and inability to arbitrate alternatives we were to find no other means of preventing a greater evil. But it is becoming less and less reasonable to characterize a death as a lesser evil, still less a war, and least of all official murder and torture.

If we reassert that imperialistic war and repression perpetrated on the people are crimes not only of *lèse-humanité*, but sins—that is, crimes of *lèse-divinité*—then we shall also be driven to the conclusion that wars of liberation are evil. Those that we must permit as a lesser evil, then, must be lived with a "bad conscience" — not with psychological anguish, but in a spirit of penitence. And they must not be glorified or "justified." We can no longer continue to glorify arms today, or to regard anyone as possessed of legitimate power by force of arms. Only the just execution of the popular will legitimates.

The glorification of many a so-called deed of liberation on our continent serves to legitimate the current unjust configuration of that continent. A fundamentalistic interpretation of the exodus must not be allowed to lead us to a hallowing of arms and weapons. There are no more holy wars. In the wars that we have, the goal must be to win peace.

It will take us many years to sow this new climate in our history and in our hearts. Without a hefty dose of the violence of life, it will be impossible to sweep away the violence that leads to killing. The beatitude of the poor, and of those persecuted for their fidelity, must be complemented by that of those who toil boldly for peace. This is how the daughters and sons of God will see the sovereignty of God effective among us. This beatitude will be attained by a gradual adaptation to the methods of the creator, which, despite the logic of the established order, are the most realistic, because they are the methods that are most congruous with our reality as God founds that reality. It is not temerarious to assert that this path is also the profound yearning of our peoples; and that our sensation of our growing strength proceeds not only from listening to God in prayer and attending to the events of our recent history, but also from listening to our "afflicted people," as they were called by Archbishop Romero — that organizer of the people, that champion of dialogue at all cost, that blessed builder of peace.

5. CREATING IN LATIN AMERICA AND CREATING IN THE WORLD

I began by asking why nothingness prevails over being in Latin America, qualifying "nothingness" as unjust privation, and "being" as unjust privilege. From this interpretation of what prevails today I now move to the question of whether it is possible for being to prevail over nothingness. The question of a passage from nothingness to being is a question concerning creation—in this case, a question about historical creation in Latin America today. We answer that it is possible, under two conditions: that of a personal transformation (conversion of the old human being), and that of the process of liberation for the construction of a new society (the path to the new eschatological humanity). Both processes are gradual, however, as they encounter the grossest resistance, both on the part of the established order and on the part of its introjected human model. Furthermore this gradual process of historical creation is inscribed within coordinates that determine the backdrop of Latin American history, inasmuch as, like it or not, our history is part of the history of the West and of universal history itself. And they are coordinates of today, arising as they do out of new technological conditions and the way these conditions are channeled, namely, by way of decisions sprung from a worldview of technology and an ideology of progress, of which ideology these new technological conditions are consciously felt to be the privileged vehicles. Let me now attempt to characterize these conditions, summarily, in the light of the faith in creation that I have been developing, and then examine the challenge they pose to historical creation.

(a) Coordinates of History as a Dilemma: To Create or to Destroy

The first coordinate is the possibility of nuclear holocaust. It has been less than a half-century since we acquired the nightmarish power to do away with the human species. A nuclear holocaust would be total human uncreation effected by human beings themselves. Henceforward humanity's survival partly depends, at least negatively, on human beings themselves, and not only on nature and (ultimately) on the creator of nature.

The second coordinate is the real possibility of gradually doing away with natural life, and accordingly with human existence, in free interaction with nature. The plunder of nature is reaching the limits of availability of various natural resources that are indispensable for human life, and in particular, altering the biosphere to the point that a state of irreversible deterioration may now be impending. We human beings enjoy a two-edged opportunity—either to humanize nature in such a way as to increase its potential, and our own as well, beyond our wildest dreams—or to use our relationship with creation in order to destroy that creation. Are we on the threshold of an artificial life, of an equilibrium (ecosystem) produced by human beings in isolation from nature (whose elements will now have become hostile to us) and maintained in viability only by an act of our collective will? Henceforward the survival of nature on earth depends not only on the creator of nature, but on ourselves, as well, who can either enhance nature, or damage it gravely and irreparably.

The third coordinate is the possibility, recently become reality, of human genetic "engineering." This means the direct effect of the human being as creator (or destroyer) on the human being as creature. Intentional genetic mutation is not value-neutral. It has two potential directions: either the security and open-ended improvement of human beings as creatures (however we are to understand, at each successive moment, the end that ought to be secured, and what constitutes improvement, with the attendant risk of error in parameters or execution); or massive genetic manipulation (Huxley's scenario), which will entail our utter perversion as creators and degradation as creatures. Henceforward humanity must choose between constitution in the image of God, with self-transcendence throughout the quest, or constitution in our own image, possibly even entailing constitution of a part of humanity in the image of beasts or robots.

At the present moment, Latin America is the mere object, not the subject or agent, of these possibilities—the object of wills not in solidarity with us, but dominating us. We are currently helpless even to defend ourselves against these forms of possible (and now partially real) action—destructive action—to be exerted upon our continent. The most that we can say is that this activity is beginning to be understood and resisted.

In all three cases, the level of creation is reached as a result of a certain type of human activity—an activity that attains absolute or relative "ceilings," an activity of persons "who know what is good and what is evil" (Gen. 3:6), which somehow makes human beings "like gods." Where can this activity possibly intersect with our Latin American project of historical creation? In a like context, does our project not appear outmoded, and altogether a secondary enterprise? Will not a consideration of this overall climate inevitably be the source of discouragement when it comes to waging our battles?

No, on the contrary; and I shall attempt to demonstrate not only a connection between the two processes, but precisely the importance of succeeding with our project if the overall process is to be rehabilitated and satisfactorily reoriented.

I have said that all three cases attain the level of creation. But attaining the level of creation does not mean attaining the act of creation. The act of creation is attained only if the adequate alternative is selected. Otherwise, one attains only the contrary of creation—destruction, degradation, and condemnation. Creation means the creation of life. No other "creation" merits this sacred name. Creation is properly divine. The creator is God. In God, power and goodness are one; hence God can only produce life; hence all that God posits in creation is good. We human beings can come to be creators only when we accept ourselves as created—that is, only when we choose ourselves as good, as the guardians and facilitators of all creation at the heart of a "cosmic democracy," and not the wielders of anything like an unjust dominion over creation.[29]

It is against this background that our Latin American project of creation in history unfolds.

(b) Strength in Weakness

As we have indicated, the starting point of this project is not only our condition as non-people, but also the experience that we have accumulated in the liberation processes. In these processes, we have felt it in our bones: One does not come to be a people by defeating internal and external enemies politically or even militarily. So many changes are necessary in the manner in which we produce and distribute material life, in social relationships, in our deep aspirations, and so on, that they will be tantamount to a radical transformation of humanity, a new birth, a veritable self-creation. I have described the present as a *kairos,* as the hour of God, not only because it is the hour of creation, and God is the creator, but also because this is the hour of death, as well, and we have mightily sensed the passage of God. As the bishops said at Medellín (see no. 6), Latin America is living its paschal hour: God has come to deliver and adopt a people. I have asked at what moment we are in this passing of God, and answered that it is night: black, stormy night, but not without signs of dawn.

National security regimes are falling, not overcome by armed might, but collapsing under the weight of their inability to respond to the challenge of the moment, and even more so under pressure of the dignity of their victims and the family members of those victims—an unarmed dignity, but an unbending one. The population is becoming increasingly more organized, daily more aware of its identity and interests, and daily more capable of attaining both. Our peoples have become more competent, more dexterous in their splicing of ancient knowledge to the acquisitions of the modern world. A part of the church institution supports our hope and promotes popular participation in the decision-making processes of society and politics. These are but a few of the signs new eyes have seen, and new hands have wrought, in this night. These signs, along with so many others, are gradually composing a new context, a new atmosphere: that of the violence of life as an alternative to the violence that leads only to death. I believe we are in the presence of a historical concretion of Jesus' response to Paul: "Strength is made perfect in weakness" (2 Cor. 12:9). Helpless against the military and the police, debilitated by an almost total want of resources, we are gradually manifesting the strength of persons who have resolved to live—not at any price (not at the price of submission and degradation, the price that our political, economic, military, cultural, and even, not rarely, ecclesiastical elite has been willing to pay), but in a worthy and participatory manner.

Till now, the more visible element may have been our weakness; but I believe that the strength made perfect in that weakness, and always present in seed, has at last begun to sprout, and is growing stronger, and hope that it will spring into bloom in these years. "And all this is the work of God" (2 Cor. 5:18). This is the news that the prophet felt in Babylon, and it made an evangelist of him, because it was God who was accomplishing it: God was creating, and sending the prophet to proclaim this to the people (Isa. 43:19). Paul relays this news to the Corinthians. Something has happened of which they must be apprised, and they must themselves become a new creation (2 Cor. 5:17). And this is in substance what we proclaim today as God's creation in Latin America. And we announce this news as gospel to the world. In 1973, a group of Brazilian bishops put it very simply: "We are coming to understand by practice that this people is the good news of Christ to our world."[30] It is the paradox of the beatitudes: eschatology begins in history.

(c) International Guild of Life

Against this backdrop, in which the existence and creaturely dignity of humanity teeter on the brink, the power of God, being made perfect in weakness, is the only thing our peoples possess with which to resist the aggression of internal colonialism, imperialism, and their own internal antagonisms. But besides being the only thing they have, it is precisely this that makes them so courageous. For it has to be said that, in this hour of merciless aggression, of polarization, and spirit of partisan identification, when the mighty are no longer satisfied with unjust domination of the anonymous, but require that all the oppressed bear the stamp and image of their class and degradation (see Rev. 13:16–17), the value of the dignity that answers neither with genuflection nor bestialization is beginning to be recognized by those in the imperialist countries who themselves have not bowed to the beast. In a worldwide situation marked by sin, the children of light are gradually recognizing one another. And this time they are not delivered to an apocalyptic combat. They suffer only the violence of testimony (Rev. 1:16; 6:9; 19:10), not the torrents of the exterminating angel or the bloody riders of justice. In this hour of total uncreation, and shameful resignation to what appears as clothed in strength, the international guild of those who stand on the side of creation is also being forged. This spirit (the life-giving Spirit) must be constantly embodied in time and place. Without it, we hold, there is no salvation. This is what our creator requires of us today.

CHAPTER II

Israel: From Liberation to (Re)creation

1. STATE OF THE QUESTION

The proposition "God is creating in Latin America today" is an expression of our reading of the signs of the times. This proposition is a conclusion drawn from many premises, among which is a biblical faith in creation.

Biblical scholars have been struck by the relatively late date of the creation accounts. Apart from the Yahwist texts, which do not include a narrative of the creation of the universe, these accounts would be: Second Isaiah, the Priestly Document in Genesis, and certain psalms of doubtful date but without any convincing signs of great antiquity.[1] This faith has a long, pathetic history. For the people of Israel, as for us, faith in Yahweh as creator was a point of arrival, the term of a journey sown with sweat and tears—or rather, a gospel that sowed the night of catastrophe with light.

To be sure, the people of Israel held various worldviews throughout the ages, and they shared them with neighboring peoples. These were religious conceptions and asserted the divine origin of the world and the sovereign activity of God in that world. But none of this entered into the first Israelite professions of faith. God simply came forth to meet Israel in history. Or, more precisely, it was this liberating encounter that founded

Israel as a people. Israel felt that God was with them, and that
it was God's repeated intervention that molded them as a people. In this dialogue, Israel came to know itself and God. Then,
through that relationship, Israel came to know other peoples,
along with the material world to which it felt bound by so many
ties. Israel's creed was historical, then. In Yahweh's revelation,
the meaning of history had been disclosed to them. Their God
had "happened to them" as savior. Thus Yahwism was a salvation religion, and only from a point of departure in history
could Israel arrive at a salvific faith in creation. More important
than rummaging around in Israel's surrounding cultures to
ascertain the origin of such and such a biblical representation
of creation in the Bible, then, is a search for the answer to the
question of how Israel welded that representation to its salvific
faith, a faith based on historical events.[2] Let us briefly retrace
this path, since, even apart from the fact that it constitutes the
substrate of our faith, it will also shed abundant light on our
own journey as God's people.[3]

2. HISTORICAL SYNOPSIS

(a) The God of Israel Promises and Fulfills

The oldest biblical conception of Yahweh is that of a tribal
god. It is taken for granted that other gods exist. But Yahweh
has chosen Israel, and Yahweh's saving solicitude has been demonstrated in both a personal commitment to the people and a
record of living up to that commitment. The Lord is God
because the Lord saves. The Lord is the God of Israel because
the Lord saves Israel at the expense of other peoples.

In the last book of the Law, we find an extremely condensed
formulation of Israel's bond with Yahweh, the Lord:

> When the Most High assigned the nations their
>   heritage,
>   when he parceled out the descendants of Adam,
> He set up the boundaries of the peoples
>   after the number of the sons of God;

> While the Lord's own portion was Jacob,
> His hereditary share was Israel [Deut. 32:8–9].

Thus do the people sing the liberation that constitutes their foundation as a people:

> Sing to the Lord, for he is gloriously triumphant;
> horse and chariot he has cast into the sea.
>   [Exod. 15:21]

This is the origin of the historical creed, the origin of Yahweh's legal title to Israel: "I the Lord, am your God, who brought you out of the land of Egypt, that place of slavery" (Exod. 20:2).

The conquest of the promised land would confirm this view of a strong, jealous tribal God, conqueror of the gods and their peoples. Such is the God of Israel celebrated in the ancient victory hymn sung in honor of Deborah, when God had "humbled the Canaanite king, Jabin, before the Israelites" (Judg. 4:23). Israel had chosen new gods, and so "war was at their gates" (Judg. 5:8), "when I, Deborah, rose, when I rose, a mother in Israel" (Judg. 5:4), and the Lord "went out from Seir . . . marched from the land of Edom," and "the earth quaked. . . ." Now the people of Israel "recount the just deeds of the Lord, his just deeds that brought freedom to Israel" (Judg. 5:7, 11).

Throughout all of this history, the people's self-concept is founded in, and indissolubly linked to, faith in their God:

> My father was a wandering Aramean who went down to Egypt with a small household and lived there as an alien. But there he became a nation great, strong and numerous. When the Egyptians maltreated and oppressed us, imposing hard labor upon us, we cried to the Lord, the God of our fathers, and he heard our cry and saw our affliction, our toil and our oppression. He brought us out of Egypt with his strong hand and outstretched arm, with terrifying power, with signs and wonders; and bringing us into this country, he gave us this land flowing with milk and honey [Deut. 26:5–9].

The apogee of this concept of God is to be attained in the age of David and Solomon. Now the promises will have been fulfilled: Israel is sovereign of the land, free and powerful. And David will pray:

> What other nation on earth is there like your people Israel, which God has led, redeeming it as his people; so that you have made yourself renowned by doing this magnificent deed, and by doing awe-inspiring things as you cleared nations and their gods out of the way of your people, which you redeemed for yourself from Egypt? You have established for yourself your people Israel as yours forever, and you, Lord, have become their God [2 Sam. 7:23–4].

Who God was had been revealed. The image of the God who had brought the promises to fulfillment had been realized, and was therefore fixed. Thus Solomon, when he blessed the Temple, could pray: "Blessed be the Lord who has given rest to his people Israel, just as he promised. Not a single word has gone unfulfilled of the entire generous promise he made through his servant Moses" (1 Kings 8:56).

Israel had confidence in its God. On the basis of their own experience, the people could tell Yahweh: "Great are you, Lord God! There is none like you and there is no God but you, just as we have heard it told" (2 Sam. 7:22). They had no need to go running after any foreign god; nor did they acknowledge any, any more than they acknowledged any political or military power over themselves. Since the fall of Ramses II, no great power had arisen in the Near East, and so the power of the confederation of Israelite tribes had waxed apace. Israel had become a rich and mighty state.

(b) The God of Israel and the Gods of the Empires

But the rise of Assyria in the eighth century changed the situation radically. Assyria rapidly came to dominate the scene. The Kingdom of Israel offered resistance, and was swept away forever. The invaders reached Jerusalem itself, and the holy city had to bow to their might. Judah was transformed into a vassal kingdom. And Yahweh, the God of Israel, was subjected to conquering gods: Assyrian gods were placed on the main altar of the temple itself, while Yahweh was thrust aside, to occupy a mediocre position among the idols, reflecting the diminished status of the erstwhile sole God of Israel.

Judah had been wounded in its national pride. But it suffered still more deeply from its wounded faith, which had been undermined to its foundations. In the Syro-Ephraimite war, Achaz had not wished to put God to the test, out of a lack of faith as well as for fear of the demands that a divine initiative would entail for his policy. Thus it was the enemy who raised the question of the power of Israel's God, and the Book of Isaiah places it on the lips of the Assyrian general who is urging Achaz to surrender:

> Do not let Hezekiah seduce you by saying, 'The Lord will save us.' Has any of the gods of the nations ever rescued his land from the hand of the king of Assyria? Where are the gods of Hamath and Arpad? Where are the gods of Sepharvaim? Where are the gods of Samaria? Have they saved Samaria from my hand? Which of all the gods of these lands ever rescued his land from my hand? Will the Lord then save Jerusalem from my hand? [Isa. 36:18–20].

Does our God have the power to save us? Here is the question that shook Israel to its depths:

> O God, our ears have heard,
>   our fathers have declared to us,
> The deeds you did in their days,
>   in days of old [Ps. 44:2].
> How long, O God . . .? [Ps. 74:10]

Thus did many of the Israelite faithful pray. Others thought the hand of the Lord had been shortened (see Isa. 50:2), and began to follow other, more powerful gods, the conquering gods. Still others sought to remain faithful, but did not know how to interpret this national defeat. "The Lord has forsaken me; my Lord has forgotten me," they cried (Isa. 49:14). But most of the people did not even dare pose the problem. Traditional religion had been converted into a culture and an ideology, which bestowed security and meaning. In these ruinous circumstances, then, they preferred to leave this little piece of reality intact, and systematically reject any questions.

(c) A Judgment upon God's People

It was the prophets who posed the question of faith in all its raw significance. They picked religious practices apart, showing that they were not sacred, that they were not conducive to an encounter with the Lord, but only served to prop up a false sense of security in the nation, a sense of security without foundation in fact. And they systematically went about dismantling these false securities.

Even before the catastrophe, the prophet Amos had warned the Kingdom of Israel, so proud in its imagined might, and so secure in its notion that Assyria was yet far off:

> Woe to the complacent in Zion,
>> to the overconfident on the mount of Samaria.
> Beware, I am raising up against you, O house of
>> Israel,
>> say I, the Lord, the God of hosts,
> A nation that shall oppress you [Amos 6:1, 14].

Rites defend nothing:

> I hate, I spurn your feasts,
>> I take no pleasure in your solemnities;
> Your cereal offerings I will not accept,
>> nor consider your stall-fed peace offerings.
>> [Amos 5:21–2]

> Seek good and not evil,
>> that you may live;
> Then truly will the Lord, the God of hosts,
>> be with you as you claim! [Amos 5:14]

Amos tells Israel: This god of yours does not exist. This god you bribe with religious festivals is an idol. This god who closes his eyes to your sins in return for promises and offerings is an invention of your own. This god indissolubly joined to Israel by tradition, though it be the most glorious of traditions, does not exist. Then Amos strikes at the heart of the Israelite faith: the exodus is no exception, no privilege:

> Are you not like the Ethiopians to me,
>   O men of Israel, says the Lord?
> Did I not bring the Israelites from the land of Egypt
>   As I brought the Philistines from Caphtor
>   and the Arameans from Kir? [Amos 9:7]

The Lord has liberated not only Israel, but other oppressed peoples.

Of course, the Lord is specially attached to Israel — but not, as so many think, in order to save them:

> The eyes of the Lord God are on this sinful kingdom;
>   I will destroy it from the face of the earth. . . .
> By the sword shall all sinners among my people die,
>   those who say, "Evil will not reach or overtake us."
>   [Amos 9:8, 10]

The allusion is to a historical act of judgment and destruction to be wrought by God in Israel by means of Assyria. Obviously, God has power over Assyria, as well.

The God of Amos is not a tribal God. Yahweh's sovereignty extends to all peoples, and the whole universe. God's concern is not for those who offer divine worship, but for those who live humanely and do justice. And Yahweh's interventions in history are precisely for the purpose of defending the cause of the oppressed. It is in this perspective that Israel ought to understand its history with God, and not as the exercise of a preeminence. As Israel has been transformed into a tyrannical state, then, the Lord will intervene once again — but this time to strike this people down, and judge the prideful and powerful. Hence the prophet's terrible warning: "Prepare to meet your God, O Israel!" (Amos 4:12).

The reign of Jeroboam II may well mark the economic and political apogee of the Northern Kingdom. A secularized Yahwism, transformed into a naturalistic, ethical, and political religion sacralizes the established order and lends a sense of security to its practitioners. The sanctuary of Bethel is "the king's sanctuary and a royal temple" (Amos 7:13). The priest of Bethel therefore persecutes the prophet. He need not inquire into the truth of the other's oracles. His criterion for their delegitimation is that they contravene law and order. Official religion cannot assimilate Amos' message, nor does it allow itself to be called into question by that message, and Amos disappears by order of the king, at the instigation of Bethel's priest, as "the country cannot endure all his words" (Amos 7:10).

The problem lies in two totally opposed forces. Official religion has no more living words; it exercises a function of mere attestation, and has become simply a sacred commerce, a business. The priest confers legitimacy, and in return receives money and social prestige. He acts in the name of the god of the past, a mute, tamed god, a god he claims to serve, but in reality a god he owns. Amos speaks in the name of a living God, who has waylaid him and turned his life upside-down. His is the God of an unfinished history, whose hands are ever on that history, keeping it open and unpredictable. Amos discovers the true meaning of God's past actions, which are sovereign actions. And he proclaims the imminent intervention of Yahweh once more, since the people have ignored this God. The one who has acted is above all the one who acts and will act:

> The lion roars—
>   who will not be afraid!
> The Lord God speaks—
>   who will not prophesy! [Amos 3:8]

God has snatched Amos from his comfortable existence and sent him to prophesy catastrophe.

It is not easy to grasp the profound reversal implied by the prophetic message. God was the one who had fulfilled the promise made to Israel's forebears. Come what might, the possession of the land seemed secure. It had even come to define Yahweh: According to the historical creeds, Yahweh was the one who had rescued Israel from the house of slavery and had established the people in possession of the land of promise. This is what the people celebrated in worship, as they returned thanks to God along with their firstfruits and other sacrifices. How could these persons assert that the covenant was conditional, and that if Israel broke it, through a neglect of their personal relationship with God, and therefore by a renunciation of justice and mercy, the Lord would actually expel them from the land and become the God of another people? Israel was not just a people who at some moment or other in their history had adopted the Yahwist religion. Israel was the people of promise, the people of election, the people of God. How could God, who had molded them, ever destroy them? Official religion cried: Leave God alone! And the king interpreted: I shall not put the Lord to the test. But the prophets insisted on transferring the focus of attention to the present (hence the call to conversion) and the future (the coming catastrophe as God's own deed). And so they revitalized the past, understanding it as the moment of God's salvific initiative and the people's response, the time of a living relationship that should never have died. For that current, living relationship is Israel's only foundation: "Unless your faith is firm you shall not be firm" (Isa. 7:9), where "be firm" means to dare to live by the current word of God.

One after another, the prophets rose up to urge Israel to mistrust their false securities. Foreign gods were of no avail, they cried; nor was it of any use to practice all the minutiae of Yahweh's religion without changing one's life. Israel must dare, for good and all, to put God to the test. Israel was in peril—let Israel be converted to God, then, and see whether God had power to save them. Let them trust in God, and see whether Yahweh was a God to be relied on. Isaiah urged this decision on King Ahaz (Isa. 7:1–16), but the king chose religion over faith. He was unwilling to rely on the possible historical activity of a living God, and preferred to hold to the security of ancestral promises in exchange for sacrifices and offerings. Then the prophet predicted the country's destruction:

On that day
The Lord shall whistle
for the fly that is in the farthest streams of Egypt,
and for the bee in the land of Assyria.
All of them shall come and settle [Isa. 7:18–19].

Or in an image more terrible still: "On that day the Lord shall shave with the razor hired from across the River [i.e., with the king of Assyria] the head, and the hair between the legs. It shall also shave off the beard" (Isa. 7:20).

Isaiah's God is a God who acts in history. God wishes to save. But salvation is not an act of magic; nor does it mean saving someone from external enemies alone. The salvation willed by God is founded on an interior buttressing. God wills the strength that metes out justice, the abundance that bestows true peace. God wills integral liberation. Isaiah's God says: either a social transformation as foundation of victory, or destruction. The leaders, however, think: Neither shall we change our behavior, nor will the God of David permit that Jerusalem and its temple be destroyed. And so Isaiah ends his life prophesying to the king: "Behold, the days shall come when all that is in your house, and everything that your fathers have stored up until this day, shall be carried off to Babylon; nothing shall be left, says the Lord" (Isa. 39:6). Nor will the pillage of Judah be due solely to the weakness of Judah. It will be a deed of the Lord. He will whistle for the invading horseflies; he will be the one to fetch the razor from across the Euphrates. Why? Because "this is a rebellious people, deceitful children." They "put [their] trust in what is crooked and devious, and depend on it" (Isa. 30:9, 12).

For the prophets, an appeal to God's activity of old will not be enough. For them, the Lord acts today, by calling the people to conversion, and when they abandon God, God judges them. Assyria, Egypt, and Babylon are instruments of God. They are not the enemies of God; nor have they overcome God. They are God's vassals, and they execute the divine orders to chastise an impious people:

Who was it that gave Jacob to be plundered,
Israel to the despoilers?

Was it not the Lord, against whom we have sinned?
In his ways they refused to walk,
his law they disobeyed [Isa. 42:24].

Of course, this is no act of divine caprice. It is motivated by
Israel's infidelity.

If you would hearken to my commandments,
your prosperity would be like a river,
and your vindication like the waves of the sea;
Your descendants would be like the sand,
and those born of your stock like its grains,
Their name never cut off
or blotted out from my presence [Isa. 48:18–19].

From the status of a tribal God who rescues Israel alone,
God has ascended to the status of the God of universal history,
judging Israel by means of other peoples. For the prophets, this
God has no competitors. This is the Lord (Amos 9:6). Neither
the peoples nor the sea nor the mountains are obstacles for
Yahweh: "It was I who made the earth, and man and beast on
the face of the earth, by my great power, with my outstretched
arm; and I can give them to whomever I think fit. Now I have
given all these lands into the hand of Nebuchadnezzar, king of
Babylon, my servant" (Jer. 27:5–6). Now Yahweh is no longer
one of the "sons of God." Yahweh is the most high, the only
God, the creator. It is a terrible thing, then, that Yahweh should
be precisely the one to hand over the land of promise to Nebuchadnezzar. The servant, the chosen one, is no longer Israel!
Now he is the enemy king, who does battle with Israel. The
reversal is complete. Who can bear it? How can this be assimilated?

(d) The Lord Will Do Something New

The God of the prophets is not characterized mainly by judgment. Not even in Amos is judgment the final word of God. The
God of the prophets continues to be Yahweh, the God of liberation. The prophets are traditional. Therefore they lash out

against traditionalists, who have imposed a closure on the foundational time and thus have ignored the God of liberation, whom they confine to the past and to whom they appeal for the consecration of their unjust order and the prevention of present liberation. The prophets rise up against a profession of faith transformed into an ideology that serves as a cloak for evil and injustice, and against a rite that claims to seal a covenant between the God of liberation and an anti-people. The pathetic element in the prophets is that it is the God of liberation who sends them to proclaim a judgment of condemnation. Hence the prophets' suffering, which faithfully mirrors the suffering of God. The Lord and the prophets are the only ones who do not will the death of the people, or who see that for the salvation of that people the only effective medicine will be catastrophe. But they proclaim catastrophe in order to establish a firmer salvation. Beyond judgment, then, indeed by way of judgment, salvation is the act of God par excellence, and the prophets proclaim this. Indeed, it is this act of God that defines prophecy. And it is of such weight that it snaps the salvation history of Israel in two. Von Rad writes: The prophets' "point of departure is the conviction that Israel's previous history with Yahweh is over, and that he wishes to initiate something new."[4] And he explains:

> The prophets strive to convince their contemporaries that Yahweh's earlier salvific institutions had lost all value for them, and that if Israel wishes to be saved it must dare to stride forth in faith to meet a new, future salvific action on the part of Yahweh. This conviction of a breach with the past places them basically outside salvation history as Israel has understood it thus far. The prophets' message has its center and its remarkable explosive force in its shattering of Israel's earlier existence with Yahweh and its opening of the historical horizon to a new activity of God with his people.[5]

(e) Salvation through Judgment

To be sure, the breach for which the prophets call is, in their eyes just as in Yahweh's, the path to the maintenance of fidelity.

It is not a matter of switching gods. It is a matter of responding to God's initiative. But it is too late to escape catastrophe.

For Hosea, "return" means receiving life from the Lord, but through death:

> Come, let us return to the Lord
> For it is he who has rent, but he will heal us;
> he has struck us, but he will bind our wounds.
> He will revive us after two days;
> on the third day he will raise us up,
> to live in his presence [Hos. 6:1–2].

"History suddenly plunges into an abyss, to disappear, and a shoot of *non-history* springs up, to be the stalk of a new history."[6]

> For the people of Israel shall remain many days
> without king or prince,
> Without sacrifice or sacred pillar,
> without ephod or household idols.
> Then the people of Israel shall turn back
> and seek the Lord, their God [Hos. 3:4–5].

The eternal one, once more installed as Israel's God, requires Israel to renounce its rejection and negate the negation: They shall call their brother " 'My People,' and their sister, 'There is Compassion' " (Hos. 2:3). Between catastrophe and salvation, one as sure as the other, comes the mystery of nothingness.

Hosea had engendered *non-offspring,* who, in the near or distant future, would be transformed into *offspring.* This is the *return* in Hosea: the passage from negative to positive, the appearance of something where there had been nothing, resurrection after death.

From the entrails of Isaiah arise two beings: The one is non-offspring (Ready for Plunder, Ready for Booty—Isa. 8:4); the other will come to be offspring (A Remnant Shall Return—Isa. 7:3). For Isaiah, as for Hosea, there is a sacking and a return. But they will be simultaneous. In the same generation some will be annihilated, and others will become a remnant. Catastrophe will befall all, and only some will survive. And in any case, for both groups the catastrophe is in the future. Jeremiah and Ezekiel, on the other hand, prophesy from the midst of catastrophe itself. To prophecies of peace that close the people's eyes, in various manners and degrees, to catastrophe, Jeremiah and Ezekiel tirelessly oppose the utter certitude of ruin. But both foretell, with even more assurance, salvation.

Jeremiah's joy renounces no suffering, no tears. He will keep on, drawing his very sustenance from all these trials and all these renunciations. His strength comes from the torments that encourage and exalt him. Those who will share in his song of joy and hope are those who, as he, have known suffering, and these are the poor and abandoned, the disinherited and the hungry, those who die in the desert and the living dead.

Jeremiah could not even descry the first faint glimmer of day. His good news drew its sustenance from the tremendous experience of the sheer fact that it was past midnight. Jeremiah penetrated the days of nothingness that Hosea had glimpsed. And he could not emerge from them. And yet, in penetrating them he won the unshakable certainty that there would be a resurrection: "I will hand over this city to the Chaldeans. . . . I will gather them together from all the lands to which in anger, wrath, and great rage I banish them. . . . They shall be my people, and I will be their God" (Jer. 32:28, 37–8).

Two events, separated by months, by years, by centuries, by millennia—catastrophe and return—despite all, coincide, are adjacent, mutually intimate, simultaneous. Two sentiments, distant from one another by all the bulk of a contradiction—grief and gladness—couple nonetheless. That *nonetheless* would have been no more than a stubborn wager, had Jeremiah not heard it from the very mouth of God. Jeremiah's theocentrism reaches its climax in that *nonetheless*. State and Temple can crumble; yet the covenant abides, thanks to the existence of every Hebrew. God had once been Israel's space. With Jeremiah, God becomes but Israel's time.

(f) Historical Creation

Throughout this painful history, it becomes ever clearer that God's most proper activity is salvific action. But to save after catastrophe is to create. Ruin is the historical translation of nothingness. Hence the naturalness with which expressions reminiscent of creation spring to the prophets' lips. The decisive element, however, in the biblical notion of creation is simply "the fact that God's activity causes something new to arise, something that did not previously exist in this way."[7] Jeremiah puts it simply: "The Lord has created a new thing upon the earth" (Jer. 31:22).

The inevitability of catastrophe is not owing to the will of God, but to the obstinacy of those responsible for the people. It is the only way to bring these leaders back to reality, to disillusion them. It is the exposure of Israel's true condition, which religion had made it possible to conceal from Israel's own eyes. There are three capital texts that constitute a synthesis of the direction of the Lord's intervention.

Hosea says:

> I will make a covenant for them on that day,
>   with the beasts of the field,
> With the birds of the air,
>   and with the things that crawl on the ground.
> Bow and sword and war
>   I will destroy from the land,
> and I will let them take their rest in security.
>
> I will espouse you to me forever;
>   I will espouse you in right and in justice,
>   in love and in mercy;
> I will espouse you in fidelity,
>   and you shall know the Lord [Hos. 2:20–22].

And Jeremiah:

> The days are coming, says the Lord, when I will make a new covenant with the house of Israel and the house of Judah. It will not be like the covenant I made with their fathers the day I took them by the hand to lead them forth from the land of Egypt; for they broke my covenant, and I had to show myself their master, says the Lord. But this

is the covenant which I will make with the house of Israel after those days, says the Lord. I will place my law within them, and write it upon their hearts; I will be their God, and they shall be my people [Jer. 31:31–3].

Ezekiel:

For I will take you away from among the nations, gather you from all the foreign lands, and bring you back to your own land. I will sprinkle clean water upon you to cleanse you from all your impurities, and from all your idols I will cleanse you. I will give you a new heart and place a new spirit within you, taking from your bodies your hearts of stone and giving you hearts of flesh. I will put my spirit within you and make you live by my statutes, careful to observe my decrees [Ezek. 36:24–7].

This historical action of God, announced by the prophets, is the source of what I call creative action. It is the appearance of new human beings and new social relationships. It is not a raising or lifting from without, an exaltation of which humanity would be the object alone, and not the agent. On the contrary, it is a human action. It is the action by which God makes us active. God places the divine Spirit within us in such a way that our most intimate, most free activity becomes the action of God. And the content of this action is victory over selfishness, and the full humanization of human relations: a heart of flesh.

Religious relationships and moral norms are no longer to be something external and foreign to us. In the covenant to come, God will place the divine law in our very hearts. The law of our heart is the very law of God. When we obey our deepest inner pulsations, we shall be obeying God, as well: Morality is naturalized and religion humanized.

This creative action, which penetrates humanity's very sources, and re-creates them, reaches the depths of the God who reveals these depths. This action reveals the primacy of God's faithfulness over the infidelity of the people. And it gives the reason for God's faithfulness: the divine love. Here the prophets allude to the most human symbol of love: God's creative action is a marriage bond. "I will espouse you to me forever; I will espouse you in right and in justice, in love and in mercy."

The tenderness of the divine mercies will ultimately triumph over both the oppression of the mighty and the discouragement of their victims. It will transform our heart of stone into a heart of flesh, and will transform this flesh into a lifegiving spirit.

This is the inner core of the prophets' message: God is on the point of acting. God is about to re-create humanity. If the people respond, history will swell: God will be revealed as creator and we as created creators. Indeed, God's love will ultimately triumph not by overcoming us, but by bringing it about that our own humanity triumphs in us.

The historical density of these assertions, and the urgency of their formulation in terms of creation and creativity, are clear from the circumstances of the Babylonian exile. It is the exile that has given us the splendid vision of the dry bones and their resurrection (Ezek. 37:1–14), to be embodied once more, and just as splendidly, in the prophecy of Second Isaiah.[8]

3. THE GOOD NEWS

Israel has ceased to be a people. The last descendant of David has died in obscurity in Babylon. The covenant between God and the people of God, which had been the basis of Israel's existence, is a shambles. Israel no longer has a Temple, a priesthood, or a sacrifice. The nation no longer even lives in the Lord's land. Not only has it ceased to exist as a political entity, but even as a social body it is only a disheartened remnant, with precious little hope for the future. In these conditions, how can the people approach the Lord in search of salvation?

On the other hand, the Jews are living at the heart of the world. Defeated and subjugated by Babylon, they are also fascinated and molded by that power. And the might of the oppressor is due, in the general opinion of the time, to the power of its divinities. In these conditions, the prophetic question of the power of Yahweh surfaces. But laboring under a terrible sense of guilt, and dazzled by the power of the Babylonian divinities and the magnificence of their religious ceremonies, how can the

Jews ever dare to ask Yahweh to come and challenge the power
of these giants?

Their religious manifestations consist mainly in lamentations
over present conditions, the recollection of the grandeur of their
past, and observance of the Law.

It is in these circumstances that the great prophet arises. He
comes forward as an evangelist (Isa. 52:7)—the bearer of tidings
of salvation. And salvation is liberation from Babylon and return
to the land in completely renewed conditions of life. And the
book begins:

> Comfort, give comfort to my people,
>   says your God.
> Speak tenderly to Jerusalem, and proclaim to her
>   that her service is at an end,
>   her guilt is expiated [Isa. 40:1–2].

The judgment of the Lord is over and past. Now comes God's
liberation. The right attitude for us to have, then, is to abandon
discouragement and open up to this historical novelty. This novelty says, to Babylon: There is "none to save you" (Isa. 47:15).
To its gods: "Bel bows down, Nebo stoops . . ." (46:1). "You are
nothing . . ." (41:24). To Israel: "Fear not, for I have redeemed
you . . ." (43:1). "Go forth from Babylon . . .!" (48:20). To Jerusalem: "Let her be rebuilt . . ." (44:28). To Cyrus of Persia: "The
Lord's friend shall do his will against Babylon and the progeny
of Chaldea" (48:14).

But this good news is couched in a basic formulation that
sums up all the good news that ever was, as it constitutes its
root. The prophet is sent to proclaim this plain, unadorned news:
"Here is your God!" (Isa. 40:9).

And the presence of the Lord means abundant life. If the
Lord comes, it is for salvation. If it is the Lord, liberation is
being wrought. To be sure, the Lord has judged, as well, but
rather through his presence/absence, which causes death:

> In an outburst of wrath, for a moment
>   I hid my face from you;
> But with enduring love I take pity on you [Isa. 54:8].

(a) Creation-Salvation

But how can the people be made to sense that Yahweh has the will to save Israel, or indeed the power to do so? For the prophet, the adequate answer to this question lies not in the past, but in the future, which is already under way. Precisely now, the Lord is about to show all of the strength of the divine arm and all of the tenderness of the divine heart.

But this does not mean there are no present and past facts to proclaim this strength and tenderness. And it is here that the prophet recalls the creative-salvific activity of God in the polemic with the gods of Babylon and the crushing of the people. With reference to the power of the idols and the Babylonian empire:

> To whom can you liken me as an equal?
>   says the Holy One.
> Lift up your eyes on high
>   and see who has created these [Isa. 40:25–26].

This is the first of fifteen occurrences of the verb *bara* in Second Isaiah. *Bara* is the technical term employed in the Bible to designate the creative act, and Second Isaiah may be the first to use it.[9]

> For him, the creation of the universe is not precisely the first of so many other deeds of creation-redemption, but an ongoing quality of all divine activity. . . . Hence, in his book, creation appears ever more clearly as a historical deed of salvation that continues throughout the ages and ultimately issues in the era of the Covenant.[10]

In view of the prostration of the people, then, which suggests, "My way is hidden from the Lord . . ." (Isa. 40:27), the prophet responds by evoking Yahweh's creative power. He sees God at this very moment creating "the ends of the earth" (40:28), and giving "strength to the fainting" (40:29). This gives him a sense of faith: "They that hope in the Lord will renew their strength" (40:31).

It is this power of God's, which fashions and molds all, nourishing and consolidating it, that distinguishes Yahweh from the idols. The idols gleam bright and terrible, but it is only human beings who have fashioned them and clothed them in their splendor (Isa. 40:18–20; 41:23–4; 44:9–20). It is Yahweh who is the universal source of life and salvation:

> Thus says God, the Lord,
>   who created the heavens and stretched them out,
>   who spreads out the earth with its crops,
> Who gives breath to its people
>   and spirit to those who walk on it:
> I, the Lord, have called you for the victory of justice,
>   I have grasped you by the hand;
> I formed you, and set you
>   as a covenant of the people,
>   a light for the nations,
> To open the eyes of the blind,
>   to bring out prisoners from confinement,
>   and from the dungeon, those who live in darkness.
>   [Isa. 42:5–7]

Here we see, in inextricable interpenetration, the Lord's pristine deed and imminent act: the creation of the cosmos, and the re-creation of the human world in the fullness of life and justice, God's creation and ours, to crown with historical liberation the divine gift of life and salvation.

Even the expression "I formed you" is the one used in Genesis to denote Adam's creation. Now the prophet uses it again, to denote the election and historical constitution of the people of Israel:

> Remember this, O Jacob,
>   you O Israel, who are my servant! ...
> Thus says the Lord who made you;
>   your help, who formed you from the womb. ...
> I will never forget you [Isa. 44:21; 44:2; 49:15].

For all of these reasons, von Rad says:

In Second Isaiah we stumble on a tradition that no prophet had ever referred to: the creation of the world by Yahweh. ... Now, there is a special circumstance in the ideas of Second Isaiah concerning creation. He does not see creation as a sealed occurrence, utterly apart from historical events. He seems not to distinguish the two very clearly. Creation, for him, is the first of Yahweh's historical marvels, and a special testimonial of his salvific will. Second Isaiah provides the convincing proof of this "soteriological" conception of creation when he speaks at times of Yahweh as creator of the world and at others of Yahweh as creator of Israel.[11]

In chapter 46, the backdrop is composed of the rites of enthronement of the Babylonian god Bel-Marduk. There we have the dramatic account of the fashioning of the world, which was simultaneously the fashioning of the gods and the birth of the empire. This had all taken place in the midst of a mortal struggle with chaos, and must be ritually repeated every year lest the delicate equilibrium of the cosmos and the empire get out of plumb. Gods like these, the prophet says, "must be borne up on shoulders, carried as burdens by the weary" (Isa. 46:1). With Yahweh, just the opposite is the case:

> Hear me, O house of Jacob,
>   all who remain of the house of Israel,
> My burden since your birth,
>   whom I have carried from your infancy.
> Even to your old age I am the same,
>   even when your hair is gray I will bear you;
> It is I who have done this, I who will continue,
>   and I who will carry you to safety [Isa. 46:3–4].

Yahweh is no burden to Israel. On the contrary, it is Yahweh who has carried Israel from the beginning, by means of the divine creative action. But this is easy for a God who is no idol, and who never grows tired or weary. This is the basis of Yahweh's faithfulness, and the foundation of our faith: Yahweh's creative action proceeds from an invincible love. This God, then, can say, in all tranquillity, and with absolute assurance: "I shall be the same."

But when the prophet uses the word *creation* with reference to Israel, he is thinking especially of the passage through the Sea of Reeds:

> Was it not you who dried up the sea,
>   the waters of the great deep,
> Who made the depths of the sea into a way
>   for the redeemed to pass over? [Isa. 51:10]

It is astonishing how readily the prophet moves from the primordial separation of the waters to the dividing of the waters for the liberation of Israel from the hand of Pharaoh. For him they are simply two different aspects of the one historical act of God's creation-and-salvation.

(b) Now They Are Brought into Being

After all, this prophet's great proclamation is that this historical act, still incomplete, is on the point of being resumed:

> From now on I announce new things to you,
>   hidden events of which you knew not.
> Now, not long ago, they are brought into being.
>   [Isa. 48:6–7]

> See, the earlier things have come to pass,
>   new ones I now foretell;
> Before they spring into being,
>   I announce to you [Isa. 42:9].

Hence the prophet's longing for the coming of this new creation:

> Let justice descend, O heavens, like dew from above,
>   like gentle rain let the skies drop it down.
> Let the earth open and salvation bud forth;

let justice spring up!
I, the Lord, have created this [Isa. 45:8].

What the Lord created is of such power that it casts all that
is old into shadow. In order to know God, and in order to know
human beings, one must look primarily to the future:

> Thus says the Lord,
>   who opens a way in the sea
>   and a path in the mighty waters,
> Who leads out chariots and horsemen,
>   a powerful army,
> Till they lie prostrate together, never to rise,
>   snuffed out and quenched like a wick.
> Remember not the events of the past,
>   the things of long ago consider not;
> See, I am doing something new!
> Now it springs forth, do you not perceive it?
>   [Isa. 43:16–19]

What does this act of historical creation consist of? The
prophet is certain that it will come to pass, but he respects its
novelty. He does not set about anticipating it, then, or reducing
it to a projection of the present. What can be described are its
implications in terms of modification of the present situation:
Babylon and its gods will fall, the Israelites will return to their
land, and Jerusalem will be rebuilt. But he knows that the events
proclaimed, while constituting a most remarkable historical
change, do not exhaust the potential of this creative act on the
part of Yahweh. After all, what the Lord is actually proclaiming
is that, through these events, a new Israel will be born, and
through Israel, a new humanity and a new universe.

(c) Creation of Paradise

This historical and cosmic recreation is portrayed by the
prophet in the image of the exodus. Just as Yahweh prepared
a people of God on the journey through the desert to the land
of promise, so now the people will be transformed on this new

historical pilgrimage. They will be transformed precisely in their act of converting the earth into a paradise, their conferral of eschatological historicity on the primordial paradise.[12]

The Lord's reply to the "poor and needy" in search of help is not a mere spiritual counsel. On the day of glory God will transform human beings' whole reality, "that all may see and know, observe and understand, that the hand of the Lord has done this, the Holy One of Israel has created it" (Isa. 41:17–20).

> In the desert I make a way,
>   in the wasteland, rivers.
> Wild beasts honor me,
>   jackals and ostriches. . . .
> Thus says the Lord who made you,
>   your help, who formed you from the womb. . . .
> I will pour out water upon the thirsty ground,
>   and streams upon the dry land. . . .
> They shall not hunger or thirst. . . .
> Sing out, O heavens, and rejoice, O earth,
>   break forth into song, you mountains.
> For the Lord comforts his people
>   and shows mercy to his afflicted.
> [Isa. 43:19–20; 44:2–3; 49:10, 13; see
> 43:21; 44:1–5; 49:9–13; 51:11; 52:11–
> 12; 55:12–13]

(d) Creation-Liberation: The Servant of Yahweh

This new creation is a historical act. In other words, it does not occur by God's laying hands on things and turning everything topsy-turvy without human intervention. Yahweh works historically, by stirring to action human beings who, in implementing their own designs, consciously or unconsciously accomplish the divine work. For the prophet, this is the case with Cyrus, king of the Persians. It is he, rather than the people of Israel, who will be the strong right arm of the Lord. This cooperation between God and human beings, although occurring beyond the borders of Israel, can be so profound and meaningful that the prophet actually bestows on Cyrus the name which Israel reserves antonomastically to David and his eponymous successor: the Anointed One, the Messiah.

> Thus says the Lord to his anointed, Cyrus,
> whose right hand I grasp. . . .
> It was I who made the earth
> and created mankind upon it;
> It was my hands that stretched out the heavens;
> gave the order to all their host.
> It was I who stirred up one for the triumph of justice;
> all his ways I make level.
> He shall rebuild my city
> and let my exiles go free
> Without price or ransom,
> says the Lord of hosts [Isa. 45:1, 12–13].

It will not be Cyrus, however, who will bring this complete re-creation to its culmination. Second Isaiah speaks of a personage called the servant of Yahweh — Yahweh's child and favorite, the elect of God, the perfect, conscious divine instrument. Doubtless the servant is the new Israel, the Lord's people, purified by God and obedient to the divine ways. But he is also, in the midst of the people, a special individual, who by reason of his absolute fidelity to Yahweh and to the people is the living link, the covenant between God and God's people — indeed, between God and all peoples.

This figure is the needed historical ballast for the new exodus depicted by the prophet not as a mode of life unencumbered with difficulty, but only as the end and fullness of the journey. Various passages (Isa. 42:2–3; 49:4–7; 50:4–8; 51:7; 52:14; 53:2–12) speak of the tragic side of this figure. Yes, he will ultimately triumph, but only after being subjected to calumny, contempt, persecution, imprisonment, torture, and finally, an ignominious death, all because he will have been a champion of justice and loyalty, because he will have answered for others, and borne the burden of our sins. This figure in the poem shows us that historical creation is inevitably liberation, and that one gives life only by bestowing one's own life.[13]

4. ISRAEL AND LATIN AMERICAN CHRISTIANITY

This summary has shown the movement from the promise fulfilled to the historical act of judgment and salvation—from sacred history as past, to be celebrated and preserved, to its revelatory relevance for present and future. Here God's action is present as creation. It bears all three marks of creativity. Its proper subject is God, who operates with utter, irresistible sovereignty (although the divine plans are implemented through instruments); the action is novel and surprising; finally, it is a salvific, life-giving action. The creative action occurs in history, then; it is always occurring, but at times it appears in an especially visible, striking, decisive way. It occurs always in the same, lifegiving way. And it occurs as God's personal, free expression not only as self-revelation, but as self-bestowal. This activity of God's is neither intramundane nor magical. It follows a historical processuality, and can be observed only by faith, although the word that proclaims it and the heart that awaits it help discover it when it occurs and endorse it with their response.[14]

Surely it would not be an exaggeration to say that the history of Israel's arrival at faith in creation through faith in salvation parallels Latin American history in many ways. Of course, the details are different. And of course our reading of the Old Testament is done through the lens of the Jesus event. But saving these differences, surely the main lines of the two histories are parallel:

(i) Israel sprang up as a people in the conquest of Canaan, convinced that they were a chosen people, to whom God was delivering that land. With time, the conquerors fused with the native populations, and a syncretism appeared at all levels, including the religious. There was always an insistence on the importance of maintaining the purity of Yahwism, however, and Yahwism eventually came to constitute the substrate of the entire culture. Yahwism's institutional apparatus was a fundamental part of the state, enjoying various degrees of autonomy depending on the era and the persons involved.

Today's Latin America originated with the constitutive encounter of the native peoples of this continent with a Christian people that believed itself chosen by God for the grand mission of the evangelization of the New World. This encounter took on the political and military guise of conquest, and the economic form of colonization. But for more than a few missionaries, evangelization was so substantive that it, too, took on political, economic, and cultural forms. With time, the conquerors fused with the native population, and a syncretism appeared at all levels, including the religious, although the religious institution was always watchful in maintaining a purity of faith. Eventually Christianity impregnated the culture and the institutions of Latin America to such an extent that we can speak of its radical Catholic substrate. And the church institution formed a basic part of the power structure, although with varying degrees of autonomy, depending on ages, places, and persons.

(ii) In this state of affairs, Yahwism (or Catholicism) tended to regard itself as sacred, in the sense of set apart from life and history. Yahwism (Catholicism) was not open to discussion. It was part and parcel of the patrimony—of an original deposit to be safeguarded and defended at all costs as the sealed font of life. Thus understood, religion tended to be expressed primarily in custom—that is, in rules and guidelines (ideological, institutional, cultural, and moral references) which endowed the group with an identity and maintained its cohesion. The religious institution was distinguished by a strict separation of priests and faithful. The priestly word was reduced to a gloss on a gloss— to the interpretation of the religious institution. And its social function was one of simple endorsement of whatever was handed down by the hierarchy.

(iii) Under these conditions, an appeal to God's currency or novelty—any attempt to "try God out" in the present, in the current historical experience of God's presence, word, and will—becomes suspect and indigestible, non-assimilable. The gospel has given way to Christian doctrine (or the Torah) and ecclesiastical discipline, and any attempt to restore its primacy tends to be regarded as a threat.

(iv) Any proclamation or experience of God that goes beyond the maintenance of the basic order as summed up in the law and order of the present, any suggestion that faith involves response to and acknowledgment of God's creative and current action in history, calls established religion into question. It calls it into question from within, inasmuch as the God who "happens" is the same God who has already "happened," and who seeks to accomplish the same divine work and deed. But, while transpiring in the same spirit, God's intervention is not reducible to a mere restoration. It involves historical novelty.

(v) This breach with the past occurred with the rise of prophecy. Through the prophets, God appeared as the one who creates in history, the one who opens history up, but not in a magical way—in this case, it was through catastrophe. Established religion in post-exilic Judaism accepted prophecy in principle, but with such obtuseness that it constituted it an office. Of official prophets Jesus said "that they build the prophets' tombs . . . and thereby fill up the measure of their fathers who killed them" (Matt. 23:29–32). This same historical breach is occurring in Latin America today, largely through the impulse of its Christian being, which seeks to resolve, or at least attenuate, the contradiction between evangelization and colonialism that pervades its history as it marked its birth and institutionalization. In its most current expressions, the Latin American church has recognized the prophetic warning: We live in a situation of sin, and the church institution is not outside this situation. But at the moment of drawing the conclusions from this theological judgment, part of the church institution vacillates or retreats, while, even more significantly, the rest of the power structure seeks desperately to prevent the church institution from changing its social locus.

(vi) It is no exaggeration to speak of our peoples' situation as one of catastrophe. Like Jeremiah, many Latin American Christians (including priests and prophets like him) can testify to their experience of blackest night and the shadows of death. And, again as with Jeremiah, this terrifying experience of the dark night inspires in them not merely fidelity, but hope, and even joy. The psalmist asks: "Will the shades rise up to thank you?" I can personally testify that many people, old and young alike, reduced by the established order to mere shadows of themselves, are rising up to give thanks to God, and fortified by faith, rise up in quest of life in the name of Jesus of Nazareth. "Will you work your wonders among the dead?" (Ps. 88:11). In

Latin America today, so many torture victims, families of the "disappeared," peasants, laborers, and settlers expelled from their lands, their work, and their houses; union activists, members of neighborhood committees or human rights groups, servants of the word threatened and harassed; so many who hunger, are naked, subjugated, ill, and suffering, can prophesy, from their own experience: "But your dead shall live, their corpses shall rise; awake and sing, you who lie in the dust. For your dew is a dew of light, and the land of shades gives birth" (Isa. 26:19). Such is the gospel of our almighty God, the creator of all, who stands with us in Latin America today.

PART TWO

FROM CHAOS AND COSMOS
TO FAITH IN CREATION

CHAPTER III

From Ambivalent Experience to Faith in Goodness

1. STATE OF THE QUESTION

(a) From the Experience of Creation to That of De-creation

The Latin American people, including myself, have had experiences of creation. We are witnesses of the fact that where sin abounds, grace abounds the more, and that strength is accomplished in weakness. The shape of our world is one of death, but the night has slowly crept past its darkest hour. And so to us, this is a moment of salvation.[1] It is the hour of the peoples. Even our massacres attest to this. The suffering of our continent gives the lie to any rhetoric of mere optimism, for surely nothing, not even the most promising future, could justify the sacrifice of such an enormous number of persons. But the way in which this suffering is confronted does give reason for hope. A believing, oppressed people relies on God. It stands firm (see Isa. 7:9), and so has an experience of a creative God. And if neither hunger, nor unemployment, nor political dismemberment, nor repression has been able to shatter our peoples, then what can separate us from this hope? Death, where is your victory (1 Cor.

15:55)? Our people say, "You never lose hope as long as you have faith." This is not voluntarism or fanaticism; nor does it show a perfect grasp of our long, uneven historical journey. It is theory, then. Indisputably, there is historical creation in Latin America; there are new human beings here, and the seeds of a new society.

But precisely in this experience of life reborn and hope recovered, we have also experienced the stark, violent contrast of the deeds of the powers of oppression and the forces of death. It is not a matter merely of the "passivities of the real" (Teilhard de Chardin) or of the contest between being and nothingness, inertia, exhaustion, of the temptation to routine and resignation. It is a matter of a contest with other powers among us and within the established order. Does every noble effort, whether individual or collective, social or cosmic, not inevitably "wind down"? Do we not always have to begin anew? Does repression not surely rear its ugly head ever and again, whenever attempts are made in the direction of liberation, producing a situation that seems worse than the one it replaces?

We wonder, then, how far our power of self-creation, and creation of history, extends. More radically, we wonder how far the creative power of God reaches.

Does not this struggle, which Paul felt within him (Rom. 7:14–22), as well as in the history of the cosmos (Rom. 8:19–23), express a certain insuperable dualism?

(b) Two Powers?

Our option is for life to the limit, to the hilt, in all abundance, and for all. We do not accept the sacrifice of some to the power of others. We place our bets on boundless life, as shared gift. And nevertheless, as we proclaim this gospel, there are those who regard themselves as our enemies, and ourselves as members of a band of hooligans. We try to be builders of peace; and yet, without wishing to, we find ourselves on the battlefield of a war to the death. Despite our best intentions, must we not confess our inability to conjure away a certain insuperable dualism? Would it not be more honest to accept this as a fact, and work within the factual?

As the storm clouds of World War II loomed, Freud presented human life and history as disputed by Eros and Thanatos, which he saw as eternal and indestructible powers. In his attempt to universalize his experience by way of a scientific approach, he had no other choice but to adopt the old myth of the eternal return.

Today, the euphoria of the nineteenth century—the myth of progress—would seem to have withered and died. We experience development as an ideology[2] to which people's actual lives are sacrificed, and whose most comprehensive and symptomatic expression is the arms race, a contest that fills the developed peoples with terror and prevents them from enjoying the comfort for which they have sacrificed so much of their humanity. Most people feel trapped in a suffocating morass of dilemmas. The alternatives proposed by their leaders all seem unacceptable, and, prostrate with frustration and disillusion, they prefer to keep their mouths closed and their heads in the sand.

Can we help recalling the ancient wisdom of Ecclesiastes? Everything in due course. We must recognize the times in which we live. Live these times to the hilt. Surrender to them. The challenge addressed to us today is not to force new schemas on things, but to accept the polarity and alternation of human affairs, and of all things created, as a given, a fact, and go on from there. Humanity has not been granted the power of determining its times and seasons. Time has other rulers, suprahuman and infrahuman. Let us accept the determinism that looms over our limited destinies, and play the game of life not with nostalgia, but with realism and passion.

Were this schema to express the truth of the matter, the most that could be said is that, if the hour of resistance is over and done now for the Latin American people, then the silent, fecund hour of building and planting is at hand. Let us take advantage of it, for it will be limited, and then, right on time, it will be our enemies' turn. There may seem to be some opportunity for historical creation at the moment; but the tide of history will sweep away all that we have built, as, each day, the sea destroys our footprints in the sand. In this schema, an individual, a human group, even a people, can choose its life with an enormous determination to force things, fate, and the measure of things, in protest against a situation that is degrading and unjust. This would be a heroic deed, and one that will be celebrated in song and saga. But its price will always be death.

Our question, then, bears not only on the extent of our power of self-creation in history, but, more radically, on the extent of God's own creative power. Is it an irresistible power, as Amos, Hosea, Isaiah, Jeremiah, Ezekiel, and especially Second Isaiah prophesied? Or is it limited by the fragility of creation — or even by some rival power?

(c) The Mystery of Iniquity

We must confess from the outset that we have personal experience of the power of death as irresistible. For us, the "mystery of iniquity" (2 Thess. 2:3), that favorite theme of apocalypticism, is not, as perhaps it was in the 1970s, an irrational figment of the imagination utterly to be discarded in a sorely needed process of demythologization. With all due allowance for its fantastic (and, for that matter, merely allegorical) visual imagery, we must admit that its brutal presence and authentic shape are so graphically discernible today that our own tendency would be precisely to embrace it in all its realism. How easily we could be seized and immobilized by this reality! The critique of fetishism that prevails in our society has become remarkably obsessive. Might it not actually suggest the victim's secret fascination with its own ritual sacrifice?

Our experience will never be adequately expressed by the series of problems that plague underdevelopment (including cultural, psychological, and spiritual underdevelopment), or by the problems of the opposition of classes in the productive process, with their political and ideological expressions, or even by the notion of personal sin (individual or social). It is not a matter of denying the responsibility of these causes, however, or even of adding to the list. At the level of examination — the scientific level — there are no further causes. But these historical agents wreak such catastrophe that it would appear that the effect overflows not only the subjective will of those who create them, but the very deed they do. It is as if the mechanisms involved acquired an autonomy of their own, and simply went berserk, firing at random. The evil perceived is not only quantitatively greater, but qualitatively more monstrous than anything that could issue from those sources. Above all, it is an evil that seems to fail to maintain any relationship with ends or purposes. Hence the measureless grief and profound discouragement of its victims—the grief Jesus must have felt in his agony in the garden (Matt. 26:38).

Must we not conclude that the power of God is less than irresistible? That if God creates, another destroys? That our history is sealed by a struggle of the gods?[3]

As I observed in the introduction, Christian faith in creation is a victory. It is indeed one that must extend beyond the polarization that is so prominent a feature of our cultural horizon. What, then, chiefly composes this horizon of ours?

2. COMPONENTS OF OUR HORIZON: COSMOS AND CHAOS

In general terms, I call this conflictive polarization of our horizon "cosmos and chaos," since each bloc's qualification of itself as good and the other as evil is built first of all on a parameter of the order that makes human life possible (at least in terms of the system's understanding of "human").

I shall describe the first two pairs of opposites in terms of the way they are usually understood in our milieu. They make up the system of coordinates in which our peoples have always found themselves, forced there by outside and enemy wills rather than by any freedom of their own to determine their own place. The third pair describes the historical subject or agent which, by way of self-imposition, draws the other coordinates.

(a) North-South

The shorthand "North-South" refers to the developed countries on one hand and the Third World on the other. This polarity can also be expressed in other antitheses, emphasizing other aspects of the opposition as defined in the North and frequently internalized in the South: civilization versus barbarism, progress versus backwardness, enlightenment versus routine, light versus darkness, Christianity (or post-Christianity) versus paganism. This same antithesis is reproduced within each individual country of the North-South polarity. Specifically, in Latin America it stands for the oppositions between bourgeoisie and people, educated and illiterate, whites and natives (or blacks or mestizos), city and country, capital and province, and so on.

In the beginning was the South. From thence the North emerged. Civilization springs from barbarism, we hear, cosmos from chaos, and the order generated will be a precarious one, in ceaseless need of renewal and restoration. Cosmos is interior to chaos, and hence never quite accomplishes its task of cloaking over its lawless host, of conquering the interior darkness, which, at least as residue and seed, forever lurks in the so laboriously established order itself. If civilization arises from barbarism, it will have to avoid contaminating itself with it. *Mestizaje,* mixture, is always degradation. In the face of this perilous possibility, the only solution is domination: Either dominate the barbarians or be barbarized. There need be no war, as the South lacks the power of the North. Repression will do. The order of civilization is just the right medicine for the barbarians. Violence comes only out of the South; what the North provides is justice.

With enlightenment, backwardness yields to progress. The civilized understand the barbarians, then, but not vice versa. Hence the legitimacy of tutelage and protectionism, and the uselessness of spending a great deal of time attempting to show the Third World the advantages of submitting from the outset. Animals, children, and the uncivilized always reject the yoke. But this is only because they do not understand the yoke. The yoke is the only way to bring them to reason.

Northerners preach one god: reasonable, luminous, and humane. Here is the god who *annuit coeptis,* who nodded assent to the Northern enterprise. "In God we trust," then. Here is self-styled Western Christian civilization. Side by side with a religion like this one, the gods of the South are but grotesque, sanguinary idols. The truth of this Christianity is attested by the prosperity of the nations that proclaim themselves Christian. Hence the confidence of these nations in the god who fosters their undertakings.

(b) West-East

The shorthand "East-West" designates the polarity between what remains of the Soviet bloc and the liberal democracies of the developed West, along with their respective spheres of influence. With increasing reluctance (hence the need for invasions, destabilizations, and economic and political wars), Latin America still falls within the zone of influence of the United States, the undisputed leader of the Western bloc. Any exceptions, subjected to "economic sanctions" and ongoing harassment, serve only to prove the rule. As the West understands it, this opposition could be characterized in terms of democracy versus dictatorship, tolerance versus repression, person versus party (and state), liberty versus totalitarianism, open world versus closed world, Christianity versus atheism.

As in the foregoing case, this opposition is reproduced within each member country of the power bloc. In Latin America, for those who style themselves the representatives and guardians of Western Christian civilization, the "communists" are the Marxist-Leninists, the socialists, the revolutionaries (who call themselves humanists and Christians), workers' movements and organizations, defenders of human rights, and so on. Growing sectors of the church institution are, in this acceptation, "communist," and therefore naive tools of Moscow or the Eastern bloc.

In the past, the East was almost like the West (although barbarism still persisted there, among the masses as among the ruling classes). But then the East rose up in its pride and embraced that heresy of the West, that diabolical perversion of right order and hierarchy, communism. The diabolical had always lurked in the West. But now it was hypostatized, and laid claim to world sovereignty. Will the evil from without succeed in overcoming and subjecting Western Christian society? Will evil manage to penetrate the citadel of good, and corrupt it utterly? Poverty and injustice are communism's natural allies. If the poor and downtrodden have neither a decent life nor any understanding of the ideological wiles of the East, especially if the number of these poor continues to grow, the socialist temptation will be irresistible. But if this society is converted to Westernism, it will become the right hand of God. It will be invincible. If the West prevails, this will be because it is in the West, for all its sins, that the finger of God is discernible. If conversion fails, conquest will do. When all is said and done, the inevitable outcome of this schema will be war, since the East has the strength of the North. (After all, it is part of the North.)

But will this not surely be a holy war? The sins of the West are human sins. Who does not long for wealth, for power, for pleasure? As society is organized, and with life so short, is it not normal that selfishness should be so much in evidence? But the East rejects God, and deifies the party and the state. Surely God will be with those who place their trust in him?

If this is the meaning of this war, there is no room for neutrality. Tolerance is criminal weakness. On such an enemy, only overwhelming superiority will be of any effect, since reasoning has no value in its eyes. Tolerance has a meaning in our eminently fluid, versatile society. But it would be shameful resignation to the mind of that one-piece machine, that fetish whose only aspiration is to world domination.

(c) Established Order versus Recusants

The established order is first of all the state—not the state in the narrow sense of government, or even in the sense of the bureaucratic apparatus of government, but in the seemingly vague, and yet so effective, sense of the general will as power. The reference is in the first place to the apparatus of state, business (especially multinational corporations and the media), and the army. But secondarily, intermediate entities come under the umbrella of state, especially religions. The antithesis of the established order will be constituted by the marginalized, victims of discrimination, rebels, and any organization whose aim is the establishment of another order. The first to come under this heading are the absolutely poor, especially when they come to understand that they are impoverished; secondly, there are those who are neglected in the institutional distribution of power, when they do not wish to sue for their rights within the established framework; then come the crowds of the unemployed, the abandoned sick, those living alone, and the living damned: addicts, homosexuals, the colored poor, and so on. Finally, there are those who, for ethical or ideological reasons, abjure the established order and either fight to build another or simply refuse to play the game.

In an abstract (componential, contractualist, or functionalized) society, the danger of disintegration and anomia, even of war waged by all against all, is obvious. This danger finds an adequate counterweight only in the constitution of the state as Leviathan (Hobbes). But this mortal deity (for indeed it is a deity) must put to death anything that transcends it, even if only symbolically. It must redefine the value and the frontiers of life and death. It fulfills the function of nature for the individual who has been withdrawn from nature and transformed into a cultural being. It demands the surrender of everything, and then returns what it judges to be just, now in the form of institutionalized ownership endorsed by law (Rousseau). The manner of determining the nature of the just is beside the point (whether by the general will, by the dictates of one's social betters, or by experts). What matters is its absolute, transcendent value — to the point that anyone unwilling to submit to freedom (justice) voluntarily will be forced to be free (legally free: a citizen of Leviathan).

This order is fond of proclaiming itself a-theistic. It justifies its claim by its abstract condition. Religion is personal (that is, private). What it is actually proclaiming, then, is: With me, everything; without me, nothing. In other words, Leviathan understands itself, and not God, as the source of life within its order, as the creator of life, and especially, as master of life (Baal).

All three of these models function jointly in our society, creating an all-pervasive polarization. One very important sphere of their influence is to be found in the schemas of sensibility, and in the symbolic archetypes. These are diffused not only in a conceptual, operative way, but in a visceral, subliminal way, as well — in television advertisements, fashions, customs, soap operas, comics, and so on. Let us attempt to sort out some of their underlying traits:

Humankind's division into good and evil is absolute and unquestioned; it requires no argumentation or explanation. The good are the ones on our side; the evil are the others. The evil resort to brute force, even if they occasionally enjoy some technological advantage. They are primitive. They are less well organized, more massified. They are inferior. Eventually they fall into torpor and are defeated—although, at times, in their revolts or invasions, they cut a wide swath through the midst of precious lives. Their victims are the price we must pay for the reestablishment of order.

The good are white, urbane, modern, technological, and very controlled. They know their superiority, and can therefore affect tranquillity and confidence; but the normal order (the established order) is always in danger, and resources are all focused, in an inflexible, orderly manner, on the banishment of the danger.

The evil are different. If they are beautiful, their beauty is a barbaric one. More usually they are ill-proportioned, inharmonious, greedy, needy, vulturelike. At first glance they are capable, powerful, invincible. But they have structural weaknesses, and these will prove their ruin. They would like to snatch the paradise of the good for their own, but they will never succeed. They are many, but their place will always be in the exterior darkness.

Ultimately, the good are the wealthy, and the poor are evil. War, then, is the only prospect, and we may as well resign ourselves to this fact. The "others" will never be exterminated. Or at any rate exteriority—poverty, marginality—will never be eliminated, so that outsiders will crop up everywhere and always. Nor can the "others" ever be converted; they cannot come over to "our side." The reason is very simple. Ours is an order stamped with finitude, with scarcity. Places are limited. We, the chosen, readily come to believe that our order is the natural one. The threat from without, which must be exorcised, convinces us that victory, while costly, will be well worth the sacrifice. And the first thing to be sacrificed is criticism of the established order. The second is isolation, and a refusal to make a commitment to safeguard the order that benefits all who live within its borders.

It is certainly not temerarious to assert that a part of the church institution, in its uncritical acceptance of so-called Western Christian society as Christendom (although it criticizes its abuses) — understanding Christendom as the result of an evangelization of culture that through a process of centuries has succeeded in penetrating the several elements of that culture, and even more so its constitutive nucleus — readily opts for a perspective of chaos versus cosmos, and within this perspective aligns itself with North, West, and the established order. The result? War without quarter against non-jurors — against the East and its internal agents, and against all that is regarded as barbarism. And we have, in a very literal sense, a church militant.

(d) Fetish versus Numinous

Harassed by these enslaving, highly ritualized polarizations, we may be seriously tempted, however unconsciously, to "buy" the chaos-versus-cosmos schema, and simply throw in our lot with the excluded, chaotic member. But if we take this approach, we promptly collide with a fourth representation of the chaos-cosmos background: the fetish versus the numinous.

The fetish would be the extreme form of chaos — Saturn devouring his children. As the executioner is an incarnation of evil, the victims, as such, will be sacralized as well. Hence their numinous character in our minds. Some of the more common characterizations of this representation of the cosmos-chaos horizon are: the United States versus Latin America, the bourgeoisie versus the people, a consumer society versus a popular culture, the organizations of the system versus popular organizations, the right versus the left.

An apocalyptical, fundamentalist Christian consciousness will reinforce these polarizations, but will thereupon proceed to add new ones: the bourgeois church versus the popular church, the church of officially endorsed movements versus the church of the base communities.

The condemned member will suffer extreme marginality and injustice, and will be excluded from the possibility of ever emerging from its misery. Here, life is experienced as profoundly irrational and ruthless. It is not easy to discover meaning under such conditions. Hence the propensity to adopt an oversimplified view, characterized by stark contrasts. There can be no politics—no mediations, no "paths." The dilemma is that there is only life and death. In this situation, an interpretation of Marxism as both mechanistic and voluntaristic (which terms are not contradictory, but complementary, in practice) seems to solve the problem of meaning, and offer an extreme solution. If to this is added a social interpretation along the lines of Christian millenarianism, the result is a truly explosive mixture.

It goes without saying that the appearance on the scene of this polarization reinforces the seeming justice of the previous three, bestowing legitimation and a "fine-tuning" on their mechanisms. And our polarizations become a ravenous, insatiable spiral.

3. EVALUATION OF THE CHAOS-COSMOS SETTING

(a) Not History but Theomachy

In a chaos-cosmos setting, the only salvation is a precarious one, never definitive, always under threat—and hence militant, sectarian, and self-repressive. Why? Because the creation of humanity is unfinished. And the reason it is unfinished is not that the process of hominization is still open, or that human beings must struggle with obstacles that endanger the process and can even cause it to collapse, but that the person is here insubstantial—something belonging to the West, the North, the "mortal god." Violence is original, primordial. Chaos comes before cosmos, and abides at its heart still; therefore, it cannot be transposed. More than this, violence is sacred: the forces of good against the forces of evil. We persons are steeped in violence; we are the battlefield of a contest that transcends us. Our mission as human beings is to enter this sacred military service. This is holy war. Our enemies too are personal beings—absolute and inviolable. At bottom, perhaps despite themselves, they are servants of the forces of evil. Hence one may placidly destroy them. There is no such thing as sin (or if there is, it is an effect, not a cause). There is only the war of the gods. There is no history; there is only theomachy.

(b) Roots of Polarization

Do not these schemas, thus described, coincide with the description of the situation set out in the opening chapter? The first three shape the setting in its dominant, overriding aspect; the fourth, in its recessive, buried aspect; and all four, the entire horizon. Our Christian faith in creation, it must be stressed, tells us that our horizon corresponds only to a distorted form of reality. These schemas force reality. Accordingly, from our faith in a creator who is concerned for creation, and who abides within creation, unfolding as love, we cannot accept that this polarized setting should express the original constitution of reality. Consequently, neither can we place ourselves at either term of any of these polarities.

Nevertheless, if these polarities factually characterize our situation, we cannot say that this is a mere chimera. Even in its alienation, it could not exist unless it were to be founded somehow on possibilities of reality—in this case, historical reality as a concentration of the various modes of reality.

The first explanation of the chaos-cosmos setting might be based on the limitations of cultures, especially in their organizing expressions. Cultures can deviate from their most creative direction, and instead of interacting, dynamically and simply, with their medium, allow themselves to be borne along by an instinct of self-preservation. This shift in direction implies a self-absolutization, as the institution now lives simply to stay alive instead of seeking justification in the performance of its function. It moves from the relative to the absolute, from conflicts at the heart of life to a war to the death. The non-assimilated, if it cannot be ignored, must be subjected or destroyed. And precisely to this end it is stripped of all value, even demonized.

But our polarization rests on a foundation sunk deep in the constitution of reality. It has aspects that are humanly conformed (relative cosmos), and others that are deformed, or inhumanly conformed (relative chaos), in every culture, in every human group, in every person. There are even cultures that, on the whole, can be qualified as more cosmic, just as there are others that must be regarded as more chaotic. Or again, one and the same culture can, at a given moment, be either more chaotic than cosmic, or vice versa. Nor will this evaluation be established solely on the basis of its ethical elements. A great many aspects must be taken into account: its dynamism and its capacity for order, with its consequent development or progress in the integral sense in which *Populorum Progressio* understands these terms, and so on. To be sure, this fluid hierarchization of socio-historical reality, which, of course, does not coincide with the three schemas we have analyzed above, need not engender polarization. In and of itself, it would rather stimulate emulation, interaction, and assistance. But the tendency described in the foregoing section generates the temptation to cling to the booty of the acquired (see Phil. 2:6), and this is the source of our polarizations.

But the ultimate root of this polarization lies in the fact that good actually is the engendering force of dynamic order (St. Augustine), and evil actually is the begetter of chaos. If these forces were subjects, and if their nature were homogeneous, albeit under opposite signs, the chaos-cosmos setting would indeed express the constitution of reality. The good creative God would be a limited being, incapable of stamping all reality with the divine seal and thereby saving creatures. And creatures would have been created to assist this God in what is really an impossible undertaking: universal salvation. Thus, reality across the board—divine, cosmic, and human—would be a death agony.

(c) Understanding This Setting

It must be admitted that reality bestows plausibility on this representation. Indeed, it is difficult to demonstrate its radical inadequacy. Nevertheless, from our faith, we Christians assert that neither good nor evil is an original, absolute, intramundial agent. Evil is the disintegrating tendency, the fragility, the personal incapacity of a group or an age. It exists more positively when it is a thrust toward inertia or destruction. It exists more expressly when it is a decision taken by groups or individuals. But in none of its versions does it transcend the incidental level in individual and social agents. It characterizes none of these agents adequately or substantially. Good exists as adequation, as vitality, as symbiotic relationality, as capacity to extract life and to give of itself as love. But on none of these levels does good totalize a subject. It is in this sense that "no one is good" (Mark 10:18).

Good and evil exist, then, but they do not constitute adequate and opposite subjects. On a scientific level of observation and analysis, good and evil must be seen as either human acts or the results of human acts (individual and social), or else experienced as such in their capacity as circumstances of nature that favor or oppose the realization of persons and cultures. In the first case we have ambiguity; in the second, partly our lack of dominion over nature, and partly nature's indifference to the human species, even though the latter is part of nature, and of course we experience this indifference alternately as benevolence and malevolence, even though it is actually only chance and necessity, whose effects on us are now positive, now negative.

(d) Struggle of the Gods?

Nevertheless, after this scientific demythologization, conceded in its entirety, we still experience reality as a struggle of powers. Marx, for example, shows us the secret of merchandise: The rift between social producers and private consumers prevents the latter from recognizing their contribution to the value of merchandise, which therefore seems to them to have its own value, and which is now unattainable owing to the withdrawal of surplus value. The producers do not recognize the work of their hands, their creatures, and must now deliver up their very lives in order to possess them. But with this mechanism exposed, why is the problem not reduced to one of means of production? Why does merchandise continue to be a fetish? Analysis has laid all of its parts out on the table—why does another, deeper drive put it back together again?

It is a commonplace that we continue to speak of "sunset" when it has been centuries since we have held geocentrism theoretically. We shall have to do away with the current mode of production, yes. But we shall also have to explain something: Whence this religious fascination, this worship of vanity, that sucks the vital sap of myriads of human beings, and that in so many revolutionaries provokes blasphemy, the hypnosis of fetishism, and the fabrication of new fetishes?

4. OVERTHROW OF THE CHAOS-COSMOS SETTING

(a) Faith as Victory

I should like to suggest that only a faith in a creator God, an almighty God-with-us, can break the spell of the chaos-cosmos schema. To begin with, where the life and death of humanity is decided, the religious dimension appears. This is a human dimension, and as such, an ambivalent one. It can be oriented to idolatry (and blasphemy, which is idolatry in reverse), or to the worship of the living and true God.

But faith in God can come only from God. The existence of this grace cannot be proved. It can only be testified to, and ultimately, authenticated by practice. Thus, only liberation from the chaos-cosmos setting "proves" the victory of this faith.

For us, this faith is bestowed on us in Jesus. By his death we know that God is with us, actually preferring us in some sort to the divine Son himself. By Jesus' resurrection we know that the one who is with us is the almighty creator, for whom death itself is no obstacle. And so that one is our savior, in whose sight there are no powers or rulers. That one is sovereign of all—not as a proprietor (Baal), however, but as the transcendent creator, who is a stranger to all necessity. The world, and ourselves in it, are the free unfolding of this love on the part of our God.

If we live by this faith, the chaos-cosmos horizon opens out. Good is now a transcendent dimension (God over all and God in all), while evil is an intrahistorical product. They are not two symmetrical poles. But we speak of living a faith, not of professing a doctrine. The result of living this indispensable faith is a relative atheism—atheism with respect to the divinity of the chaos-cosmos setting. Our good news is the proclamation that one can live in the open air.

We can cut our affiliation with their organizations, close our ears to their slogans, ignore their fashions, repudiate their leaders. They decree our political death, and behold, we live. We toil in their factories, in their fields, in their offices, in their hospitals, in their schools and universities. We toil there, however, not as their slaves, but as apprentices in the management of what will belong to us all one day. This system had held itself out as a god of life and death. It demanded our acknowledgment and submission. Today we are this god's atheists, and behold we live. This is "big news," and it is ours. We have discovered the limits of this system. The system is not almighty. Indeed, the power that will bring it down tomorrow is already present in seed. We have experienced the presence of this new power as a power that delivers us from the fear of death. Living in that fear, we had spent our lives, squandered them, as slaves. Now we know that our poverty can enrich others, and that in our weakness is made manifest the strength of God as salvation for all who dare to withdraw their fealty from these powers of death to live in our hope.[4]

(b) From Theomachy to History

But here a question arises. Will the victory of our faith while we are still in enemy country effect more than solidarity among ourselves? Will it change the chaos-cosmos setting as well? Unless we have this comprehensive change at least to an appreciable extent, our only choice will be war (cold or hot) and violence (within the individual, among individuals, and among groups and institutions), and there will be no opportunity for humanity to bridge the gap between the victims and their executioners. Our faith responds with the hope that the one who raised Jesus from the dead will not only transform our mortal bodies, but will create a world where justice dwells. For this one is our almighty God, our creator-with-us.

But the full identity between the liberator and the creator will appear only at the close of history. Meanwhile, our "understanding of the reality corresponding to the biblical idea of God . . . may be characterized as a historical understanding."[5] In history, faith experiences God the creator, but the absolute irresistibility of the power of this God-with-us will emerge only at the last.

Faith in the creator-with-us, then, ought to lead us also to moderation in our *pathos* and in our conceptualization of our historical struggle for liberation. History, when sufficiently dense, assumes an idolatric dimension. It can also have a sacred dimension. If this dimension becomes substance, it will be removed from history, and seem now a fetish, now an image of God. This is not to deny the existence of these seeming fetishes and sacraments. But they are neither fetishes nor sacraments; they are ambiguous historical realities. This is what they are in themselves, and this is what they ought to be taken for by individuals and groups, even when they are acting as fetishes or sacraments. It is more convenient to deal with them as representations than as insuperably ambiguous realities (though some are more evil than good, others more good than evil). When a project is being implemented, the temptation to sacralize it, and to demonize what opposes or resists it, is all but irresistible.

Obviously the fetishistic dimension of a person, institution, or historical event is to be denounced, and the sacramental dimension proclaimed. Ex-President Reagan would be a prime candidate for the former process, and the Christian base communities will readily qualify as examples of the latter. But Reagan is also a person for whom one ought to pray, and was president of a nation which he interpreted, as it were, and which must be understood in relation to its circumstances. Similarly, the base communities can be the scene of power struggles, sectarianism, complacency, inertia, and a host of other limitations, all of which preclude their sacralization. We have a powerful tendency to oversimplify things. But our faith in the creator-with-us impels us to do justice to every aspect of reality. This should not lead us to perplexity and paralysis, of course. On the contrary, it ought to incline us to seek out channels of openness instead of entrenching ourselves in sealed blocs. Obviously it is easier to do this in the open air than in the Tower of Babel.

(c) Faith in Creation

In conclusion, we affirm the struggle because evil really exists, and it must be overcome. And we affirm it because good is deeper within us than we are within ourselves, so that we must transcend ourselves in order to possess it. But this struggle is not our death agony, because the most profound truth of all is the solidarity of our creator with us, and the absolute power of our God. Evil can go as far as to kill the body, and therefore we must fight with all our might to eradicate it. But even in the worst of cases, we are utterly in the hands of God. And the power of God is irresistible: Not even death stops God, for God is creator.

The chaos-cosmos setting is not sacred. That is, it is neither primordial nor eschatological; it is historical. No cosmic structure is divine; no kind of chaos is irreducibly antidivine. Every order has limitations and negative elements; every disorder has positive elements and is a candidate for salvation. No human being is only good; nor is anyone only evil.

Nevertheless, there are divergencies and confrontations. These must be acknowledged, in their relativity. There are paths that lead to life, and paths that lead to death. One must choose. The paths must be managed. They must be straightened out. This is a serious business. Lives are at stake, our own and others'. But all of this must be done without mutilating reality. Reality must be respected for what it is.

Faith in creation is adequate response to God's position in reality and adequate cooperation with the divine creative activity upon that reality.

God sides with the poor and oppressed. God judges the wealthy, the oppressor. God calls for conversion. However, God desires not the death of sinners, but rather that they be converted and live. God abhors nothing of the created; otherwise there would have been no creation. God creates out of free will, out of love. God creates by the divine word of benediction. What exists, then, is blessed, good, primordially good, only good, transcendentally good: not only good in principle, for the creative word of blessing resounds everlastingly. God is uttering that word now; and that word of God upon us is more determining than our own word.

Those who accept this as their setting, and as *the* setting, refuse to accept the notion that the established order is an expression of the truth of things. Faith in creation is thus protest, and hope, and principle of a transforming activity.

CHAPTER IV

Israel: Faith in Creation as Victory

1. STATE OF THE QUESTION

We live our lives in a strongly polarized setting. We have to deal with the all but irresistible temptation to explain reality as an eternal struggle between opposites. This temptation becomes compulsion when contending powers demand we blindly conform, allow ourselves to be molded by their slogans, join their struggles. In this context, our faith in creation can only be regarded as a victory. In worshipping God alone, we reduce these oppositions to the relativity of history, to realities embraced by the will of God, which we make our own, for universal reconciliation. This faith generates new eyes, to see the "cosmic democracy."[1] It gives us new hands, to transform all of these antagonistic contrasts into salutary antitheses and symbiotic varieties. But this victory requires a great deal of patience, and frequently takes the form of a hope against hope.

Our faith is a present experience; but it has biblical roots. From a point of departure in our own situation, then, let us strike a dialogue with the first chapter of Genesis, which was composed at a moment of great need, and of national prostration and disenchantment.[2] It represents the victory of a robust faith, then—one which could communicate serenity and hope.

This dialogue is also an explicitation of one of the presuppositions of our earlier propositions.

2. TEXT AND CONTEXT

This will not attempt to be a comprehensive study of the text of Genesis 1, of which there are many,[3] but a concentration on those considerations bearing most directly on our objective.

While the text may have been established only in the Persian era, it is undeniably an expanded version of a document with a very rich prehistory. Generations of priests had developed this composition in terms of the faith of Israel. The notion of God and God's relationship with the world, gradually molded all down through Israel's history, could not be expressed in terms of the surrounding culture. Thus, the creation accounts of Israel's neighbors had to be modified to suit the originality of the Yahwist faith. This could be accomplished only in a long, difficult struggle with neighboring religions, a fact evinced in the text's ambivalent echoes of Babylon, Canaan, and perhaps Egypt.[4]

First, there is the tripartite conception of the world held by Israel's neighbors, and altogether acceptable to Israel.

The universe has three levels: sky, earth, and subterranean abyss or water. The earth is a flat disk afloat on the waters. Stretched over the dome of the sky is the divine abode. The entire structure rests on a number of pillars. The heavenly bodies move across the breadth of the sky. Rain, snow, hail and wind are stored in their respective chambers above the sky.[5]

There is also a similarity in cosmogeneses—in the way in which various ancient civilizations imagined the formation of our universe. There are successive stages: The first is composed of separation and division—light from darkness, earth from sky, then the waters above from the waters below; then the edifice is constructed—the firmament or vault of the heavens; then it is peopled—the heavens with sun, moon, and stars, the sea with fishes, and the land with plants and animals.

But over this common frame of reference, the composition places a polemical content with regard to religious tenets. Not that this solemn, technical, and ritualized text ever suggests the possibility of an alternative religious view to its own. But the polemic it implies can be detected from a knowledge of the cosmogonies of the surrounding peoples and of the religious situation of the people of Israel.

(a) Cosmogonies of the Near East

The cosmogonic myths of the peoples around Israel were mutually inconsistent. But traits that must have been present in them can be identified from the rejection of them in the Priestly account of creation.[6]

Among Israel's neighbors, cosmogony follows theogony, and chaos precedes cosmos. This universal principle extended even to the gods, among whom it had its application in the victory of the younger gods over the more ancient divinities. The origin of reality is so far above good and evil that it first produces monstrous divinities and later the principle of order. Evil is as old as the oldest being. Indeed, evil in its chaotic form is the past time of the being defeated by the establishment of cosmos; thus the ordering god supervenes as the future of being. But is this movement irreversible? Surely not. After all, it has been violent; disorder has been overcome through disorder. Thus there was evil not only in the beginning, but in the very defeat of primordial evil. To create order is violently to destroy the "order of disorder." Creation is essentially ambivalent, then. This ambivalence is only compounded with the appearance of human-kind—sprung from the blood of the murdered rebel god. This origin seals human destiny: to serve the conquering gods by bearing their burdens.

The dominion of the ordering gods over original reality—both divine and amorphous, monstrous and threatening—can never be complete and consolidated. It must submit to a recurring cycle. The purpose of human beings is to assist the victorious gods in that cycle. This is the meaning of the ritual of the new year—the beginning of the cycle, the moment of creation. This is likewise the meaning of the rituals associated with the cycles of nature, which attest, in the death and resurrection of nature, to the everlastingness of the combat.

The final concretion of order is the state. Hence the political nature of worship, and the preponderant role of the king in that worship. Worship means the renewal not only of nature, but of the state, which imposes order in the name of the ordering god. Those chosen by the national god as servants of that order dedicate themselves to it heart and soul; but the chosen people as a people also rehearse the life-schema of the god, serve him or her, and make use of other peoples in doing so. The original, everlasting enemy, chaos, or evil, will find its historical symbol in the enemies that the king, who is the great servant of the national god, will have the mission to destroy.

These gods, ultimately personifications of the forces of nature, will be the expression of human dependency vis-à-vis those forces — an expression of the precarious balance that we may manage to establish, of the ambivalence we perceive in each force, and of the disjunction, indeed the hostility, seemingly obtaining among them. The monstrous will be reflected in the sea and the tempest; the orderer will be linked to the uranic (the sun, the moon, lightning, and so on); while the chthonian (earth-dweller) will be the consort of the heavenly divinity, as well as a deity in her own right who must be appeased and paid in order to penetrate and harness her. Human beings will be able to live by rendering each sort of divinity its due. To serve the gods, then, is indispensable for life. But it becomes an unbearable burden.

(b) Pagan Religions in Israel

As we have no space here to paint an adequate picture of the religions of the Old Testament people of God, we shall have to make do with a detail of that great fresco. I propose to focus on the extirpation of idolatry under Josiah in 629 B.C. (2 Kings 23:1–25). This event is most meaningful for our purposes, in view of the exceptional nature of the means employed, together with their scant success, evincing how deep were the roots that Yahwism was attempting to tear up.[7]

Jerusalem, Judah, and Israel were inundated with idols,

priests, and rites. The cults were ancient ones, established by kings of old in conformity with the customs of the land or of neighboring peoples.

Of the wide variety of cults, two stand out in bold relief, not only in the passage at hand, but throughout the entire prophetic, Deuteronomic, and Priestly literature. The first is the Canaanite cult of Baal and Astarte. These cults had a priesthood, as well as sacred prostitutes and temple slaves. They were fertility cults, and their ceremonies could be frenetic and orgiastic. The second is the Assyrian and Babylonian cults "to the sun, moon, and signs of the Zodiac, and to the whole host of heaven." Like those of Baal or Astarte, these cults were practiced in high places and sought to influence human destiny—which is why its priests were fortunetellers.

The costly, inexorable tone of these religions, which raised their devotees to the heavens and then dashed them to earth again, reached an extreme in the cult of Molech, to whom parents sacrificed their young children. At Jerusalem the crematorium was in the Valley of Ben-hinnom. These cults had invaded the Temple itself, where worship was offered to Baal and Astarte with the use of sacred prostitution. The adoration of the heavenly hosts had its symbols both within the Temple and at the entrance, where great horses were represented drawing the chariot of the sun.

The cult of Yahweh had thus become just one among many, and not always the principal one. Loyalties were divided, then, and so were human beings. In fact, even the cult of Yahweh was now a way of understanding and practicing religion deriving no longer from Yahwism, but from the invading religions themselves. Both the fertility gods and those of heaven are cyclical, and thus themselves subject to necessity, mutually limited, and therefore imposing on human beings, whom they reduce to their service. As nature divinities, they are amoral, and so they can be bought with offerings, although the basic intent is to assimilate their rhythm and share in their glory and their demise. But there is no ethic in their glory, nor any compassion in their demise. Religion symbolizes the iron law of nature. Does this leave any room for the call to history, to liberation, to personal loyalty, to hope?

(c) The Account in Genesis 1

In striking contrast with this background of the creation myths of surrounding peoples, and the religious practices of most of the Jewish people themselves, the Priestly account of creation, in its historical context, is absolutely unique. We are struck by the victory it represents: that it should have been conceived and redacted at all, let alone actually winning over the people.

God, sky, earth. Thus Genesis 1 sums up the whole of current existence. But it adds, by way of explaining the relationship of the three: God has created sky and earth.

Before there was sky or earth, there was only an amorphous chaos—darkness, or a murky abyss. God summoned light to exist, and light existed. Then God separated the light from the darkness, and fashioned the vault of heaven to separate the waters below the vault from the waters above it. In the seas this vault reached down to the waters below, and so the continents appeared. By the word of God the earth put forth the vegetable world, and the seas were peopled with living creatures. And on the vault of the sky, to measure times and seasons, God placed two great luminaries, and the stars. Finally, God created the beasts of the earth, and the human being. God did all of this. Such was the origin of the sky and the earth. Facing God, only chaotic, gloomy passivity. There is nothing more. Except God's word. God makes light. God divides, forms, orders, and distributes. God populates and blesses. And God verifies that all is good. God and God's word accomplish all of this. God and the serene, irresistible divine majesty. Nothing opposes God. Only God and creation, God and the divine deed exist. There is nothing more. By God's word were made the sky and the earth.

From the very outset, our narrative is in open conflict with the myths of the neighboring peoples, and the key of the divergence lies in its conceptualization of God.

3. CREATION AND THE DIVINE SOVEREIGNTY

(a) The God of Genesis 1

The first great contrast to be observed in the Genesis account is that there are no elements of a theogony, nor therefore of a theomachy.

The first chapter of the Bible narrates the birth of the sky and the earth, these alone. Not the birth of God. God is not born. The God of the Bible has never lain entangled in the confused mass of beginnings. God did not have to burst free of the abyss. In order to exist, God had no need to slip the suffocating embrace of sky and earth. God has wrested no one's supremacy by violence. God has had no other gods or monsters to combat. God has no need to stay on the alert against possible acts of vengeance on the part of defeated rivals. God is jealous or envious of no one. God has no need to create human beings for the sake of any service they may render. God has no need of anything whatsoever. God makes all things willingly, and effortlessly, purely for love.

Nor does God spring from the dark forces of the beyond. God has no competition. God does not even reign over other gods. These gods do not exist. There is only God, the Lord.

Nothing is known of God previous to the moment of creation. Indeed, the problem does not harmonize with the biblical perspective, "which has no wish to know God except from his creative act."[8] And this is the case not only because any knowledge of God apart from, or therefore antecedent to, creation is impossible, but first and foremost because it betokens a lack of faith to pretend to a knowledge that is always tantamount, in the mythologies, to a dominion over the divinity.

But this knowledge is also impossible because: "Nothing that has been created is contemporaneous with God. As creation has been accomplished totally in the time of history, none of its elements existed in the non-time of God. God's exteriority in relation to his creation is genuinely absolute."[9]

And the reason for this is that, for the author of Genesis 1, regardless of what other Semite peoples may have thought, God neither emerges from nature nor is part of its process. The author conceives of God as "outside the cycle of natural forces. He is none of them, nor even the sum of them all."[10] Hence the divine liberty vis-à-vis creation. Creation is not the emanation or reflection of the divine nature, but a product of its personal will.[11]

But if creation by word bars any naturalistic conception of the divinity, as well as all pantheism, then deism, too, is precluded: The arc of God's saving word spans an infinite distance, actually penetrating creatures more deeply than does their own existence. "This is the primordial miracle: that God would constantly address his word to creation across the abyss of formlessness and nothingness."[12] Truly we live by the word that issues from the mouth of God (Deut. 8:3).

(b) God's Sovereign Mercy and the Experience of the Covenant

Genesis 1 transcends its neighbors' cosmogonies in its notion of God. This notion proceeds neither from the science of the time, nor from the philosophical effort that, from China to Greece, characterized the era in which it was set down in writing.[13] So its origin must lie in the faith of Israel; concretely, it is found in the Priestly meditation on the covenant, now based on the prophetic contributions—most meaningfully, for our purposes, in Second Isaiah, but also in Jeremiah and Ezekiel, which both form part of the Priestly family of writings.

> The fact of creation is defined by a spate of words, orders, and indications coming from God. It is as if God directed Israel's fate. The omnipotent "And God said" (Gen. 1:3, 6, 9, 11, 14, 20, 24, 26, 28ff.) is as authentic a formula of God's promulgation of law as it is of the divine proclamation of prophecy. Even the judgment proclaimed by the text of Genesis—that the work accomplished by God on each day of creation is "good," or, in the case of the human being, "very good"—comes out of the experience that the God of Israel, especially as manifested in the Exodus from Egypt, has the power of absolute disposition over light and darkness, earth and sea; such elements are not, therefore, demoniacal, destructive, autonomous powers.[14]

Thus the doctrine of creation is the most extreme representation of the sovereignty of God as experienced by Israel over the course of its history. Speaking of Genesis 1:1, von Rad says: "The hidden pathos of this expression resides in the implication that God is Lord of the universe."[15] In other words, in Israel's darkest nights and deepest suffering, faith in a God of liberation could be adequately expressed only by faith in that God as creator. Indeed, against a backdrop of universal history (not only as experience, but as reflection), and in a living awareness of one's dependency on nature and such mighty forces, only a God who was creator, and free and sovereign as well as faithful, such as Yahweh, could warrant the hope of liberation.

For us Christians, this expression of faith in creation ultimately refers to the Reign of God proclaimed by Jesus. "The sovereignty of God is the exercise of the specifically divine function of God as creator. . . . The coming of such a kingdom means that God cares for human beings in order to actualize his 'dominion' in this world," which is nothing else but "the ancient love of the covenant, communion with God, in which God is still sovereign interlocutor."[16]

This is Jesus' intent when, by way of justifying his most novel proposition, in which he sums up not only his preaching but his practice, and the very core and substance of his gospel, he appeals to the creation theme: "You have heard the commandment, 'You shall love your countryman but hate your enemy.' My command to you is: love your enemies, pray for your persecutors. This will prove that you are sons of your heavenly Father, for his sun rises on the wicked and the good, he rains on the just and the unjust" (Matt. 5:43–5). Jesus has come to enable us to become children of God (John 1:12). But what else could this be but to be as the creator, whose dominion is grace and fidelity (John 1:17)?

If Christian faith in creation is cosmological and metaphysical, then what I have just said will be only an outrageous, confusing conceptual extrapolation. But if the object of faith is precisely this evangelical representation, then we need not hesitate to characterize it as a display of the love of God (Auer). The one who *divided the waters* below from the waters above is the one who causes the *rains.* The one who placed the greater luminary in the firmament is the one who *makes "his" sun shine* in a personalized way. On the basis of our rationality, we must admit that we cannot understand this proposition animistically. But in faith, we must maintain this proposition without any representation. What is creation, then? Salutary sovereignty, almighty love.

In our Christian faith, this is the first teaching of Genesis 1: God has absolute dominion over all that exists, and the content of this irresistible divine sovereignty is the existence and life of every being, together with the harmony of all creation. God's dominion is a personal covenant, gratuitous love.

(c) The Creative Act as Transcendent

A basic aspect of this sovereignty is its transcendence: "While creation is not contemporary with God, God is contemporary with his creation."[17] God is characterized by an immediacy, a parental solicitude; but all of this is beyond manipulation by creatures. God is irresistible, and faithful, while always reserving the "how" and the "when."[18] Creation is the object of faith, then, and not the conclusion of a reasoning process.[19] Not that this faith is unreasonable, or that a discreet, humble use of our reason is incapable of leading us to our creator.[20] The fact is that, while almost all peoples have had some notion that what exists has been made by some god, the notion of creation as proposed by Judeo-Christianity does not seem to be found apart from the "religions of the book."

From this viewpoint, one sees that Genesis 1 is very sober. "The Priestly Document resists the temptation to describe the creative act as such."[21] Even when (making use of the cosmogonical representations usual in his time) the Priestly author asserts that God separated (v. 4), made (vv. 7, 16, 25), or placed (v. 17), he renounces any attempt to show just "how" God did so. Thus the reference to the cosmic artisan is relegated to the status of an analogy, at most, if indeed it can be regarded as more than a simple image. Scholars have observed a tension between the creative word and God's immediate activity.[22] The latter would seem to be the more ancient representation. The fact that it was not simply replaced by the more sophisticated, refined word would indicate not only the author's fidelity to his sources, but also that he regarded the concept of the immediate divine action as an adequate characterization of God's immediacy with respect to creation, and especially, of God's personal concern. In other words, what we have in the text is a graphic presentation of the notion that what exists comes from God, and that this is why it has all been well made. Creation by the divine word seems to have been added to safeguard the absolute transcendence of this divine activity, and thus to strip the preceding representations of any connotations of a demiurgic, intramundane activity and fabrication.

Scholars find this transcendence expressed in the verb *bara*, whose grammatical subject in the Old Testament is not only always divine, but always precisely the God of Israel. Thus "no analogy is to be found between this creative activity, nor can any representation be developed of the same, since the divine activity can be represented only to the extent that it is like human activity."[23]

God is conceptualized as creating by way of the divine word and Spirit.[24] These "instruments" of creation are strictly divine. This establishes God's transcendent immanence in the act of creation, thereby precluding a search for analogies and representations of that act.

Creation implies a universal activity in the world on the part of God, and a total referral of that world to God. Thus there will be no category of thought adequate to receive it.[25] As universal, transcendent reason, the creator cannot be boxed into a cosmic rational schema.[26] The mere fact of a genuine, authentic causality does not mean that the creator, along with the divine creation, can now be picked to pieces according to a formal analytical schema superior to both.[27] The relationship between creator and creature is not a relationship of cause and effect.[28] The principle of causality is not the basic regulator of relations between creator and creation. The creator is not a cause in the sense of a link in a chain (even the first link), to be arrived at by regression along a continuum.[29] A denomination of God as first cause, by way of distinguishing this cause from intramundane, or "second" causes, "is no more than a theological figure of speech."[30] Of course, neither can we represent creation in words: "For us, it is incomprehensible how the spiritual word directly produces a material reality."[31]

Thus God's transcendence is reflected in the fact that we have no access to God's "non-time"; nor can we represent to ourselves or adequately conceptualize the divine creative act; nor is any *experience* of the sovereignty of God available to us. But this transcendence is our foundation, and we are therefore required to establish ourselves upon it (Is. 7:9), and in this sense called to *test* it. This physical test or proof of God (Zubiri) would be an act not of pretension, but of obedience.

God's sovereign transcendence of ourselves and the world (characterized in the Bible as glory and holiness), eludes specification not only by philosophy and science, but by the religious mind, as well. Not only is the sinfulness of religion as a *sacrum commercium,* on the twofold level of ritual and morality, revealed here, but also, and especially, its ridiculous futility, its vanity. Neither sacrifice nor observance of the law gives anyone a right against God. Creation is the free display of God's love. A human being addresses God out of need and desire; God responds only out of sovereign freedom. Indeed, God has loved us first. Creation is thus God's ineffable gift of self as Person. The only appropriate response to this divine bestowal is human surrender (Luke 1:38) — religion in spirit and in truth (John 4:23).

Another consequence of God's sovereignty over the world is the worldliness of reality. None of the latter is God. The universe is not divine. It is from God and in God. This is the unhesitating assertion of Genesis 1 regarding the powers. They are in the text: chaos, sun, moon, and nature. Let us say something about each of them.

4. GOD AND THE POWERS

(a) Overthrow of the Chaos-Cosmos Setting

"The earth was a formless wasteland, and darkness covered the abyss, while a mighty wind swept over the waters" (Gen. 1:2). The second verse of the Priestly account of creation is the object of the widest variety of interpretations, both as to its relation to the first, and as to the meaning and mutual relationship of its terms.[32]

If "In the beginning" has the indefinite, merely introductory meaning of "when," then chaos certainly pre-exists creation, and in either of two ways. Either chaos is absolutely pre-existent (as, for example, in Greek philosophy, or in the cosmogonies of

Israel's neighbors), or it pre-exists creation as the latter exists today, without prejudice either to what existed before this or to its relationship to God, which in this case would be of no interest to the author. The latter interpretation is compatible with the interpretation of "In the beginning" as referring to the beginning of what is real today if chaos is neither a component of this world nor the material of which the latter has been made. Some writers distinguish two creations — a first creation of chaos, and another, definitive creation of the sky and the earth — since, they argue, if God did not create chaos, its creator would have had to be neither God nor creature.

In my view, both by way of exegesis and as a Christian reading supported by tradition, it is appropriate to read "In the beginning" as it was read and interpreted by the writer of John 1:1. That is to say, we think that "the concepts employed in v. 2 are cosmological topics familiar to Priestly erudition."[33] What we have, then, is a representation. Its suitability, and even necessity, derive from the experience of chaos (storms, ground swells or tidal waves, earthquakes, the terrors of night, the wilderness, and so on) — in a word, from an awareness of the precariousness of the natural order.

> Chaos constitutes a perpetual threat to creatures. Here is a primordial experience of man, and something that puts his faith continually to the test, a test that faith in creation will have to surmount in the grand manner. Thus v. 2 teaches us to understand the miracle of creation from a point of departure in its negation; hence it begins by speaking of the formless, the unfathomable, whence the will of God has stirred creation and over which God constantly maintains it. For the cosmos stands in constant need of this creative and sustaining will.[34]

That this is the meaning of verse 2 would seem clear from the account of the Flood, which is likewise part of the Priestly corpus; the Flood is understood as an un-creation, but not an absolute one. The account of the Flood can also contribute to an understanding of each term and its relationship: *Chaos* would be the generic word (for which we should have to extract *tohu*

from its more specific traits, retaining only the condition of unin-
habitable void), and the other two terms would constitute
"description." Thus we should preserve the unity of inspiration
of the accounts, since, as has frequently been remarked, the
Yahwist account begins with a populated, watered desert, while
the Priestly account has in mind a flooded zone to be dried out
and supplied with channels. Thus we should have a dark, watery
mass, without any horizons, and shaken by tremendous churning
movement.[35]

At all events, the text makes it quite clear that chaos neither
offers resistance to God's activity, nor even serves as raw material for God's construction of the skies and the earth. Chaos,
then, experienced by the human species and perceived as an
everlasting threat, appears in our account as bereft of any power,
even of resistance, vis-à-vis God. It does not coexist with God
in the divine "non-time." Nor is it in any way God's rival.
Granted, "the creator's relationship with this chaos is not precisely determined."[36] God never creates it, or blesses it, or, still
less, exorcises or struggles with it, as God does in the poetic
writings of the Old Testament. But is not this "imprecision" a
most forceful expression of that residue without which we should
find it difficult to do justice to our experience, a residue that we
could never conceptualize in clear and distinct terms and yet
cannot disregard — hence the "justice" of these symbolic expressions as asymptotic lines or limit concepts?

God is the sovereign, to be sure. But is not our cosmos a
precarious mesocosm wedged in by us between the unfathomable abysses of the surpassing great and the immeasurably
small? The keys of the universe elude us; but is this only because
they have not been made to our measure? Is it not rather that
the universe is not "in itself," or properly "its own," so that
creation will be a "miracle," in the strictest sense of the word,
not just the miracle that the universe should exist at all, but also
the miracle that it should maintain relatively stable forms of life,
reaching all the way to homo sapiens, and that it should still
endure? Do we not continue to adhere to the notion, which we
hold in common with the ancients, that God is sovereign even
over chance and necessity? From our very science, our technology, and our politics, which have done so much to discover and

conceive regularity and establish stable orders, does not the lurking presence of the chaotic become even more evident and more disconcerting to us than it was to our forebears? Are we not all modern Atlases, bearing the world on our shoulders by means of a titanic effort? The ancients cast this care on the divinities of bygone times. But one of the results of the mundanization of the universe has been that we must bear its weight ourselves, as the place where we live. If von Rad, as an exegete, concludes that "the theological thinking of Genesis 1 moves not between the two poles of nothingness and the created, but between those of chaos and cosmos, instead," then must we not say that the concept of creation in our time can only be conceived as a victory over the threat of the chaotic—a threat more and more present to us the more we subdue the earth?[37]

If we fail to maintain the divine sovereignty over chaos as transcending every historical subject, then we fall into theomachism—that is, the chaos-cosmos setting. Any self-proclaimed cosmos demonizes exteriority, so that nothing will remain but a struggle between blocs, each of which will pre-contain its own depersonalizing framework.

Only faith in the almighty God-with-us who transcends all from within can deliver us from the anguish which leads us to define ourselves by the effort to endure, a definition that we express in war to the death.

(b) Overthrow of Astral Religion

Severino Croatto states of the Priestly creation narrative: "It is a unit, with its *theological* climax in verses 26–28 (man's creation) and its *telos* in 2:1–4 (the divine archetype of the Sabbath), but with its maximal *tension* in verses 14ff. (the creation of the stars—those regulators of the life of the cosmos in the mythologies, as they determine the calendar of cultures and of human activity in the "priestly" tradition)."[38]

Croatto's point is well taken. The disproportionate length of the pericope, its central position, the importance it ascribes to the creation of light on the first day, and the care with which it specifies the function of the stars in human affairs (something no other work does), all indicate the tremendous force of the belief to which it is opposed, and the danger this posed to the faith of Israel. Not only for neighboring peoples, especially Babylon, but for Israel itself the course of the stars determined the fate of individuals and peoples, and the sun, the moon, and the stars were actual names of divinities whose beneficent or malign influence brought life or ruin, and especially, the sequence of whose apogees and settings locked the course of human events in series issuing in glory or death. So people saw themselves stripped of their subjectivity. They were neither center nor source, but mere force field. Living was knowing what one had to do and doing it. Hence the anguish, the fear, and the sense of the inexorable that pervaded the life of the ancients. The most that could be done was to try to conjure the danger away — redeem life in exchange for something precious.

The basis of this religion will lie in an agricultural people's genuine dependency on sun and soil, as well as on the discovery of the cycles of various crops, which coincide with the appearance and disappearance of certain planets. It will also embrace the cycles of the moon, which coincide with the ideal rhythm for pruning and certain other agricultural tasks, not to mention woman's periods and everyone's state of mind. For the farmer, it is vital to know when each task must be performed, and to this purpose calendars must be invented, based not only on the moon and the sun, but on the position of the stars and planets. This science is vital for the life of the people, and therefore sacred. But from here it is only a short step to the sacralizing of its elements. And instead of placing these at the service of human beings, it is human beings who feel themselves to be prisoners of a "denaturalized" knowledge elevated to the status of religion.

But the text of Genesis demythologizes everything it possibly can. First it detaches the heavenly bodies from light, relegating them to a more modest, derived function. Second, it omits their names, referring to them generically as luminaries. Third, it deprives them of any influence on human destiny. Their role is to light the earth and distinguish day from night. They have no influence on life. They merely mark seasons and years. This modest function, however, does have a religious specification in the proclamation of festivals. "This emphasis was to be expected in the Priestly Document, where salvation history is refashioned into a liturgical history."[39]

And the "luminaries" do preserve one trait of personality and power: their finality is to rule (in the sense of governing or dominating) the day and the night. Still they have no influence on human destiny. And especially, it was God who made them and placed them in the firmament for this purpose. Thus the luminaries are things made by God. They are God's creatures.

The perception of a relationship between the stars and human fate outlived Old Testament times. The intertestamentary apocalyptical literature is obsessed with these heavenly signs. Jesus was often asked for a sign "from heaven" — a demand with which he consistently refused to comply (Mark 8:12; Luke 11:29–32; 12:54–6; John 6:30–36; Matt. 4:5–7; Mark 15:31–2; 1 Cor. 1:22–5). True, these terrible portents do appear in the synoptic apocalypses; but here, even in circumstances of such cosmic commotion, faith casts out fear (Luke 21:25–8).

Paul, too, warns his churches against "any empty, seductive philosophy that follows mere human traditions, a philosophy based on cosmic powers rather than on Christ" (Col. 2:8). Or again, "No one is free to pass judgment on you in terms of what you eat or drink or what you do on yearly or monthly feasts, or on the Sabbath" (Col. 2:16). God has toppled the "principalities and powers" (Col. 2:15). True, "while we were not yet of age we were like slaves subordinated to the elements of the world" (Gal. 4:3). But now, with the Messiah, we have died to the elements of the world (Col. 2:20) — in which case: "How can you return to those powerless, worthless, natural elements to which you seem willing to enslave yourselves once more? You even go so far as to keep the ceremonial observance of days and months, seasons and years! I fear for you; all my efforts with you may have been wasted" (Gal. 4:9–11).

St. Thomas devotes a considerable amount of space to this subject in his *Summa Theologiae*. First, in treating of the works of the fourth day, he discusses all of the objections about the place of this day in the whole series, and strongly emphasizes that the stars are made for the sake of human beings. Then he acknowledges the power of the stars as "moved movers" of the heavenly bodies, and even concedes their influence on the human body and hence indirectly on the understanding. But he emphatically refuses to admit that they might have any power over the freedom of the human will—provided, of course, that the will determine itself, and not be determined by the passions; hence the saying, "Who rules his passions, rules the stars." Any direct influence on the human will is attributable to God alone.

This Christian understanding has always been maintained in the church. It is not a consideration that would be somehow secondary to the core of Christian faith, but is part and parcel of the very heart of that faith. It is strictly and ineluctably implied in the doctrine of the subjection of all "powers," like all the rest of the hierarchy of creatures, to God, with neither earth nor sky, but humankind occupying the highest station in that hierarchy.

Our world, too, is filled with astrologers and fortunetellers. Today more than ever we need a faith in the creator-with-us, who delivers us from the fear of determination and blind fate and restores us to the joy of a precarious freedom.[40]

5. THE CREATOR'S STAMP

(a) Sovereignty of God and Unity of the Universe

The power of the stars is paltry in our text, in comparison with the power of nature: "Let the water teem with an abundance of living creatures . . ." and "let the earth bring forth all kinds of living creatures." Earth and water bring forth life. Such is the generative power of nature.

The Priestly text acknowledges the existence of "powers." Faith in creation does not mean an idealistic assertion of freedom, or an attempt to evade the human condition. The subject of faith, on the contrary, is constituted by persons who accept their earthliness. In fact, it is faith itself that enables them to make this humble, joyful, and grateful act of acceptance.

But the structure of the account indicates the hierarchized unity of reality, and human beings' place in that hierarchy, with supreme energy.[41] "Just as Gen. 2:4bff. [the second creation account] establishes the human being as the center of God's activity, so Gen. 1:1ff. [the first account] establishes him at the peak of the cosmological pyramid."[42]

The upper strata of the pyramid of creation depend on the lower, yes; but the lower are for the sake of the upper, and humankind occupies the pinnacle. Humankind depends on everything else; but everything else is for the sake of humankind. The element of dependence is expressed by the text in the need for food, that most primary of all needs, which symbolizes the power of nature over humankind. The human purpose of the lower strata is conveyed in God's consignment of the earth to the care of human beings, with our consequent duty and mandate to subdue it.

According to the Priestly account, then, the primordial structure of creation consists not in polarity and a contest of contraries, but in a mutual symbiotic union, a unity in hierarchized variety. Our dependence on nature need not engender resentment or hostility. Our commission to subdue it comports no denial of the dignity of creatures, and in no way sanctions their pillage and destruction.

The foundation of this unity is not to be sought in some external regulation of the machinery of the cosmos (as with deism), and still less in any rationalistic harmonization of the immanent principles of things (as, for example, with the pre-Socratics). The Israelite conception of the unity of the universe "basically draws its inner strength from an experience of Yahweh's right to unlimited authority. Only such an experience could maintain this conception in the face of the contradictions that prevail throughout the universe and its history."[43] It is the experience of the covenant, then, that establishes the experience of the oneness of the universe: It is only God's faithfulness that could found, in any being, a unity reconcilable with the independent self-identity of each and the irreducible variety of all. It is not a matter of reduction to a system, then (the unity in question is a natural one, a oneness of nature), but of a common, graduated sharing in God. What experience of this unity do we have? Once more, we must emphasize faith as victory. Subjects that conceive themselves as individuals in competition with other individuals, and in a relationship of subject to object where nature is concerned, are incapable of grasping this unity of creation.[44]

> Even in the Old Testament, creation never actually comes to be the mirror in which the wise providence of God is reflected in all evidence and, as it were, rationally. Creation is rather the testimonial of a mysterious, hidden God; and if an individual Israelite manages to discover in creation and its order the wise and just God, creation nevertheless remains, for all the rest, a source of terror. . . . Thanks to the priority of the covenant, man can nevertheless look creation in the face.[45]

We do not admit, then, that war is the father of all things (Heraclitus), or that the dynamic structure of reality is dialectical in its most radical and comprehensive configuration. And although the biologists of evolution of the past century saw the biosphere under the figure of the struggle for life, this was less an insight based on nature than the projection of a phenomenon of human society upon the natural order.

A faith in the oneness of creation forbids us to resign ourselves to this fierce, polarized world, and invites us to reconcile humanity in the bosom of a "cosmic democracy."

(b) Sovereignty of God and Goodness of Creatures

The unity of the universe as grasped by faith is not equivalent to the philosophical grasp of reality as a single dynamic, articulated structure. Faith sees a common, varied, and hierarchized participation in God, in which creatures consist, severally and conjointly, in God. This is the radical meaning of the "good being" of creatures (see vv. 4, 10, 12, 18, 21, 25) and of creation as a whole (v. 31).[46]

The first thing to be taken into account in our text is that it is not the narrator who enthusiastically proclaims the goodness of the works of God, nor is it creatures themselves who glory in their goodness, but God who *sees* that they are good. In view of the structure of the text, this divine weighing or appraisal expresses the satisfaction of the artisan with the result of each step in the production of the artifact, as well as with the final outcome. The distribution of the work by days reflects the image of the work week, through which the artisan accomplishes a project in a workshop, in tranquil, orderly fashion, in perfect control of the artistic process and without any resistance on the part of matter or tools.[47] The exclamations of admiration in the text translate the adequation of the artifact to the idea that has inspired it and the end for which it is intended, the perfection of its execution, and the harmony of the whole. Creation is good, then; nothing has opposed the divine realization, which God has had the power and ability to execute to the divine taste. The things produced are consistent. They "make sense," severally and as a whole. The chaos-cosmos setting (evil-good, meaningless-meaningful) has not been created by God. It is a purely intrahistorical situation. It did not exist in the beginning, nor need it be definitive.

This does not mean that we must close our eyes to the polarizations of the current scene. The intent of the text, on the contrary, is to urge us not to resign ourselves to these polarizations. Genesis 1 summons us not to optimism, but to a sharing in the faith that God once had, and still maintains, in creation, that this faith may be transformed into a hope that evil will eventually succumb and reality will gleam once more in its pristine splendor. For the moment, creation is "subject to failure," inasmuch as we human beings cause it to serve contrary ends to those for which it was created. But as Paul says, "it cherishes the hope of seeing itself delivered from slavery and decadence." Meanwhile, we, too, groan inwardly, "as we await the rescue of our being."

Here and now, for us, this means that the liberation process ought to maintain a fervent aspiration for its self-consummation in a process of reconciliation.[48] Granted, this will not be furthered if we turn our back on our problems. But still less will it be furthered if we forget our universal destiny to salvation (1 Tim. 2:4), based on God's judgment on the divine deed of creation, a judgment expressing not only the divine wisdom and power, but an irrevocable communication of the divine love. Enemies must be combated with the thought in mind that they are not originally or definitively evil (if this qualification has any meaning), and that they, like ourselves, are intended by the creator to form part of the one community of God.

PART THREE

EVIL IN CREATION

CHAPTER V

State of the Question

1. A SPECIFICALLY JUDEO-CHRISTIAN PROBLEM

By our faith we profess that the world, and ourselves within it, exist as an unfolding of the invincible goodness of God. The concept of creation is a representation of the absolute sovereignty of a wholly good God, a sovereignty that places and maintains us in existence by the divine word of truth and grace and by the divine Spirit, the gift that gives life. It is in this precise sense that we define ourselves as creatures, and cherish the conviction that to be creatures bespeaks our uttermost depths, tells what we strictly are, not only what all we different beings have in common, but what each of us is in our irreducible individuality. To be creatures is not a generic condition. It is the outcome of God's call, which names us—gives nature its names according to its species, and calls persons by their own names.

From this viewpoint, to see the world and ourselves within it as creation is to pronounce upon it the same word of blessing as originates and maintains it. To see the whole universe as creature is to profess the original, indelible goodness of all that exists. In the beginning—that is, in the most genuine element of every being (in Christ)—there is no evil-and-good, but "all was good."

From a point of departure in the chaos-cosmos setting that wraps us all around, imprisoning us nearly to the point of deter-

mining us, we have arrived at the further shore of faith in creation—faith in an unrivaled Good who has made all things good.
By faith, we have dismantled the metaphysical pretensions of
the chaos-cosmos setting. But then experience posited it once
more, and indefectibly. For us, faith is victory over this setting.
But will this victory not be converted into an agony? Will persons
of faith not have to acknowledge that they are Sisyphus, the
Titan who was obliged to resume his task ceaselessly because
time and time again, close as he might have come to succeeding,
he had failed? Will not the presently invincible existence of evil
cry, "Lie!" to faith in a wholly good creator?[1]

For those who would hold the anteriority of chaos to cosmos,
while the existence of evil may be painful, even tragic, at least
it is perfectly understandable. After all, cosmos can never spread
so far as to fill chaos, whose circumference is infinite and therefore nowhere. This is the fact. But if all is originally good, then
how did evil come into the picture, and come into it so radically
that we cannot imagine a world without evil? If creation is our
representation of the sovereignty of a wholly good God, then
how can we profess that sovereignty to be irresistible? If God
were not entirely good, it might be thought that the creator takes
no interest in creation, or even is beyond both good and evil—
or, finally, that God is evil, or somehow the enemy of creation.
But if God is both almighty and all good, then where did evil
come from, and how does it continue to exist?

This state of the question has two vectors. Along the first, we
confess that this statement of the problem is specifically Christian. Only in the sight of our almighty God do we discover the
non-naturalness of evil. Only before God does evil reveal all its
intolerable scandal. If we feel evil to be something revulsive, it
is because we believe in a creator-with-us. But while our faith
rips the mask from evil's intolerable face, evil, in turn, will make
faith problematic: Drowning in the morass of a triumphant evil,
the believer exclaims, "How long, O Lord? How long?" and the
Son of God cries out with a mighty voice, "My God, my God,
why have you left me helpless?"

Evil, suffered or committed, tends to take the wind out of
our sails, tempts us to accept its fatality, demands we bow our
heads and confess that this is how life is and that there is no

remedy for it. Then the only choice is the rebellion of the desperate, the complicity of those who seek their place in the "kingdom of this world," or the inhibition of those who would like to sneak off with as little dirt on their hands as possible, taking hopeless refuge in their inner fortress. True, our faith refuses to accept that this situation expresses the constitution of reality, and recognizes that reality to be violated, to groan with the agony of being forced to serve a vain purpose, a purpose that contravenes its nature, serving evil instead of good. Our faith shows us that the truth of beings lies trampled underfoot by injustice. But that same faith groans inwardly, deep within our own being, at the experience of the prostration of this world and of ourselves within it. If "this vale of tears" is not the world created by God, has the enemy crept into the field while God slept and sowed bad seed that yields only corruption (see Matt. 13:24–30)? Finally, does not Jesus himself posit two principles, one of good and one of evil, and thus define this history of ours as a drama? Where is the invincible sovereignty of the wholly good?

2. A THIRD-WORLD PERSPECTIVE

In the First World, it is possible to harbor the illusion that evil is a mere privation; or else that evil constitutes merely the passivities of the real;[2] or again, that evil is but the trail of footprints left by a sustained effort of integral development; or that evil is no more than the series of dissonances that enhance the harmony of the whole.[3] In the First World, evil can seem a circumscribed, regionalized thing—a chaos wafting above the daily round, from time to time seeping down through the cracks, but ultimately conjured away so that all is normal again. Inevitable evils, like death, are rendered invisible. Others are objectified, and pursued without quarter by research and technology. And still others are naturalized as ingredients of the human condition, or tolerated within certain limits, or approached by way of their conversion into virtue: evil behavior for a part, but good for the whole.

Evil can thus appear as "lesser evil," since the developed world is founded on the negation of the constitutive relations of personhood: the negation of solidarity with other peoples, who not only are not helped as sisters and brothers, but are cruelly oppressed, and the negation of religion, a re-linking with the author of life. Without transcendence, evil ceases to be mystery and is transformed into sheer dysfunctionality or limit.

But when you see the peoples of Latin America, you cannot trivialize evil. It is difficult enough not to think of it as a voracious, insatiable fetish. From the midst of our situation, then, we assert that a theology which fails to take the measure of this reality, a reality evil in all its dimensions, is not only in-significant — non-signifying — but irresponsible. It is itself an expression of the evil it undertakes to approach so obliquely.[4] Nor therefore may theology permit itself a method of analogy of similarity, dissimilarity, and eminence; nor again that of a dialectic of the Platonic type, which proceeds from the positive to supreme positivity. Theology, in content and method, must descend into hell, and not only into the conceptual, mystical hell beyond the grave, but to that of the "damned of the earth," the living hell of "this vale of tears."

3. EVIL GIVES GOD THE LIE

When all is said and done, the enormous weight of evil could seem to offer no other alternative than the denigration either of God or of human beings. Unless we are of the clan of the satisfied, or of the solitary, how can we escape this dilemma? Unless we are blind to the fact of living at the cost of others, or aloof from these others lest the very sight of them offend us, then how can we not criticize God or lose faith? After all, is not an expression of contempt for human beings ultimately a speaking-ill, a cursing (*maledicere*), of their creator? To lay responsibility for evil at the doorstep of human freedom, besides being exaggerated and incorrect, only moves God's responsibility one step further away. Is God not the author of this frail liberty of ours? Why have we not the ability to make a flower, when we can so easily trample one under foot?

Even if God were only the author of our freedom and our final judge, and history were the hour of human beings alone, it would still be extremely difficult to explain evil. But if "the

Father works until now," then where is the power of this good God? Thus not even the notion of sin exculpates God, for God is not an impartial judge, but the judge who justifies sinners.

Evil triumphant contradicts the Christian God. This is how St. Thomas sees things. On being asked whether God exists, he begins: "It seems not." And his admission echoes down the ages, with all its virulence: God is "the infinite Good. Therefore if God existed there would be no evil. But there is evil in the world. Therefore God does not exist." St. Thomas' own reply to this difficulty has this to be said for it, that it faces the problem squarely: "As St. Augustine says in the *Enchiridion:* 'God, being the highest good, would by no means permit the existence of something evil among his works, were he not so powerful and so good as to draw good from evil itself.' For it pertains to the infinite goodness of God to permit evil to exist that good may come of it."[5]

4. GOD'S PATIENCE AS WITHDRAWAL

According to Thomas' argument, if God does not draw good from evil, that is, if God does not ultimately transform evils into good, then God is not sufficiently mighty and good to be our God. But is it altogether evident that God is drawing good from so many evils? Can we really say that those who do not see that God brings good out of evil are blind, or full of ill will? If we cannot say this, then it is not evident that the Christian God exists; and now faith will be based on the hope that God will ultimately transform evils into good. True, at times, from our personal experience, we intuit the law of the cloud and the silver lining. On the other hand, there are also many evils that appear incurable, and a great deal of useless pain. Indeed, at times all history seems to be issuing in catastrophe.

If, in spite of this, we maintain faith in an almighty and all-good creator, this faith—nourished, of course, by the sacrament of historical events—will ultimately take the shape of a wager. Unless indeed our faith is to cheat us in the end, only at the term of history will it be clear to all that our God exists. For the moment, there is nothing to lead us to believe that this history of ours could issue in such a culmination. The term of history should rather be its judgment, its condemnation; then perhaps it could be transfigured and saved. Thus an atheism arising from the suffering of the evil of the world would actually be more Christian than a profession of faith in a God whose existence could be reconciled with the existence of this evil or who could be asserted to be aloof from it.

If God has not yet drawn good from so much unredeemed evil, it is because creation is a drama, and not simply the artisan's tranquil labor, as represented in Genesis 1. The drama of creation has not reached its dénouement. Cosmos has not yet overcome chaos. From out of this situation, only a faith become hope can call the reality that today enslaves us distorted, and reserve the name of "reality-unqualified" for what we descry only in hope.

But in this statement of the case, too, our faith is in a hidden God (Isa. 45:15). While our situation negates God, our God does not reject the rejectors of God. Our God forces no one. Our God is a God who has patiently slipped away, withdrawn from the scene.[6] Our God has been rejected.[7] This is why history, and the nature it brings us, are not an epiphany of God. For faith asks us to trust in this hidden God. "I am who am" (Exod. 3:14) is the nameless name of the delivering God. There is only one way to trust this God: by respect and reverence.[8] God must be allowed to be God. " 'The exact time is not yours to know. The Father has reserved that to himself' " (Acts 1:7). " 'As to the exact day or hour, no one knows it, neither the angels in heaven nor even the Son, but only the Father' " (Mark 13:32). Ours is but to be patient witnesses of this crucified love until it comes.

But this difficult, trusting hope does not dictate the undertaking of any hasty theodicies. God has no need of being defended. This is the time and moment of God's patience, the patience with which God protects us; the case is not the other way about. We are delivered, too, from the Promethean tension: We are no Titans, to bear the weight of the world on our shoulders. That task is God's. Our own assignment is a more particular one: " 'The poor you shall always have with you' " (John 12:8). Messianism died with Jesus;[9] now there is only concrete service. The truth of our life is at stake here. Here, and not the utopias of a land without evil, is the meaning of our struggle with evil. "The world where justice dwells" (2 Pet. 3:13) is the term of our hope, not of our historical projects. Even the most revolutionary of our historical projects can but aspire to that just world. We may strive to pass from a situation that is more evil than good to one that is more good than evil. Finally, this hope delivers us from the spell of evil. It desacralizes evil, and thereby prevents it from pilfering the horizon of our awareness and concocting the theophany of an upside-down god.

CHAPTER VI

Inculpable Evil

1. UNDERDEVELOPMENT AS EVIL

Although we stand in the sight of a wholly good God, we need not run for cover, or fill the winds with excuses. Trust overcomes our shame, and we confess our sin. But precisely from a point of departure in this confession, which brings us to the light of truth, we can do no less than confess that the evil we have suffered is far worse than that which we have committed. Indeed, at times the very evil we commit is occasioned, while not caused, by the difficulty of our lives and the injustices that weigh us down.

A great part of the evil of our Latin American situation is due to the underdevelopment of productive forces, institutions, and individuals. Still today, the cycle of floods and droughts shreds the lives of millions upon millions of human beings. We have not yet succeeded in subduing the earth even this far, even to this minimal degree. In many zones of our continent, people must slave to exhaustion merely to eke out their painful existence. Many die before their time, live diseased lives, and have no qualifications for a profession or trade. And is not even a goodly part of our age-old oppression to be explained as a series of brutal, primitive solutions to the problem of low productivity, and accordingly, of scarcity, which no one has discovered a way to solve more efficiently and intelligently? Is it not this stalemate that has forced the migrations to the cities, which has so thoroughly jumbled not only human geography, but the whole of Latin American culture? The migrations express the enormous latent life-energy stored up in traditional societies; but they also represent apocalyptic suffering, and an incalculable cost in human lives. The utter lack of any planning, any organized reception for the migrant multitudes, doubtless reflects the ruthlessness of those who govern us. But it also betrays their utter incompetence. The migrations are more than a sacred drama. They are the historical epic of our peoples, which the future will have to regard with deep respect. But meanwhile, is daybreak not terribly long in coming? Is this not an exceedingly difficult journey? Where are there any routes, any signposts? The storm bursts upon our heads, and our feet slip. We lumber along in the dark, speechless, scorned, and set upon by enemies. On the other hand, would it not be an impossible task *in the best of cases* to provide services to so many barrios, and employment for their population?

And yet—awash in the capitalist system, if merely on its periphery, in countries regarded by the United States as its "own back yard"—are we governed by anyone who actually has a great deal of choice? The opprobrium that brands the administration of nearly all democratic governments, and, in the national security regimes, amounts to the crime of *lèse-humanité,* falls back on the heads of our rulers and their accomplices (the bankers, the business tycoons, high-ranking military officers, and bureaucrats). But are not they themselves the by-product of this situation of semicolonial underdevelopment?[1]

There would be no point in attempting to paint more of this picture. For that matter, no description could adequately portray the situation. What I have already said will suffice for an understanding of the fact that a goodly portion of the evils that surround us are occasioned by the fact that we are still the "least ones." In such conditions, what is the meaning of our faith in a creator-with-us? How can we say that this God loves us, and has done all things well?

2. ARE WE ALTOGETHER TO BLAME?

In fact, the Latin American perspective makes it very easy to plumb the depths of the glorious, agonizing drama of history.

Humankind has devoted by far the greater part of its long journey on this planet to a search for something to eat and a little piece of land on which to dwell in relative security; to trying to live in community under some minimally objective and rational social regulation; and to striving after an individual life less threatened by disease and less radically eviscerated by the requirements of the clan, a life that might be in some sort projected as gladness and creative freedom.

Have not humanity's enormous gains been made at the price of bearing heretofore unimaginable tensions, and shattering solidarities to their very marrow? Obviously, in all of this, we must confess our sin; but is it not equally obvious that life has left us precious little choice in the matter?

In a barrio, for example — to cite just one set of circumstances among so many — will not a consideration of evil as sin be a luxury to which few can aspire? Can the sufficient deliberation and full consent to an act against life and the God of life that constitute the conditions for mortal sin be imputed to many of the persons who commit materially grave acts in these environments? Are these acts, which doubtless effect some kind of dehumanization and death in other persons and in those who commit them, genuine humanly acts? Or are they mechanical impulses — sheer issue of the flow of passion? In a barrio, will not a rhetoric of "contempt for the creator and turning to the creature" cast the burden of guilt on persons already overburdened by life?[2] And above all, will it not be untrue?

This is not to deny the possibility (and reality) of sin in these environments. To do so would also be denying the possibility of grace there. The problem lies in a verification of when the level of sin is reached and when it is not. And it seems reasonable to say that not only much of the evil that comes upon us from without, but much that emerges from ourselves, as well, is hardly to be imputed to us as sin. Thus, while our confession of sin is indispensable for an adequate grasp of evil, it does not account for all evil, either in the world or in ourselves.

3. INCULPABLE EVIL AS TEMPTATION

From the objective distance between sin and other types of evil, and even more from the possible prevalence of these latter, a grave temptation arises: to abandon the image of God as creator-with-us, together with our own image as creatures in a loving religious bond with this God, with our brother and sister creatures, and with creation as a whole. This temptation is complex. For instance, we might regard the creator as an "evil god."[3] Then we shall make our basic attitude one of greed. The correspondence between these attitudes rests on the notion that if God is not with us, but is indifferent, amoral, or even hostile, then there can be no trust—no basic trust in existence, in the sacred sources of life. Once we dissolve the religious bond that founds and maintains all things, the only alternative is an existence reduced to the sheer effort of survival, a clinging to life at all cost.[4] If we yield to this temptation, our constitutive links are broken and we become wolves to one another. Now the only prospect is oppression or submission: war.

This temptation against the creator-with-us, as against humankind and the material reality that supports that humankind as creature of God, has been the pitfall not only of the dualisms of so many religions, but of Western modernity as well, which began by labeling the creator a tyrant and enemy and has ended by decreeing the death of God—qualifying, accordingly, the human person not only as absolute self-end, but as self-cause.

If the temptation to proclaim an evil god and give ourselves over to greed arises from the shattering fact that evil cannot always be imputed as sin (although this evil is always aggravated and further poisoned by evil as sin), the temptation will exist as long as there is evil. As we foresee no possibility of the substantial attenuation of evil, it would be poor apologetics to attribute everything to sin and deny the existence of inculpable evil and the temptation it comports.[5]

4. HUMAN CONDITION AND HISTORICAL CONDITION

The evil just summarily described is not in itself what has come to be called the human condition in the abstract. We Christians do not regard it as evil that we must die, that we suffer illness and infirmity, that we become exhausted when we exert ourselves, or that we experience needs. We do not regard it as evil that the years we spend preparing for life, and then our declining years, are so protracted in comparison with the time of our prime of life. We do not even regard it as evil that we must struggle to understand, or that we err—indeed, and this is still more painful, that our misunderstandings engender confrontation, disappointment, and loneliness. We regard none of this as evil, although these things too are our sorrow and our torment, and incline us to ask God: Why did you make us this way? The human condition comports a disproportion between awareness and desire on the one hand, and our material condition on the other; and there is something unnatural about the conjunction of the two in one and the same living being. The human person is not tidily proportioned, as a beast is. No, we hold our treasure in earthen vessels, and we are as aware of its value as of its insecurity.[6] This incommensurability can shatter us. It is a temptation. But we do not call it evil, because we are making no attempt to be gods, and we accept the being that God has given us.

The evil to which we refer—inextricably interwoven with, but distinct from, sin—does not pertain to the abstract human condition, but is rather part of what we might term humankind's historical condition. And it is this that we do not see as clearly pertaining to the being that God has given us, nor indeed would we find it acceptable if this were to be the case. After all, dying at an advanced age, after a full life, surrounded by one's children and grandchildren, is a very different thing from dying alone, or in frustration, or before our time, or by a violent death. To fall ill and then to recover is a very different thing from being ill all one's life long. Having needs is very different from suffering hunger frequently and being without a fixed dwelling or elementary services or stable employment. It is not the same thing to suffer some misunderstanding, as to be absolutely unacknowledged by society at large. And when all this is not exceptional, but precisely the state of vast elements (indeed the greater part) of humankind, when evil springs up on all sides from want and privation in all its many forms, along with the temptation to greed and discouragement—then human beings are tempted to become wolves to one another, and to conceptualize God as the wicked god, the enemy, the one who is jealous of human greatness and our rival.

5. PARADIGM OF THE WILDERNESS[7]

(a) Insecurity and Want of Faith

It may be a help to us in examining this situation to consider the sojourn of the Israelites in the wasteland. There the problem of thirst arose.

> After traveling for three days through the wilderness without finding water, they arrived at Marah, where they could not drink the water, because it was too bitter. Hence this place was called Marah. ... The people grumbled against Moses, saying, "What are we to drink?" [Exod. 15:22–4].

> The whole Israelite community ... encamped at Rephidim.
> Here there was no water for the people to drink. They quarreled, therefore, with Moses and said, "Give us water to drink." Moses replied, "Why do you quarrel with me? Why do you put the Lord to a test?" Here, then, in their thirst for water, the people grumbled against Moses, saying, "Why did you ever make us leave Egypt? Was it just to have us die here of thirst with our children and our livestock?" So Moses cried out to the Lord, "What shall I do with this people? A little more and they will stone me!" [Exod. 17:1–4].

> Besides thirst, there was hunger: "You had to lead us into this desert to make the whole community die of famine!" (Exod. 16:3); "Now the people complained in the hearing of the Lord" (Num. 11:1); "The Israelites lamented again, 'Would that we had meat for food!'" (Num. 11:4); "The people complained against God and Moses, 'Why have you brought us up from Egypt to die in this desert, where there is no food or water? We are disgusted with this wretched food!'" (Num. 21:5).
> This is the literal situation of no small part of humanity, and

it symbolizes the precarious condition of all of the peoples of the world. It is a situation that provokes insecurity, fear, and desolation. And it calls forth a restless spirit, murmuring, and rebellion, against the authorities and against the Lord.

This attitude on the people's part is referred to time and time again by the Psalms, the prophets, and the Wisdom literature. It is regarded as the paradigmatic expression of a lack of faith in God's promise, and a want of a proper response to God's gifts (see 1 Cor. 10:1–12). But while not denying the justice of this appraisal, must we not also admit that such precarious conditions call for heroism, and that heroism is not a normal attitude for large numbers of people over great lengths of time? God was with Israel in a very special way, and this circumstance might surely call for an equally special faith in God's saving protection. But are peoples and individuals always guilty when, in situations of prolonged precariousness, they fail to make the discovery of this omnipotent God-with-them and posit the act of trust and surrender that would be objectively in order? Is the death of so many hungry, thirsty, and defenseless persons typically due to a lack of faith on the part of the victims?

(b) Insecurity and War

The insecurity of life is also the occasion, although not the cause, of fear and mistrust among peoples. This is what sparks wars. In the wilderness, the Israelites encountered other tribes that, in the exceedingly straitened circumstances of the wilderness, had nonetheless achieved some degree of insecure equilibrium. Could these tribes have been expected to welcome with open arms these newcomers, who were destabilizing their living space? Sihon and Og, tribal kings, offered resistance. Israel crushed them. "Not a survivor was left to [Og, king of Bashan] . . ., and they took possession of his land" (Num. 21:35). The command to exterminate these tribes was attributed to God (see Num. 21:34).

Then the Israelites moved on and encamped in the plains of Moab on the other side of the Jericho stretch of the Jordan.

Now Balak, son of Zippor, saw all that Israel did to the Amorites. Indeed, Moab feared the Israelites greatly because of their numbers, and detested them. So Moab said to the elders of Midian, "Soon this horde will devour all the country around us as an ox devours the grass of the field" [Num. 22:1–4].

It would have been useless to resist. So the threatened people proposed an alternative. The two peoples should intermarry. But the Israelite leaders rejected this solution, which would have meant the end of the identity and the destiny of their people, and placed on Yahweh's lips the terrible words: " 'Treat the Midianites as enemies and crush them, for they have been your enemies by their wily dealings with you' " (Num. 25:17–18). After the victory Moses ordered: "Slay, therefore, every male child and every woman who has had intercourse with a man. But you may spare and keep for yourselves all girls who had no intercourse with a man" (Num. 31:17).

The people of Israel advanced, exterminating everyone in their path. Arriving at the borders of the land of the Canaanites, they dispatched scouts, who returned enthusiastic about the fertility of the soil, but intimidated by the fortitude of its inhabitants. "We cannot attack these people; they are too strong for us," they said (Num. 13:31).

At this, the whole community broke out with loud cries, and even in the night the people wailed. All the Israelites grumbled against Moses and Aaron, the whole community saying to them, "Would that we had died in the land of Egypt, or that here in the desert we were dead! Why is the Lord bringing us into this land only to have us fall by the sword? Our wives and little ones will be taken for booty. Would it not be better for us to return to Egypt?" [Num. 14:1–3].

We are told that Yahweh grew angry with their lack of faith: "I will do to you just what I have heard you say. Here in the desert shall your dead bodies fall. . . . Thus you will realize what it means to oppose me" (Num. 14:28–9, 34).

Let us grant that Israel had sinned by failing to trust in the promise the Lord had made to them. But is the situation of this people not a pitiful one? Here they are, caught between an inhospitable desert and the Egyptian empire on the one side, and on the other the robust, fortified Canaanite states. Henceforward they will be obliged to choose between faith and death: "Unless your faith is firm you shall not be firm!" (Isa. 7:9). There is no natural, neutral space to settle in.

Still more pathetic is the situation of the nomads who see this fleeing, starving, fanatical horde swooping down on them with a faith that renders them invincible. Some suggest they should take cover and let the marauders pass, rather than propose that the peoples merge into one. Would this not have been the wiser, safer course? Can these peoples have been exterminated for their sins?

What we have here is the terrible law of iron: war to the death. In the abstract, an alliance would have been possible. But was this a realistic alternative? Scarcity begets greed, and makes it difficult to recognize our fellows as creatures of necessity like ourselves, deserving to be dealt with justly. If life is so precarious that there is no room for everyone, what else will human beings ever do but have recourse to armed might, brute force, and, consequently, extermination or slavery?

(c) Paradigm of the Desert

Humanity has passed by far the greater part of its existence on this earth amidst the terrors of the wilderness. Here the most elemental impulses reign. A people is driven to regard both God and all other peoples as deadly enemies. This is not to say that this people has no free choice. But let us face the fact: Faith and justice would be heroism here. The Bible answers that God does not ask a Promethean heroism of us, but merely obedience. But is obedience not just as heroic? Very well, then, let sin be one of the causes of evil. But do not a great many evils occasion (not cause) sin? In any event, we can scarcely overlook the evidence: The human condition is *unnatural.* Life is precarious. There are only two alternatives, greed and faith.

6. PARADIGM OF EDEN

(a) Toil in Genesis 2 and 3: Genuine vs. Experienced

This *unnatural* situation is illuminated if we compare chapters 2 and 3 of the Book of Genesis in their respective references to human toil and dominion over nature.[8] In Genesis 2 we read: "The Lord God then took the man and settled him in the garden of Eden, to cultivate and care for it" (Gen. 2:15), and "the man gave names to all the cattle, all the birds of the air, and all the wild animals" (Gen. 2:20). But Genesis 3 says:

> Cursed be the ground because of you!
>   In toil shall you eat its yield
>   all the days of your life.
> Thorns and thistles shall it bring forth to you,
>   as you eat of the plants of the field.
> By the sweat of your face
>   shall you get bread to eat,
> Until you return to the ground,
>   from which you were taken [Gen. 3:17–19].

Obviously the situation described by the Yahwist in Genesis 3 is the one actually being experienced in Israel. But it is equally obvious that, from the standpoint of Israelite faith, this situation does not seem genuine to the sacred writer. It seems artificial. What was "in the beginning"—that is, what was according to God's plan—should express the truth of reality. But this is not the case. In other words, the situation experienced is not *natural.* The natural thing would have been the acknowledgment of creatures by humankind, a corresponding acknowledgment of the human race by creatures, and, in this cosmic harmony, the human race's solicitude for creation—its cultivation, that is, its humanization. The natural thing would have been culture, the source of life for human beings and the finalization of nature. This was what God saw, and God "found it very good" (Gen. 1:31). Genesis 2 visualizes this plan of God's. To someone with the eyes of faith, the actual situation is experienced as evil, and

not merely as the human condition (to which work, and responsibility for the world, do pertain). The unnatural element, the
evil, consists, according to Genesis 3, in the hostility prevailing
between the human race and nature, with the consequent situation of insecurity in which humankind finds itself.

(b) Walled Gardens

If the author's only experience is hostility and insecurity, then
how is it that the text visualizes a situation of harmony and
fruitful toil as genuine? For many, the answer is: by the mental
operation that consists in negating what negates persons in the
situation as actually experienced. And of course this is the mechanism that has generated the utopias—which is why they are
simply the reverse of the respective situations in which they were
dreamed. But how are we to distinguish between a mere infan-
tile projection of desires and a discovery of the genuinely
human? How are we to distinguish between what belongs to the
human condition, and evil, that is, some privation of that condition?

And why should there not be hostility and insecurity? The
answer is a product of the option we make for faith in a creator-
with-us. But this option is more than a simple wager. There are
historical mediations that make it positively plausible. These
gardens, these preserves of harmony and fruitful toil, of culture
as the humanization of the human being and the earth, actually
exist. The garden of Eden is not pure fantasy, but real possibility.
It is not a challenge for an uncertain future, but a reality at
hand, within sight. But such gardens are not Adam's; nor do
they belong to the "common people." If any such dwell there,
it is as servants of the furrow. For the ordinary run of mortals,
these are walled gardens, jealously protected by armed guards
with shining swords. Even as the Yahwist was writing, there
actually were gardens full of tame animals and fruit trees, all
profusely watered and carefully cultivated, just as in the sacred
account. They belonged to kings and their mighty retinue, who
thought of themselves as having become as gods. They belonged
to the self-styled images of God and their familiars—individuals
few and far between on the face of the earth, with the rest of

the inhabitants of that earth constituting its dust indeed. In the face of this situation, the Yahwist takes a position. Insecurity is a curse on human beings. It is not part of the human condition. The evil of insecurity is bound up with the sin of those human beings who think that they have become God.

(c) Paradigm of Eden

Once more we find the evil of insecurity inextricably bound up with sin. We acknowledge the sin. But does doing so make the evil of insecurity reducible to it? In the time of the Yahwist, an unjust appropriation of goods prevailed on the basis of a human deification. But did the objective conditions exist in which this injustice could be overcome by way of a shared abundance? Was there room for all human beings, present and future, in these Edens? Is it not the disproportion between the development of productive forces and the needs of humanity that occasions (without causing) the sin of exclusive appropriation, expropriation, and marginalization?

7. DEVELOPMENT AS BLESSING AND CHARGE

(a) God's Plan

All that has been said thus far brings us to the subject of development for the defeat of insecurity, that source of evil and sin. Development without justice does not eliminate insecurity. Justice without development (in great numbers and over a prolonged period of time) is inviable, besides failing to deliver human beings from the evil of insecurity, the source of so many temptations.[9]

In the Book of Genesis (1:28; 9:1–3, 7), human dominion over the earth is the object of God's blessing and mandate. In other words, God has placed human beings on earth to transform it into an Eden. After their fecundating toil, the earth gives of itself, and achieves its fullness. The passage from less humane to more humane conditions of life, as the fruit of human toil, is obedience to God's mandate, then, and grace, the fruit of the divine benediction.[10] Lived as grace and obedience, as conformity with God's project, the effort of development overcomes the temptation to self-deification and becomes a sharing in the activity of the creator.

(b) Eden and Babel

The myths of Babel and paradise are not antithetical poles. They are not culture and the natural life, respectively. Both are culture. The point of the respective accounts is not to depreciate culture and exalt the natural life. Both represent the humanization of culture through human toil. The point can be stated in the form of a question. What concept of human beings underlies the cultural project — human beings with intimate ties to God and nature, or human beings without bonds and without measure, aspiring to self-realization through a breach of all limits? The difference rests on different concepts of culture. Is culture a blessing and a commission from God, or is it anticommunity, a totalitarian human project?[11] Human beings are cultural to begin with. There is no "noble savage." In fact, there is no utter savage.

The problem lies in the orientation and meaning of culture. Shall we move toward Eden or Babel? Babel stands for a strongly hierarchized and massified society, whose planners and controllers dominate those who execute the supposedly common work. The leaders cultivate fame, and reach the very skies on their pedestal of numberless ants who live only to work for them in exchange for the right to live. We see a mighty development of productive forces, but its purpose is the power and glory of the leaders, not the life of each and all. Eden represents a biophilic culture. Eden cultivates the full potential of human being and earth together, in a symbiosis, with time and space for a gratifying leisure.

(c) Culture as Ambivalence

Only through working justice shall we ever defeat the element of fetishism in the ideology of progress. A fetishism of progress merely alienates the people of the developed world, while exploiting, marginalizing, and seducing those of the underdeveloped countries.

The first step in working justice will be to recognize the objective need for progress if human life is to exist.

The immense effort deployed in food production, health and hygiene, communication, and science and technology (prescinding from the intentions and representations of its protagonists, as from the concrete structures within which the effort is exerted) has not been without the concurrence of the creator, and thus constitutes a material participation in the divine plan.[12]

Work, then, as a human way of meeting needs, has been established by God (as charge and blessing) as one of the motive forces of human history. Work is based on the non-naturality of human beings—on the unbridgeable gap between people and their needs and desires. This gap is a source of anxiety and fatigue, but it also furthers the creative impulse, or self-transcendence. "Through work, man *not only transforms nature,* adapting it to his own needs, but *realizes himself* as man—indeed, in a certain sense, 'becomes more thoroughly human.' "[13] Advancement by degrees, then—process, or progress—is a characteristic of the human species.

Was there any other way to dignify human beings? We are not God. We enjoy no total, simultaneous, and perfect possession of anything. We live in time, not eternity. But neither are we reducible to an instinctive adjustment to the passing moment, to the object of our instinct. That we are cultural beings, through work—processual, demiurgic beings, then—makes for instability and insecurity. We are subject to tremendous tensions. These both endow us with life and use up that life. This does not refer to the exchange in which all living things engage with their environment, but to a need and a desire that create their object, by appropriating it in an endless process of hypothesis, trial, and error—a traumatic process, since this complex network of operations adjusts only with great difficulty to the rigidity of the instances of human need. Thus culture becomes a wager against time, and the stakes are the lives of individuals and human groups. Victory, which is always temporary, fills the strugglers with the heady glow of triumph and the beneficiaries with relief and gratitude; but many of the struggles are in vain, and the cost in terms of human lives is dear.

This is the human lot. Some sing it euphorically; others lament it bitterly; still others simply live it in its ambivalence, tasting its triumphs and bewailing its defeats, accepting the expenditure and taking fleeting respite on the plateaus. We Christians share the mentality of every temperament and every age; but as Christians we know that our purpose in life is to live it in generous response to our opportunities, which we understand as signs needing interpretation.

8. THE PEOPLE, AGENT OF DEVELOPMENT

But all this is still a matter of mere generalities. Where is the precise subject or agent of this development? Who does the developing? How do the Latin American people experience this cultural condition? From the age of colonialism down to the present day, a stereotype has prevailed. There is a song about it:

> They call me the darkie of the sugar mill:
> I hate to work and I always will—
> Work I leave to the oxen, see?
> Why should I work and let God whup me?

It is the god of the white masters who transforms the alienated labor of the slave into punishment. Work that is a source of fatigue alone, and not self-realization, "whups" you. It is a scourge. And yet black, Indian, mestizo, mulatto, and slum-white all work their fingers to the bone. They do not live to work, but work is central in their lives. The current era of the great migrations in Latin America is also the great age of popular toil. The people have no teachers, but they have learned all trades. They have built their own houses, streets, and sewers. They have learned electricity and mechanics. Little by little, in factory, shop, and office, they have become experts in what they do. They go to school at night or take correspondence courses. They are on fire with a thirst to pierce the secrets of the machine. The Latin American people do not say, like the Iberian teacher of old, "Let others invent." They frequently invent solutions in their insecure jobs, and strive to know enough to invent on a grander scale. The children of the people go to all lengths to get into the universities. Their parents will make any sacrifice to afford their children an opportunity to learn more than they ever managed to learn themselves. But the terrible fact remains: A flaming sword keeps the ragged Adams and Eves of the earth at a safe distance from the tree of knowledge. The self-deified have placed a sentry there, lest the dust of the earth become "as one of us" (Gen. 3:22).

There is difficulty in development no matter what the hypothesis, and this difficulty comports a residue of evils. All this is true; and therefore we are neither encouraged nor permitted to intone those naive paeans to progress that can waft only from the lips of those who have satisfied their basic needs and secured their lives. But it has to be said that our people have accepted the challenge of progress and will change home and hide to acquire those elements of the modern world they judge indispensable for their survival and prosperity. There is a great deal of suffering along the way, and a high social cost, a cost that ought not to have to be paid, because it includes human lives. But in the face of death—imminent death, and not a mere risk of death—the people accept the awful insult of cultural bastardization for the sake of development. A large dose of evil, then, is tolerated as inevitable, owing to our technological, institutional, and personal underdevelopment.

But, due to unjust discrimination at the hands of those who control the production of material life and of the rules of a life in common, this suffering is transformed into a bitter and bottomless ocean, from which only mute protest, insolidarity, and the loss of meaning emerge. Death becomes mortal—that is, leads to the embitterment of the heart and the slaying of the soul through evil as sin.

CHAPTER VII

Evil as Sin

1. CONTRADICTION BETWEEN GOD AND SIN

A consideration of the evil originating in the cultural, not the natural, condition of human beings has driven us to the limits of our reason and understanding. We have even managed to conjecture somehow that "this is the way it had to be." Such a consideration, however, while it may be moderately satisfactory with reference to large human groups and great spans of time, is scarcely worth much to the concrete individual wedged in between an urgent need and the lack of available sources for satisfying that need. Now life takes the shape of a question, and a wager, and can be fittingly confronted only from a point of departure in human bonds of solidarity and, ultimately, in dignity and faith.

But the ultimate opacity of the evil that so radically threatens happiness, meaning, and life itself, is rooted in its intermixture with sin. This is the evil that constitutes a frontal challenge to God as the almighty God-with-us, to God as creator.

2. ATTEMPTS AT A SOLUTION

(a) Dualism

In the face of this radically unsettling reality, many confess themselves agnostics, on the strength of the argument cited by

St. Thomas: if there were a God, evil could not triumph. And many another, in various cultures and times, has abandoned any faith in the one God, finding no other way to salvage God's goodness than to oppose to God a mighty, indestructible principle of evil.[1] Once more, we have the polarization of chaos and cosmos, in which humanity lies ensnared.

(b) Doctrine of Satan as Attenuated Dualism

The devil, as a personal, spiritual being, as the enemy of God, invested with power, the scourge of humanity and even the regent of this world, is in many popular worldviews, and cults, an attempt to maintain this opposition, attenuating it so as not to injure dogma.[2] After all, the devil is not God, but a creature who was also good at first, but who rebelled against God before being forever transformed into the enemy par excellence (2 Thess. 2:4), although an enemy ultimately subject to God like the rest of creation. This way of characterizing the devil and his functions would harmonize very well with the drama of creation as analyzed above. In the first chapter, God is the sole actor, and makes everything good: the infrahuman world, human beings, and angels. The second act has two scenes. The first scene is played out before the dawn of human existence. Some of the angels abuse their freedom, and fall from grace (2 Pet. 2:4; Rev. 12:4). The second scene is that of human history, which will thus be the history not merely of our freedom, but of our freedom as solicited by two higher wills: that of the fallen angels, who seek to drag us down to their level (1 Pet. 5:8), and that of God and the good angels, who help us not to fall into temptation and who deliver us from evil (see Matt. 6:13). In the third act, God's sovereignty is restored through an act of the divine justice, which has been delayed by virtue of the divine forbearance: those who have abused their freedom and have fallen into the snares of the devil by turning a deaf ear to God and the angels will fall into the eternal fire prepared for the devil and his angels (see Matt. 25:41); while those who have made good use of their freedom in obedience to the heavenly voices will ascend to the skies, to heaven.

The popularity of this representation springs from its felicitous reconciliation of certain aspects of the problem. Present history must be illuminated from end to end, else it cannot be discerned. The difficulty of discerning history apart from the light of eternity derives from the fact that, in history, human liberty seems tremendously diminished in the presence of the powers that seem to be history's actual protagonists: God and evil. Only the light of faith (which is that of eternity) preserves our view of the real dimensions of the struggle, and thus the minimal equanimity of which we have need if we are to play our small part therein.

Thus this view overcomes the triviality of a schema that knows no drama but that of the individual will, and so has come through the moralism of the Enlightenment unscathed. There is more in this story than a human will fortified by a salutary rearing and stimulated by the encouragement of rational social institutions. There really are powers that tear and rend. We are witness to the ragings and the machinations of apocalyptic beasts, wild animals, and dragons. Surely, without a faith assayed in suffering, we are awash in a sea of terrors.

While acknowledging the virtues of this representation, we must nevertheless rise above it, inasmuch as it presents itself not as representation but as reality. And even if it were reality, it would neither solve the problems at hand, nor fail to create others. In transferring the problem of evil from humanity to the "powers," it merely thrusts the problem one step further back: How does it come about that the almighty-with-us has created certain beings thus? And suddenly we have just lost the little understanding we had gained with our recognition that humankind, adrift in its not natural, but cultural, condition, has been delivered over not only to tremendous tensions, but to a plethora of inevitable evils, at least for the moment.

Further: This schema claims to know too much. It presents itself as capable of describing the powers and their activity in far too much detail. In my view, the apocalypses of Daniel and John are coded languages, and tell not of extraterrestrial beings, but of historical realities contemporary with their authors.[3] These languages are coded and mystified not only because they belong to the genre of resistance literature, which must be clandestine, but also because they seek to indicate that, in these historical realities (political in both cases), an authentic mystery of evil lurks. They speak indeed as if the negative element in the universe were invested with a transcendence, then; not, however, in the sense that these realities would be the work of extraterrestrial beings, but in the sense that historical, and thus ultimately cultural and human, realities can acquire a negative mass such that, in their capacity as anti-glory, they terrorize and fascinate persons, becoming a fetish that lives on human lives (Rev. 13).

Now, as already indicated, for Christians there is no such thing as a human subject, or a cultural creation, that deserves elevation to the status of a fetish. The whole of the historical is ambiguous. There are persons and cultural creations in existence whose fetishistic dimension is so dense that they appear to us as wild animals, savage beasts, dragons, enemies, Satans. Yet they are not. That is the principal element in the mystery of evil that confronts us here.

Is there nothing more? I cannot claim to be able to answer with a simple "yes" or "no."[4] But I do confidently assert that history itself is structured partially as a mystery of evil—hence the legitimacy of the representations, as long as they maintain themselves as such and do not pretend to transfer to another field the drama of history, or leave human beings almost without responsibility.

3. HOW DID SIN ENTER IN?

(a) Leap and Fall

At all events, the mystery of evil in history abides. The question overflows our comprehension. If everything primordial in creation, all creatureliness in every being, is altogether good, then how did evil take such deep root?

The answer would have to embrace two complementary dimensions.[5] In terms of the first, the answer would have to be that sin originally entered the picture just as it does today. In its ultimate reality, sin is an action establishing a leap so definitive as to be refractory to any recomposition. The leap is opaque, and thus cannot be grasped by reason. Only confession, by which one assumes before God this act as one's own, sheds a certain light on the substance of sin. In terms of this second dimension, after the confession, we find ourselves capable of recognizing a whole imperceptible process that has ultimately issued, *quasi*-naturally, in this leap into the void. This process contains components both internal and external to the operating subject. In terms of our confession that we are the author of sin, we also recognize, secondarily, something called sinfulness and temptation. This second dimension is the one that, throughout the course of history, has swollen to the point of occasionally coming to form a lethal atmosphere (the hamartiosphere). In this sense we may speak of structures and a situation of sin that render fidelity to God a matter of genuine heroism.[6] And so, although the leap ultimately always occurs as a first movement, a process in its direction is discovered that on occasion can be much more instigatory, indeed all but compelling, than at first might appear. At all events the question arises of how process or leap, fall or instant of fall, are possible.

(b) Creaturely God-lessness, the Occasion of Sin

An existence "facing-God-without-God" (the description of the first level of created being) makes it possible for us to pass to being simply without God — a passage to godlessness.[7] Autonomy as gift and charge can be transformed into aloneness and rejection, or less radically, a wandering, a deviation. The without-God aspect, even experienced facing God, is hard, even unbearably hard. Thus it can appear as unjust privation, and can occasion desolate protest, and rebellion. The paradigmatic case is that of the Israelites in the desert.

God withdraws in order to afford us room and space. This is an act of grace. It is a pathway of opportunity. Now we can transform ourselves into subject, into persons. But we prefer to remain children, dependent on the signs and wonders of a "Daddy" who is always "right there," in liberality and generosity. But God does not scurry to our side at our beck and call. Why? That we may confront our difficulties ourselves, and grow in the process. God-lessness before God makes history possible. But it is by no means clear that we persons relish this challenge.

We are afraid of the helplessness that inheres in freedom. And so we seek gods and messiahs, leaders to make our decisions for us, though we be constrained to serve them in return. At the same time, the stronger and more enterprising feel the temptation to live the deprivation of God not in God's sight—that is, with responsibility, but in the solitude that makes a law of one's own desiring and power.

And so it comes to pass that, out of a situation facing-God-without-God, complementary temptations arise: of submission (whether to a religion or a state, an idol or a leader), and of self-deification; with their two vectors: surrender to passion as the absolute, and the use of persons as means, as things, by reducing them to objects by oppression.

(c) Jesus' Murder: Sin as Un-creation

In Jesus' murder, the consequences of succumbing to these temptations are revealed in all their monstrosity. In the death of the Son of God, we see the deification of oppressors to be the mortal sin par excellence, for it was only the leaders (religious, civil, and military) who killed Jesus directly. To make oneself absolute, to elevate oneself to the status of sovereign of life and death (John 19:10–11), is the mortal sin *par antonomasiam:* it kills directly. It disfigures those who commit it, who are merely relative absolutes; it disfigures the victims they transform into objects; and it disfigures God, whom they pretend to replace, inasmuch as they ignore the fact that the sovereignty of God is exclusively *in ordine ad vitam,* so that to be as God one would have to give life and to serve, and these things alone. In Jesus' murder the sin of passion is also seen to be mortal when it takes possession of someone absolutely: Judas did not physically kill Jesus, but he delivered him up to his enemies. Finally, the sin of resignation is revealed as a mortal sin. The people as such did not kill Jesus, or hand him over to the executioner, or call for his death.[8] Indeed, a great multitude of the people accompanied him on his way of the cross with compunction (Luke 23:27). But they did not defend him. Either they did not know how to do so, or they lacked the power to do so, but in any case they resigned themselves to their own lot, and through their resignation they permitted him to fall into the hands of his enemies.

In Jesus' death it is revealed that when the human condition of life facing-God-without-God, whether owing to cowardice and a lack of perseverance, or, especially, to a lust for power, is transformed into the condition of a life simply without God, death occurs—a death that reaches persons, inanimate creation (Matt. 27:45–52), and, culminating the mystery, the very "author of life" (Acts 3:14). Thus sin shows itself to be un-creation.

Persons are born to life as persons only when they confront autonomy (the without-God) and live that autonomy responsibly (the facing-God). At this point culture as humanizing environment intervenes. The fact that "life in the open," which is inherent to cultural being, must also be lived in the helplessness of the without-God, while not the actual cause of sin in the form of submission and oppression, nevertheless surely occasions that sin. Here is the intersection of the coordinates of evil as the product of our cultural condition and evil as sin. Both evils frequently occur as inextricably interwoven. Now we see that their confluence occurs not only in events, but in structures, as well, which, if not causing events, at least occasion them.

4. DEFEAT OF SIN

(a) Withdrawal of God on the Cross: Sin as Mystery

Jesus' murder also reveals God's unbreakable decree and determination never to violate, for any reason whatever, the structure of created being. On the cross, this without-God appears to Jesus as abandonment, and he shares his complaint with God: "My God, my God, why have you abandoned me?" (Mark 15:34). God respects God's creation, then.[9] Its autonomy is maintained even at the inconceivable cost of the life of the divine Son. It is so important to God that we live the without-God responsibly (facing God) that God prefers human autonomy, though its abuse affect and wound God personally, to the suppression of that autonomy (forced submission to God) and the avoidance of greater evils.[10]

Thus, God's patience as the crown of God's love, this

supreme withdrawal in the face of the death of the Son, with the possibility of sin ever remaining open, renders history not only opaque, but, often enough, bereft of all meaning. History, then, takes the form of a question that faith alone can pierce — while leaving it intact, since the answer faith gives is invisible (Heb. 11:1ff.; 1 Pet. 1:3–21; Rom. 8:24–5; John 20:29–31). The response of faith has not yet gained historical embodiment (Heb. 13:13–14; 2 Pet. 3:13; Rev. 20:11; 21:1–5).

The foregoing posits the substance of the mystery of evil, especially in its quintessential form as sin, from a point of departure in the theology of creation. But it does not solve the mystery. There is no doubt that, while each of the evils of the historical condition is a problem, whose response must be found in history (although in their totality, as well as for each person they affect, these evils are not mere problems, but challenges, which put faith to the test and thus plunge the subject into the unfathomable waters of mystery), the evils of sin constitute not a problem but a strict mystery, so that the more adequately they are posed as a question the more they evince their condition as mystery.

(b) God's Response to Sin: Resurrection as Creation

The torture of Jesus shows us the mystery of sin in all its depths and what attitude we should take to that mystery. Above all it shows what our divine Father is doing: suffering with the sufferer (com-passion), and giving life to the murder victim.

For the Christian, the "proof" that God is creator lies in Jesus' resurrection. Here God bestows life not merely out of nothing, but out of the negation of life that is death. Here is a bestowal of life not by way of existentially neutral causality, but in protest and recompense, and in a love that goes so far as to grant to a being outside oneself one's very own life. Here is a bestowal of life that is not caprice or whim, but the gratuitous manifestation of mystery itself. And here life is given not to a single being alone, but to a universe: Jesus is the firstborn not only of humankind, but of all creation. His Pasch, then, proves the fact that all things have been made in him (in the beginning), by him, and for him. It is in the paschal moment that we come to know that our creator is in solidarity with us (not sparing the Son himself) and is almighty (restoring him to life for our salvation).

Thus, because sin exists, the creator is the liberator. By sin Jesus was murdered; and God raised him. If sin is uncreation, then existence is the most profound demonstration that God is creator, as manifested gradually in the divine self-revelation to the Jewish people, in step with the deepening catastrophe of their unfaithfulness—and then in consummate fashion in the resurrection of Jesus after his execution, which condenses "all the innocent blood poured out upon the earth" (Matt. 23:25).

(c) Jesus' Resurrection as Victory over Sin

(i) Creation is not a first, inviable attempt. God is creator, therefore—with us, and all-powerful—because in Jesus God has decreed that we human beings be able to conquer sin, and because in Jesus so many women and men of all times and cultures ("a countless multitude"—Rev. 7:9) indeed conquer sin. They conquer sin not only in being forgiven, but by actually succeeding in keeping themselves unsullied by it (see Rev. 14:1–5). We must believe that, by the grace of God in Jesus, very, very many persons have never cut themselves off from God. They acknowledge that they are sinners; they know that sin frequently springs from themselves; but they acknowledge as well that God carries the day in them, despite their own constant failures and inattention: that, despite these, they have never descended to a genuine rejection of God, thanks precisely to the preserving love of God in Jesus.

We cannot think that God made all things good, that thereupon we human beings flung all to perdition, and that, since Jesus' resurrection, a few of us have been restored to grace, but only those few who expressly accept Jesus. No, those who have had the grace to experience this process of restoration become capable in turn of recognizing a multitude of brothers and sisters of every time, language, and condition who have also had this experience—many who are with us, and many more still who are not of our group (see Luke 9:49–50).

If creation is given only in and with the temporal principle, and if Jesus' work of salvation develops only over the course of his mortal life, and subsequently, by grace, is bestowed exclusively on the church, then we shall find it difficult indeed to demonstrate Jesus' universality—which in this case would be achieved only in his universal judgment and therefore only in the life to come. By the same token, we shall have destroyed the universal character of his salvation, which will now appear as the redemption of a handful of the privileged from the midst of the *massa damnata.* Is this not tantamount to declaring that human beings must be condemned in order that glory be given to their redeemer? If so, then creation, and thus the deed of the creator, will remain relegated to the status of a first, fruitless attempt.

(ii) Creation in Christ culminates in Easter. But if creation, especially the creation of humanity, has been effected in Jesus, then the case is altogether different.[11] Now we are utterances in the Word and children in the Son, in the principle from which all things proceed and toward which they all make their way. If this is the case, then both dynamisms exist from the beginning: sin and grace. If Jesus has conquered, and is sovereign of all times despite all appearances to the contrary, then no age has ever been under the power of sin. But this is precisely what we do know in Jesus' resurrection, and we know it in faith, a faith that fashions history. History is in God's hands, however, and for us is indecipherable in its figures taken severally, to be manifested only in its ultimate resolution.

Paul's portrayal of Jews and gentiles destitute of God's grace, then, and all in the power of the enemy (Rom. 1:18–3:9), are only abstract possibilities. They abstract from the contemporary situation of the triumphant grace of Jesus. True, not a single person is just by his or her personal justice alone. Still, there have always been, and always will be, persons who are just by the grace of Jesus—by obedience to "the light that enlightens every person who comes into this world." For although "the world knew him not . . ., to those who received him he gave the power to become sons of God" (John 1:9, 10, 12).

Nothing of this militates against the dramatic character of history, or against the uniqueness of Jesus of Nazareth. On the contrary, our point of departure is precisely a meditation on

Jesus' Pasch, which forces us to emphasize the fact that our relationship with Jesus of Nazareth is antecedent to any sin. It is a relationship constituted from before the ages. Jesus' mission is not exhausted, then, in the forgiveness of sins. We all have need of him; we all long for him. Without him is only sin; with him, it is possible not to sin.

And so there is a dynamism of sin antecedent to, but also internal to, the being of each of us; and there is a more powerfully determining dynamism: that of the grace of Jesus, which is also both antecedent and internal to the being of each of us.[12] But these dynamisms enter into the world of each of us in a human way, spanning a spectrum of possibilities, ranged along a continuum of ease and difficulty, inclination, and networks of solidarity (often crystallized in structures and situations). Then they are taken up in decision as such. There are indeed powers, then, and not only the naked freedom of each individual. But the power of evil, which is strong enough to take away my life, is not strong enough to separate me from God without my consent. Jesus' power is sovereign, but only in the functionality of spirit. It has no adequate counterpart, true; but it does not impose itself from without.

Thus, God is seen to be all-powerful, and with us, in the divine power to deliver from sin, whether by pardon or preservation. We know of this power from our experience of Jesus' Pasch. There Jesus is constituted sovereign: "Jesus is Lord." And Jesus is sovereign by reason of the fact that, in every time and place, he has had subjects—that is, persons saved by him from death (in the double sense of raised and delivered from death). Jesus' sovereignty, then, is the richest meaning of the fact that all things were created through him—just as creation in Christ is the foundation of the fact that Jesus came to save what had been lost.

(d) Spirit, Victory over Sin, and New Creation

(i) Absence of Jesus and personal realization.[13] Jesus acts, we have said, as spirit; he does not impose himself from without. Jesus said to his disciples on the night of his farewell, "It is to your advantage that I leave" (John 16:7). Hence the represen-

tation of the ascension. His disciples' solitude is for their salvation. It permits them to pass from an existence with Jesus concentrated on sensible intuition ("What we have heard, what we have seen with our eyes, what we contemplate and our hands have touched . . ."–1 John 1:1) to a personal existence as witnesses, that is, as responsible agents, subjects who extend the paradigm of Jesus through their own creativity. For the disciples, the without-God-before-God is concretely identical with their without-Jesus-before-Jesus. But their aloneness is more than trial and source of temptation. It becomes their strength–the strength to don Jesus as if he were an article of clothing and then go into the world to carry forward his work and deed. It becomes their strength by the deed of the Spirit, whom Jesus bequeathed to his Father and to human beings as his last gift on the cross (John 19:30), and whom that Father, gathering it up with his murdered child, thereupon scattered across the world through Jesus raised (Acts 2:17, 33). Of this the church is a sacrament (John 20:21–3). Anyone receiving the Spirit is a "new creation" (2 Cor. 5:17; Gal. 6:15; Col. 3:10; Eph. 4:24).

In this way, through Easter, evil, especially sin, is overcome. It is overcome in its root–vanquished in the very hearts of those who receive the Spirit with faith, and in the very environments to whose shaping they contribute and whose sacrament is the church. But there still remain the existence of the human being as cultural being and the dimension of without-God, inherent to the condition of creature, as occasions of evil and sin, just as there remain structures and situations molded by those powers of evil.

(ii) From interpretation to transformation. When the Israelites were surviving in mountain caves and other refuges, hiding from the tyranny of Midian, the Lord sent his angel to Gideon who, in concealment, was grinding wheat.

> The angel of the Lord appeared to him and said, "The Lord is with you, O champion!" "My lord," Gideon said to him, "if the Lord is with us, why has all this happened to us?" . . . The Lord turned to him and said, "Go with the strength you have and save Israel from the power of Midian. It is I who send you" [Judg. 6:12–13].

Gideon asked how God's nearness can be reconciled with the fact of oppression. His question derives from a correct perception of God as liberator. Thomas Aquinas posed the problem in similar fashion in his *Summa Theologiae.* In view of the fact of evil in the world, it would seem that God does not exist, since God is all-powerful and all-good. Thomas answered that precisely in being all-powerful and all-good, God is able to bring good out of evil. We have seen that, from the death of Jesus, the absolute evil, God has drawn resurrection, forgiveness, and the sending of the divine Spirit, who renews creation. God answers Gideon that it is not a matter of asking why there is a contradiction between the divine presence and oppression. It is a matter of resolving the contradiction by doing away with oppression. But now it is not God who acts directly. God sends the oppressed, anguished Gideon forth to deliver his people — as Jesus sends forth his disciples, who had retreated into their shells for fear of repression, to pursue his way. This is the proof of the existence of the almighty good, the creator-with-us. Testimony is God's apologia. It is theodicy, the defense of God, indeed, since it is the Spirit of God who acts within the witnesses, re-creating them and thus enabling them to become agents of the good news — precisely from out of their unvanquished weakness, that thus the strength of God may appear (2 Cor. 12:9), until the day of definitive manifestation in the re-creation of all (Rev. 21:5).

(iii) From mystery to paradox. This part opened with the overwhelming consideration of the accumulation of evils weighing over the heads of the Latin American people: the conjoined evils of the stunted development of persons, productive forces, and institutions, of the sin of oppression (internal and external), and of other sins. Throughout, these evils have been seen as radical — impossible to uproot in the course of history. Is it not scandalous beyond measure that the only solution is for Jesus to send us to save the people, when we stand in such need of salvation ourselves?

So the mystery of sin is crowned with the paradox of the pathway to its solution. God has created a humanity in which evil and sin are always possible. Torture is the most insane expression of the destruction of human being by human being.

Those who condemned Jesus to death by torture intended this as a material expression of the internal deformity of this criminal and the deviations into which he had led the people, and this is why they imposed it upon him: in expiation for his sins. But Jesus offered it up for the sins of his murderers; and God, in accepting Jesus and raising him up to new life, proclaimed that this torture victim is the one who takes away the sin of the world. The one crushed and deformed to the point of ignominy is the one who glistens with the glory of God. The one who had seemed such a cripple, such a runt, the living demonstration of God's bungled creation, is the new creature, in whom dwells bodily the fullness of divinity.

And now only those who bear the sin of the world can take it away. Their lives are the solution of the contradiction between the existence of God and sin. "Who has ears to hear, let him hear, and blessed is he who is not scandalized in me."

PART FOUR

LIFE AND HISTORY

CHAPTER VIII

Reading the Signs
of the Times

1. PARADOXES OF AN EXPERIENCE OF FAITH

Two basic assertions, emerging not only from Latin American theology, but from the most genuine Latin American spiritual experience, are: God is the God of life, and Jesus is the Lord of history. Of course, these are central concepts for the Christianity of all times. But it is no less certain that we in Latin America experience them today with particular keenness and impact. And yet their profession in Latin America today is paradoxical. After all, if anything is characteristic of our part of the world, it is the unsatisfied desire for life, and historical frustration.

If God is the God of life, will the divine throne not be in the developed countries? If Jesus is Lord of history, will his representatives not be the chiefs of the powers that guide the destiny of nations?

To be sure, our peoples hold many genuine values sacred. But which of these values, up until now, has been able to save the lives of so many children who die or are crippled for life, so many women and men who die before their time or who spend their lives afflicted with the diseases of the poor, who are hungry, who find no dignified work, no place in society, no place to live, and no social security? Is there not a contradiction between our sense of life, our taste for life, our capacity to enjoy life, to give thanks for it, and to share it—and our lack of the means of life, our helplessness, up to the present, to gain the necessary elements to live the life we love? In the presence of this contradiction, what is the role of our faith in the God of life? What does it mean to affirm life in the midst of death?

The penitents of our Holy Week processions, bearing their monstrous cross, yet with glorious, radiant faces beneath their crown of thorns, have been the living image of the paradoxical manner in which our people experience the Suffering Servant as Lord of history. This is doubtless enough. But is the paradox, the *quand-même,* the affirmation in spite of all, enough? Is this the meaning of theology from the underside of history? Or is there more? What does it mean for us to profess that Jesus is Lord of history? What does this profession of faith say of Jesus, of history, and of our role in history?

Instead of responding to these questions at once, let us first situate them in the overall context of our history.

2. CAN HISTORY PREVAIL OVER ITSELF?

(a) A New Era

"History has currently made possible the destruction of history."[1]

"Accordingly, the problem no longer is whether history can eventually prevail over nature. The question is whether history can eventually prevail over itself."

"It might be said that history has recently entered upon a new era ... characterized by its real, historically real, universal unity, as well as by the possibility, likewise historically real, of having to reckon with its own end, that is, with an end that in goodly measure depends on itself and its own doing."

Standing in the shadow of the nuclear arsenals, with its vital resources virtually exhausted, our historical era will have to choose "between the opportunity of putting an end to history and the opportunity of guiding it back to more humane goals. The opportunity to put an end to history could thus be transformed into the opportunity to enter another historical stage."

"And in the face of this eventuality, not only shall we have to take certain measures—likewise historical—but we shall have to do away with a great deal of what passes for a metaphysical interpretation of history."

(b) From a Latin American Standpoint

This brutal statement of the issue has been made from the perspective of a little country caught in the throes of a civil war incited and maintained in the most turbulent region of Latin America by the United States. Writing from El Salvador, an intellectual threatened with reprisals for his commitment to the people places his struggle in the context of the historical moment. Renouncing all paralyzing metaphysical anguish (how out of place, when "we are daily led to the executioner"!—Rom. 8:36), this writer maintains the hopeful solidarity that enables him to assess, and confront in all responsibility, what is at stake in that struggle. If the United States is successful in its effort to reduce the historical novelty emerging among the Central American people to an episode in the struggle between East and West (as the 1990 election in Nicaragua suggests it may be), then there will be no "opportunity to enter another historical stage." Instead, another step will have been taken in the blind rush toward "the opportunity to put an end to history." Faced with the blindness of the current leaders of the great powers (not only the politicians, but also, and especially, the potentates of high finance, the large corporations, the armies, or the mass media), it would not seem that the problem of "whether history can eventually prevail over itself" is likely to be resolved by those who have created it, control it, and extend it.

On the one hand, then, we must expose "what passes for a metaphysical interpretation of history" for what it is, despite its positivistic and scientistic trappings, which an ideology of development and of "manifest destiny" so sorely desires to force upon us. After all, "it is one thing to recognize the character of history as creation, and something else again to regard the results of the process of creation as good."[2] And on the other hand, we must take historical means to correct this disastrous course if possible. And so we mount an effort to strike vast, organic solidarities in the developed world, especially in the United States, as well as in Latin America. And we mount an effort (for which Archbishop Romero sacrificed his life) to achieve the peace of which we have such need not only without imposing upon entire nations the drastic designs of a vanguard inclining toward sectarianism, but especially, without reducing the just aspirations of the people to an economic, political, and cultural restructuring in which they will have a role not only as beings of need, but as a responsible, creative social body.

(c) Necessity and Impossibility of Shifting to Another History

The history that began with the *Conquista* and colonialism, then, and which has superficially developed into a history of independence, of the reforms of the final decades of the last century, and of the enterprises of modernization mounted everywhere among us since the end of World War II, must become another history. Nothing less will do, if we are to have a humane material life for our peoples, or, all the more so, a co-responsible social life worthy of human beings. This is the enterprise, becoming ever more clarified and better organized, of the peoples and other subordinate segments of our culture. But as this undertaking is embodied in an age characterized by its "concrete universal unity," it collides not only with the oligarchies of the region, but with the powers that are conducting global history to its term. Thus, our life must open to another history, and it fights to achieve this other history. This is the liberation process, and it is occurring in a historical era that renders it feasible as far as the material level is concerned. But we cannot actualize these possibilities, since we are not only denied access to the wherewithal to do so, but are forced to bend our necks to a history in which there is no place for us (not only as co-responsible, but even as living beings), and which furthermore is leading us to the catastrophe its leaders are creating.

Here the problem of the relation between life and history is posed in its maximal tension, and on its most comprehensive level.

3. PRESUPPOSITIONS OF THE SCENARIO

(a) History and Judgment

This scenario implies a series of presuppositions. Today, for the first time in the history of earth, we can begin to speak of "history" in the singular, rather than merely of plural histories. History is not defined, but open. It is not open to everything at every moment; but it is open to a variety of possibilities; whereupon the choice of one possibility conditions the subsequent choice. Then the selection of a whole series of possibilities in a determined direction composes a historical configuration in which certain further possibilities are present and others are excluded. In our own era, the struggle to control nature has been such that now the problem of the age is whether history can gain control of itself or whether it will finally commit suicide. If its current direction is not decisively corrected, the odds are with death, not life.

Accordingly, the character of history as creation does not simply coincide with creation in the theological sense that we have been developing. The distance between them opens both the opportunity and the need for judgment. The necessarily historical character of the person does not coincide with assent to and conformity with the historical configuration in which that person is inserted. Spiritual discernment is a key element in the commandeering of history, if we are to walk in the light of life and expose the ideology of the figure of this world. Only in this way shall we be able to take history responsibly in charge.

(b) The Authors of History

But if at the heart of a historical configuration we must pass judgment, then obviously not all who participate in the body social are authors of this historical configuration. Its authors in the strict sense are those who have projected it, have opted for it, and have succeeded in imposing it on others. The latter are indeed its agents, in the sense that, in one way or another, they have had to participate in its execution; and among the former are agents who are opposed to the prevailing option, and participate in its implementation only under duress, and so must suffer the historical configuration as a fate and a burden.[3]

If history transpires in persons, therefore, and only in persons, then the subject of history that is the body social is not a new substantive being, but an already existing subject, and this subject is not only complex, but internally differentiated and even contradictory. Hence the possibility of a change in configuration.

Human beings fashion their lives not by way of a series of automatic responses to stimuli, but through the appropriation of a determinate system of possibilities. This system can lead to the making or unmaking of their lives—that is, to lives lived along lines of either a greater personalization, or a positive depersonalization and alienation.

The nadir of depersonalization today is based on the maintenance of a historical configuration with one's eyes closed to the certain prospect of the automatic exhaustion of vital resources and the uncontrollable possibility of a universal nuclear conflagration (not to mention genuinely inhuman oppressions and marginalizations).

As history, therefore, is absolutely open, it can lead either to depersonalization—to catastrophe—or to progressive (always partial and ambiguous, and never exhaustive) liberation. The direction of history is drastically conditioned by numerous factors independent of the will of the individuals composing the social body.[4] Nevertheless, that direction ultimately depends on the moment of decision. Thus, the current conjuncture is marked by a choice between the opportunity (inherent in the current historical figure) to put an end to history, and the opportunity (more difficult to exploit, but likewise inherent in current reality) to redirect it toward more humane goals. But if we are to seize this latter opportunity, we must take energetic historical means. We shall be required to exercise our praxis in the most radical sense, which will entail, on the one hand, the creation of capacities currently non-existent in the body social, and on the other, the actual appropriation both of opportunities available at this point in time, and opportunities that will appear in function of the new capacities to be created.

(c) Liberation from the Underside of History

Here a serious question arises. Who is to change this decisional variable within the body social? It seems highly improbable for the change of direction to be forthcoming from the authors of the current historical figure. It would be rather the principal agents who suffer it, and the instrumental agents who execute it, who would be interested in redirecting history toward more humane goals.[5] Precisely for this reason, the liberation process can be discerned, sought, and accomplished only from the "underside of history."[6] This is not to deny the presence of certain of the authors of current history (as agents, and to a certain extent as principal agents, indeed as co-authors) in the liberation process, and in the shaping of the new historical figure. But to this purpose they must be assisted, and even pressured. This proposition arises not out of an immanent analysis of historical becoming, but in all spiritual discernment, in the sense that we have already considered.

The underside of history is a historical *locus a quo* consisting of the persons of the underclasses. In Latin America, the underclasses are first and foremost the defeated, the conquered, for we are still living that phase of history that arose with the *Conquista* and colonization. Secondly, and consequently, the underclasses are the races victimized by discrimination, cultures that are despised and therefore relegated to an inferior status and condition, and the oppressed classes.

The involvement of the underclasses in the liberation process takes place in two stages. The first is that of their "no," with which they respond to the dominant ideology and initiate the historical dialogue. This "no" is a cry, an act, rather than a word. Without it, history unidimensionalizes to the point of monstrosity. The "no" of the underclasses, then, which shatters the spell of the established order and the illusion of social harmony, is the creator of transcendence, as it introduces transcendence into the prevailing figure and causes that figure to appear for what it is: deformed and counterfeit. This cry is a genuine gospel.[7] For, once it has sounded, the only alternatives are the incurable blindness of definitive depersonalization, and openness to a conversion to more humane goals.

The second stage is that of a particular manner of collaboration among the underclasses in the concrete process of liberation—the process initiated by the cry. The particularity of this collaboration consists in the fact that without an alliance with other forces, the process will not be feasible.[8] The mythologization of non-power is no solution.

> The escape from false domination will not come by way of a denial of the dimension of dominance, stressing instead some sheer "reality"—impoverished in its own turn by a consideration merely through the lens of the natural sciences. The escape from false domination will be found in the exercise of personal openness, which goes beyond the forms in which reality presents itself, in order to be delivered, from a point of departure in this same reality, from whatever happen to be its dominating forms. Let not domination by the real, then, be confused either with fear, or anxiety, or passive submission.[9]

To link the rise of the underclasses with the possibility of history's gaining control over itself, with the attendant opportunity for a genuine human life, and the qualification of this hypothesis as one of spiritual discernment, may appear to be rather a grasping at straws. For most of us, indeed, while humanity's lot is the source of an anxious and compassionate concern, the rehabilitation of the popular classes as historical subject appears even more improbable than that current history should correct its course. But were the former improbability to eventuate, our malaise in the face of what might then come to pass would not be less than that aroused by the current state of affairs. And the qualification of this historical judgment and the proposition it implies as a matter of spiritual discernment would appear to border on the insane.

4. MODERNITY AS HISTORICAL LIFE

(a) *The Traditional Human Being as A-historical Being*

The schema proposed is paradoxical, to be sure, first of all because it counterpoises the historical human being, identified with the bourgeoisie and its scientists and technologists, against the peoples of the Third World, styled traditional. Traditional human beings congeal their historical being, in order to be able to focus their efforts on living in the best manner that is possible in a given framework. Ordinary human beings (apart from exceptional cases) leave the totality to those elements charged with the task of supervising it (the authorities and the vital forces), while personally relying on what is within immediate reach. It is the latter, for them, that constitutes life. Since this life (reduced to the everyday, and glued to the given) is a cyclical one (daily rhythm, weekly rhythm, rhythms of planting and harvest, seasons of the year, local and national festivals, and so on),[10] the problem is to be able to recognize the requirements and opportunities of each moment, and to live these in an appropriate and responsible manner. The challenge is wisdom as the art of living.

But just as our political, economic, social, and cultural framework is altogether clearly defined, so is that of our individual lives and social relationships. The traditional human being follows paradigms. And to be wise is to adjust to them, to install them. Thus, to be a human being is to be an individual of a species, a member of a group, an element of a whole — each individual retaining his or her peculiarities, doubtless, and personal style, but along pre-established avenues. To be sure, the opportunity for creativity exists, but it exists only as the fulfillment of opportunities inscribed within a given culture. Self-expression along other avenues than the received is either imitation (if it is a game, or the expression of a whim) or no longer to be oneself.

(b) The Western Human Being as Historical Being

This schema has been occasionally surmounted in the course of history, by virtue of superabundant energies that it cannot contain in its framework (scientific or religious conceptions, technological inventions, revolution of productive forces, and so on) or else by reason of repressed energies to which the prevailing system is unable to do justice, and which therefore in one way or another finally burst its structures (internal proletariat, massive migration, desperate revolt, social revolution).

Ordinarily, with the achievement of certain reforms and the broadening of the established order, the traditional schema is maintained. But in the West, through a peculiar series of stages, a process has been initiated which tends to produce another schema. In the West today, human beings create society, transform nature, and create themselves. Here the traditional schema is a consciously abandoned point of departure. There are no cosmic, social, or anthropological paradigms. It is human beings who must project what world they wish, what society they wish, and how they wish to be themselves. It is they who must project, in accordance with their freedom, their capabilities and resources. In this schema, life is an accumulating combination of old projects, their outcomes, and new projects.

(c) History and Life: A New Relationship

At the origin of this historical schema are vital needs and impulses, humanity's deepest and most sacred aspirations. On one side, it is a matter of achieving life, and life in abundance; on the other, of the achievement of "selfhood"—being oneself, belonging to oneself as end, and positing for oneself the "other," other "selves." This necessary process of individuation and personalization, nevertheless, in many cases fails to take account of the basic, constitutive respectivity of the person, for which others (as such, and not as mine) are indispensable for my self-appropriation. Thus, this process gradually creates for itself a historical figure in which one tends to consider what is not oneself as mere raw material for one's own project. This divorces person from nature (which is ignored and plundered to the point of the current ecological crisis), and a social breach gradually deepens (struggle of classes and peoples, racial and cultural discrimination, North-South and East-West conflicts).

When life proceeds in function of the traditional everyday, then, it is impoverished, ultimately is defined from without, from a point of departure in the denaturing structures of its environment. On the other hand, when we plunge into history in all creativity, we find ourselves on the brink of an apocalypse, the eve of an Armageddon. Not only are we biological beings, spending our time as individuals; we have created the ability to destroy ourselves as a species.

Ordinarily we opt for one of the two terms, relegating the other to disuse. We opt for the life at hand, and come up with life within the system, and, what is more, according to its paradigms. Or else we opt for history, with a view to a fuller life, and the liberation of life; then we become rabid and hardened, withdrawing from and even despising daily life, and thereby creating new slaveries.

At this point we wonder whether there is some mediation by which we might bridge the gap between the scant resources and paltry horizon of traditional society, which kills or at least suffocates, and the insanity of a wild race to nowhere, which exalts some and crushes others, extracting all from themselves and rendering them strange and hostile.

5. AN INDEFENSIBLE FORMULATION OF THE PROBLEM: ITS THEOLOGICAL DIMENSION

Let us generalize this conception of the question, and examine relationships between life and history. By life, here, we understand the concrete reality of persons and human society. By history we understand the moment of decision in which individuals, impersonalized in the body social, not only opt among the given opportunities, and create capabilities calculated to generate more opportunities, but do so on the basis of equally creative parameters. In this framework, relations between life and history are translated into relations between human reality and freedom.

The conceptualization of the problem that we have been considering is inexcusable. In its context, freedom can do away with human reality, not only in the sense that it has at its disposition the resources for doing so, but in the precise sense that it has made options which bring us closer to this consummation each day. The discussion whether history can be necrophilic, and freedom can make its option against humanity, is not a subjective matter, that is, determined by humanity's contingent self-image. Our age has all too clearly demonstrated that the freedom that molds our current history is necrophilic. It is this inexcusable reality that bestows urgency on a decision as to what notion of reality must be the norm of history if that history is not to self-destruct.

We can frame the question in strictly theological terms. If God is not the one who has created and who will come as judge; if our God is not justified by a final declarative judgment that rewards the good and punishes the evil; if the will of God is not the death of sinners but rather that they be converted and live; if the glory of God is the human being alive; if God is shown to be holy in the act of justifying the creature; if God is, and not merely was, Creator, and the judgment of God will only be the recapitulation of creation. Then the possibility of humanity's suicide is of concern to God. Indeed, if history is the highest opportunity for the life that God has created, then could human freedom, the *chef-d'oeuvre* of God's creation, be frustrated in the end?

There could also be a specifically Christian framing of the question. If to be a Christian is to follow the paradigm of Jesus, might there perhaps be some mediation between Christian living, and this historical manner of life in which one not only selects opportunities to suit oneself, but creates the very opportunities to be selected? Christian existence is characterized by discipleship, and this is a mode of obedience. Is this mode of obedience reconcilable with the freedom that distinguishes and dignifies history? In order to reach answers for these questions, we need to address how we discern history and read the signs of the times.

CHAPTER IX

Discerning History

1. THE READING OF THE SIGNS OF THE TIMES AS A SPIRITUAL TASK

The reading of the signs of the times is an indispensable theological task. Some signs have to be interpreted. The task of interpretation has its own keys, which, besides constituting points of support, serve as controls. Hermeneutics contains its own rationality. In Christianity, this rationality moves within an altogether determining dimension: that of the spiritual. The Spirit alone is capable of interpreting God's design accurately and legitimately in the signs of the times. The prophet is the person of the Spirit. It is the prophet, then, who formulates and rigorously proclaims God's law vis-à-vis the people of God, their neighbors, or some representative person. If someone not a prophet dares to attempt to read the signs of the time, that one does so not rigorously, but by way of hypothesis, and not on the basis of conviction, but on the strength of the evidence. But no such evidence is ever conclusive. Accordingly, if concrete, positive enunciations are to be anything more than sheer hypotheses, after the manner of the scientific method, it will be because they are made in the wisdom of the Spirit—in function of the prophetical dimension that we have received. But if this dimension comes into play, its employ must be limited to the extent of the gift received, and, like all charisms, submitted to the discernment of the church.

In any event, the reading of the signs of the times is intrinsic to theology, which renders the theological enterprise a hazardous one.[1] When all is said and done, the judgment to be passed on its reading of the signs of the times must be left to the succeeding generation. (This is not to deny that, at the level of a theological production, this discourse has its own controls, and must give an account of itself.)

This is why a treatment of history and life needs to begin with a reading of the signs of the times. Two considerations recommend this method. The first is a general one, namely, that the present work is conceived in the framework of the theology of liberation. The second is that, more precisely, our theme is history; but history is what is denoted by the expression "the times"; and the need to interpret what occurs in the signs of history is a function of the ambiguity inherent to the times, to history (hence their condition and quality as *signs*). So we begin with spiritual discernment in history.

2. DISCERNING HISTORY: A POSSIBLE AND NECESSARY TASK

Discernment is possible because the Spirit operates in history; it is necessary because history is not purely and simply an epiphany of God.

That God operates in history has been the basic conviction of the Judeo-Christian faith. Thanks to the activity of God, history is liberation. To put it another way, there is history (if the historical element in history is creative openness) because God intervenes. God's intervention bestows success, victory, and peace—in a word, salvation. This intervention is understood according to two basic models: that of the heroic legends, reaching its apogee in the apocalypses and present in most of the Psalter; and the one that materializes for the first time in the account of the succession of the Davidic throne, which characterizes so many of the accounts and reflections of Israel's Wisdom literature, and is radicalized by the prophets.[2] In the first model, despite the fact that the hero is set in such bold relief, "there is no question of any human synergism." It is a matter, then, of a decisive intervention from without. In the second model, "events follow their course, without the least breach to be perceived in the earthly chain of causality. ... And yet the reader learns to see God as the hidden sovereign and guide of history."

> God acts in all spheres of life, public as well as private, in profane matters as in religious. But especially, the weight of the divine operation falls outside the sacred institutions of worship (the holy war, the charismatic leader, the ark of God, etc.) — in the very midst of the profane.

These ways of understanding God's intervention in history are founded on two different conceptualizations of God's relation to creation. According to the first way, God intervenes directly, in such a way that either God is reduced to a worldly being, or else the worldliness of the world is dissolved. If this were the manner of God's activity, there would be no room for discernment, as the overwhelming presence of God would leave no room for doubt; but neither would there be room for history, or freedom. But if God acts from within the divine transcendence, in such a manner that even the immanence of God is transcendent (God is "more within me than myself"), then God will act by means of the two divine hands: the Word and the Spirit.[3] Discernment is possible in virtue of the relationship between these two hands: the Spirit is the Spirit of the Word (who enlightens every human being coming into this world, who spoke by the prophets, and who was made flesh), and consequently the Word is pronounced in the Spirit. The Spirit alone would have left no room for discernment, but only for an ecstatic enthusiasm or trance. For its part, the Word without the Spirit is reduced to an unverifiable faith.

Historical discernment is *possible,* then, because God intervenes in history and intervenes only through the Spirit of the Word and the Word of the Spirit. But if this is the manner of the divine operation, then historical discernment is *necessary,* as well. After all, God's Word is always a human word, as well. How are we to know when the word of a prophet is only that of the prophet?[4] When is the wisdom of the wise a participation in Wisdom itself, and when is it merely the expression of *a* humanism? When does law consist of mere human traditions, and when is it the command of God? And the Spirit of God is not a worldly reality, but occurs only in human actions. Accordingly, if no human action is automatically the vehicle of the Spirit, how may we know which human actions hold their impulse from the Spirit? If the Spirit is bound to no political or ritual deed, if the Spirit is freedom, then how are we to know who is the anointed of God? Who are spiritual human beings? In particular, which works bear the mark of the Spirit? Hence the necessity of discernment.

3. A PARADIGMATIC CASE: DISCERNMENT OF CATASTROPHE

(a) *Judgment in Contradiction with Religious Sensibility*

This necessity eventually became so critical in Israel that it gradually tended to objectify God. Hence the fetishism of the Law and the Temple — lest one wonder where God is, lest one need to search for God.

The problem was radicalized the moment the prophets began to hear an unofficial word, indeed, a word that contradicted dogma: an act of Yahweh vis-à-vis the people not for their salvation but for their judgment. Jeremiah experienced the problem in all its dramatic reality, personally as well as in his struggle with the false prophets: "Confronted with concrete historical development, the true prophet finds himself in total religious insecurity. The prophetic vocation was a totally objective hearing, an attention to the events of the world nearby, as to those of the distant world of the nations."[5] False prophecy, which refused to listen, and clung to the traditional doctrine of a salvation based on election, "thus detached itself from the language of Yahweh in history and let its own desire become the author of its prophecies, thereby betraying its inability to descry a judgment weighing over the people themselves."

After rebuking the people for infidelity in their breach of the covenant, Jeremiah promises a new covenant, immeasurably superior to the first. These words, likewise inspired, are more than an expression of the need to find meaning in misfortune and a desire to give comfort and hope. But they do not detract from the seriousness of the prophet's proclamation of present abandonment by God and impending national destruction. This proclamation refers to an action of God that is not simply and adequately contained either in historical antecedents or in religious tradition. From a starting point in the activity of the God who comes, signs and congruities can be discerned. But the divine activity itself is more than these. It is a creation.

In this extreme degree, then, prophetical discernment relies neither on dogma, nor on a sharp sense of reality, but on the extreme objectification that, running counter to one's own claims and desires, permits one to receive the revelation of God's activity through the framework of history.

(b) God Judges by Discerning Catastrophe

God's activity is always a judgment. This proclamation on Jeremiah's part seems to contradict all that we have said about creation. Is God not a God of life? Is God not faithful? How can a creature of God be the ruin of the people of creation? How is such a terrible, paradoxical spiritual discernment to be understood? If it cannot be interpreted simply as a reaction of anger, rage, and desperation in the face of such great infidelity, nor even as a just judgment from which the people would emerge simply condemned for their sins—then how is it to be understood? Once the catastrophe has occurred, congruities can be sought. But it was not foreseeable; it was a novelty that neither the leaders nor the people could assimilate. Only a remnant bowed their heads. To the last moment, the majority of the people clung to the hope of a salvific intervention by God. That Jeremiah would condemn this hope could seem only the height of impiety.

In the political events around him, Jeremiah read catastrophe for his people. And he read a catastrophe that would befall that people not despite God, but because of God. A century and a half earlier, Isaiah, too, had voiced the possibility of catastrophe. But in those circumstances he had defined faith as reliance on God (Isa. 7:9b); hence his dilemma: faith or catastrophe. Now, however, how was Jeremiah to propose catastrophe *and* faith, and without offering an illusory hope, a challenge to God? Did both prophets have the same God? Can God change?[6]

Times change. The historical figure changes.[7] There are historical figures that no longer have anything to give. Not only have they exhausted their possibilities, but they render themselves positively incapable of offering solutions. There are other figures, interiorly shaken by terrible contradictions and negativities, that nevertheless contain great virtualities. These figures are created through a multitude of institutionalized decisions. In those decisions, a coincidence transpires between the operation of the Spirit and obedience to the spirit of the historical figure, between obedience to the Word and compliance with the words of divinized leaders or the absolutized human word.

At times actions performed in obedience to the Spirit are capable of opening this historical figure and saving it. But on other occasions it is too late. To be stubborn about it can be very noble, but it will be anti-historical. One ought rather to place one's wager on another, unprecedented figure — leave the dead to bury their dead and set oneself to the building of a tomorrow that will receive embodiment only in subsequent generations.

It is not necessary to imagine a God condemned, a God who has lost the game. It is enough to think of the Spirit certifying the suicide of the people in order to lead believers to an unverifiable but higher hope. The historical judgment that thus defines a time and demands a response is a creation of God. The fulfillment of the prophetic word is therefore an operation of the Word (Isa. 55:10–11), and those whose acts execute the judgment will correctly appear in the capacity of instruments of the Spirit (the immanent power) of the Word that has defined the time. This says nothing of the moral quality of these "instruments" or of their activity.

Thus God does not cause the catastrophe; but the Word of God does define the time as one of catastrophe, and the Spirit of God, through the catastrophe, publicly withdraws from a historical figure and its institutions. (Compare Isaiah's vision of the glory of God filling the Temple and shaking it to its foundations [Isa. 6:1–4] with Ezekiel's, in which that glory withdraws, leaving the Temple empty [Ezek. 8–10].)

This articulated vision of time, and this structured (composing a concrete figure) conception of the operation of God in time through the divine Word and Spirit, comprise the view that posits, in all its radicality, the urgency of ascertaining the locus of God's passage. This vision is diametrically opposed to an epiphanic conception of revelation in which God would be found fixed in spaces, times, institutions, persons, and acts — objectified in them, a God unveiled, absolutely foreseeable and domesticated, "mundanized."

(c) Jesus' Discernments

This is the problem confronting Jesus, that "pioneer and consummation of our faith" (Heb. 12:2). He had to discern his time, and he judged that God's passage there was recognizable neither in the commitment of Temple service, nor in the Pharisaic proposition, nor in the project of the Zealots, nor in the sect of the Essenes. He judged that God was passing by way of John.[8] He made this judgment counter to the judgment of the religious authorities (the Temple and the synagogue), who did not believe in John.

But in his baptism event, Jesus saw a new time opening: the Reign of God was coming, and not as judgment but as gospel. God was becoming present, and not to separate the wheat from the chaff, but to grant a general amnesty. God was coming, not in a judgment based on the law and the prophets, but in a new time, the new era of the consummation, and hence of the consuming and the transcendence, of the promise that was Judaism's very heartbeat. And so Jesus detached himself from John.

But room was left for a new discernment. This became necessary when the authorities consolidated their rejection of Jesus and excommunicated him and all that he stood for. The guests were refusing to attend the banquet. The lessees of the vineyard refused to acknowledge the rights of the lessor. They had thwarted God's plan. What was to be done now?

Jesus read that God would maintain the year of grace despite official rejection. And he continued on course, knowing that he was on the brink of failure, and of death at the hands of the authorities. He would continue to be for them the one of grace, while he combated them in pain and sorrow because their rejection closed the door to the people. They neither entered themselves, nor allowed others to enter. This third discernment left Jesus unprotected and vulnerable. "My God, my God, why have you abandoned me?" Grace would be accomplished through judgment. To Jesus fell the catastrophe, and the duty to maintain himself in it as a grace; salvation fell to the Father, who reserves to himself the time and the hour (Mark 13:32). Thus Jesus' discernment ended in an obedience that not only contradicted his will (Matt. 26:39), but would have its response only after his death (Heb. 5:7). Jesus ended his life rejecting the prevailing historical figures, but without a face and figure of his own (Isa. 53:2)—with an open proposition that had failed to make history.

Still, even without a figure of his own to cling to, Jesus did not simply curl up and die at the end. He "surrendered his spirit" (John 19:30). He surrendered it to God and to us. It was this act that sealed his freedom, and that defined him forever as the one of the Spirit. The supreme test of love and liberty was to cling neither to any historical figure nor to its failure.

In this third discernment of Jesus, the radical intelligence of an aspect of history is revealed to us:

> History is necessity only for someone who believes in the obligation to win. The law of success is the only genuine necessity. This is precisely the law from which the Spirit emancipates us. We are no longer subject to the need to win. And so we are free. Discernment is exercised upon history only when one need not win; or rather, only when, in order genuinely to win, one must know how to lose. This is the *theologia crucis.*[9]

(d) Discernment and Martyrdom

God exercised the fourth discernment in raising Jesus from the dead. But this discernment enters history only by way of the testimony of the post-resurrection appearances. This is the origin of the church, and of the Gospels born of the church to overflow it and constitute it the sacrament of the Spirit of the one who was crucified and raised again—the sacrament of the Spirit poured forth by him from the Father to the world, to all creation, to make all things new.

But the witness par excellence is the martyr. Martyrs unveil what their time conceals—the necrophilic character of a figure that styles itself salvific. But more than this, they reveal a victory over this figure: the capacity to give one's life in order to rescue those caught in this figure, transforming them into the builders of another figure, a figure reorientated to life. The fact of martyrdom, then, is a sign, especially, that, in a time marked by sin, there nevertheless superabounds the grace to refashion and recreate that time. The absence of martyrs does not normally betoken a time that is good. It indicates a time with no energies to overspill it.

Yet martyrdom is an evil. It is murder. Then it must neither be desired nor sought. Martyrdom is diametrically opposed to the planned-in-advance. On the contrary, martyrdom ought to be avoided insofar as may be.[10] The martyr reveals, in superhuman wise, that it is the Spirit who judges, inasmuch as martyrdom is the very contrary of a pre-established table of parameters. Martyrdom is radically a happening, an event, the most sublime act of freedom and love, and the victory of God and human weakness.

In our own times, just as in the times of Jeremiah, a connection has appeared between historical discernment and the activity of God. We are witnesses to the continuation of Jesus' discernment on the cross (Luke 2:34–5; John 12:31–3; 15:20–16:4).

(e) The Poor Judge the World

The martyrs, however, simply proclaim in an exceptional manner what the poor proclaim in an ordinary, daily way. The poor judge the world. This is the meaning of the majestic image of the last judgment as presented in the Gospel of Matthew (Matt. 25:31–46). If one's definitive status before God depends on one's relationship with the poor, then the crucified people are the sovereigns of history. They are the sovereigns of history because they direct destiny. And they direct it from the depths of their crucified condition, from out of their passion. Thus, a historical figure in which they are structurally abandoned to their hunger, their thirst, their nakedness, their disease, and their imprisonment is defined by the Spirit of Jesus as a necrophilic figure. Other variables are of no account. By contrast, a historical figure in which the poor begin to live is a compendium of the glory of God.[11]

There have always been poor in history. But it is an act of the Spirit when one comes to discern that the true state of a society is not measured by its gross national product, but by the condition of its people.[12] It is an act of spiritual discernment to recognize that the sense of a historical figure is revealed in the dynamics of the people. If those dynamics systematically augment the breach between rich and poor, then we are confronted with a situation of sin. That is, there is no remedy but to change the historical figure.

(f) *Judgment in Latin America Today*

This is the discernment that the Latin American church has exercised at Medellín and at Puebla.[13] If we are in a situation of sin, then God is not to be found in the established order, but in those who have no place in the same. It is in their faces that we must recognize the suffering features of Christ the Lord, with his questions and his challenges for us (Puebla, 31). "Western Christian society" is a misnomer here. Latin American society is nothing of the kind. In Latin America, faith (which does "inform" and shape the people) has been unable to be translated institutionally, as it is not alive in the elite who have fashioned and who maintain the established order. And so it is out of the very entrails of a popular faith that the cry and the struggle for liberation rise up.[14]

As in the times of Jeremiah or of Jesus, spiritual discernment translates as judgment. And behold, Latin America, hierarchized through and through, and profoundly unjust, nevertheless rises up as one entity, in virtue of its evangelization. The founders of the Latin American church were capable of recognizing the contradiction that pervaded this unity: the contradiction between evangelization and colonialism, between Christian fellowship and political, social, and cultural division. Hence their struggle without quarter against all manner of domination, that the fellowship of the children of God might be seen in all its glory, and institutionally. But with time, protest within the church was suppressed, and Latin America proclaimed itself Christendom. Henceforward the church institution would seek to correct abuses, but would accept the structural contradiction "on account of the hardness of their hearts" (Mark 10:5), and as the lesser evil.[15] This contradiction would gradually achieve the status of the normal; this asymmetry was required by reason of the primitiveness of the dominated races. Following the trauma of the nineteenth century, by the middle decades of our present century the project of the restoration of Christendom had been achieved to a very high degree. This project was complemented by that of a populist political program aimed at closing the social gap (established by a structural dualism) through integral development. As late as 1966 the Latin American Bishops' Conference endorsed this diagnosis and project. Hence the difficulty not only of assimilating, but even of understanding, Medellín's assessment, which maintained that institutionalized violence implies a rejection not only of the paschal gift of peace, but of God.[16] That was the equivalent of the vision of Ezekiel, who proclaimed that God had left the Temple. Hence the extent of the stupor and discomfiture.

This prophetic judgment, endorsed by Puebla, can be understood only as an action of the Spirit of Jesus. The Spirit always acts through anecdotes. But we condemn ourselves never to understand if we reduce that Spirit to the anecdotes. We are in the presence of an activity of divine creation. The current historical figure, then, was bound to catalyze a process that would struggle to replace it with another. And suddenly martyrdom (absent from our church since the days of its founding) returned, with its certification, as in times gone by, that the authorities with their self-styled Christianity are actually enemies of the cross of Jesus. Martyrdom has definitively disqualified the established order, and demonstrated the materialization of an opposed, creative freedom.

4. DISCERNMENT AS PRAXIS

(a) Discernment: History's Moment of Option

Discernment is a spiritual activity. To be more precise: History cannot be subjected to an exhaustive objectification. The reason for this is not only its incomprehensible complexity, but also its subjective, open disposition. So a human judgment upon a historical configuration is always creative.

It is through this creative act that the spiritual activity of discernment is brought to bear. Discernment must be a spiritual activity, as it is formally the activity of the Spirit of Jesus. But as the Spirit is not an element of this world, its activity among human activities is always intrusive. So, while requiring mediations, discernment is by no means reducible to a composition of these. It is a creative act in the strictest sense of the expression, both in the sense that history is a creative act, and in the precise theological sense that its subject is the creative Spirit. These two senses are (inadequately) distinct, and accordingly, history is not purely and simply an epiphany of God. Success is not a sign of God's favor. Success does not discern the activity of the Spirit. So discernment can be seen as a judgment in which the activity of God defines a historical figure as no longer of any utility, as "condemned," as beyond repair, as having no future. Accordingly, it is important to discern when the human activity of interpreting the present moment becomes discernment.

The limit-case of catastrophe will serve to relativize what I shall be saying since this human activity is free and sovereign, so that time alone will judge the quality of the discernment in question. When all is said and done, discernment means directing attention to God's design, which, being personal, can be known only through revelation.

(b) The Spirit as Action: Primacy of the Spirit

The great specificity of the Spirit is that it is the Spirit of the Word. Accordingly, one may expect a congruity between the words that "God has spoken on diverse occasions and in a mul-

titude of manners by the prophets" (Heb. 1:1), the wise, and
the leaders of the peoples, and the word currently in vogue.
Nevertheless, neither the (Catholic) comparative theology of
religion, nor the multiple voices of the Hebrew Bible is very easy
to harmonize, let alone to reduce to a system.

If the Spirit is the Spirit of Jesus, then it cannot contradict
him. But in a given concrete situation, how can we discern Jesus
working through the Spirit? If the imitation of Jesus is neither
possible nor salvific, then we cannot escape the equation: Jesus
is to his time as we are to ours. But in order to solve this equation
for our times, we need to know not only Jesus' time and ours,
but Jesus. Thus we beg the question; we are presupposing the
object of our quest. And yet, we cannot emerge from this hermeneutic circle. The Spirit is our doorway to (presupposing scientific and experiential cognition) the knowledge of Jesus, as
well as to the interpretation of his time and ours, so that we
may follow him.

The Spirit is our way out of the hermeneutic circle. But the
Spirit is creative breath, impetuous wind; fire that lights, warms,
and devours; dove of heaven, who hovers in self-bestowal over
all that lies below; finger that impels with sovereign force; water
of life, satiating, cleansing, and fecundating (Ps. 104:30; Acts
2:2; John 3:8; Acts 2:3; Matt. 3:16; Luke 11:20; John 7:38–9).
The Spirit acts. The Spirit is action. Apart from historical activity, then, the act of discerning history is impossible. If the Spirit
is the doorway, then the Word who is Jesus can be discerned
only in historical activity. That which, in the Trinitarian inti-
macy, is "last," in our externality vis-à-vis God is first. The Son
proceeds from the Father; the Spirit, from the Father and the
Son. But for us what is immediate is the Spirit. We begin with
the Spirit, and we end in the orbit of God; we are able to recognize Jesus as Lord (1 Cor. 12:3) and God as our Father (Rom.
8:14–16). While for God what is first is the Word (Gen. 1:1;
John 1:1), for us, in response, the first thing is action: conversion
in the Spirit of the Word of God.

There is no previous discernment, then. To pray for light,
instead of walking toward the light, is to lay claim to the power
to lift ourselves to the Spirit by our own bootstraps. One prays
in order to have the strength to walk, and to walk attentively;

only along the way will the light dawn. To interpret the gospel in order to have light, instead of walking toward the light, is to lay claim to the power to leap up to the Spirit. One interprets the gospel in order to know what to meditate along the way; this is the eating of the meat, this is the reading of the letter, that along the road will become the light of life. Prayer to God and the evangelical dialogue with the Word incite to action, and blaze trails. But discernment takes place in activity, which is subsequently explained and confirmed in dialogue with the Word and in prayer to God.

(c) Discerning History in Historical Activity

If the activity of discernment occurs within historical activity, then history cannot be discerned from outside history. This is evident as well from a point of departure in the other "hand" of God, the Word: The Word became flesh and pitched its tent among us. It has been radically historicized. The Word of God is now human word.

Anyone pretending to withdraw from history in order to hear the voice of God concerning history will hear only his or her own dehistoricized, absolutized word. There is no sacred place distinct from, divorced from, history, where God reveals the divine will. There is no temple or priesthood. The one priest, Jesus, came to us as one among many and reestablished contact with God outside the holy city (Heb. 13:12), in a place culturally cursed (Gal. 3:13)

From the Christian viewpoint, it will at times be necessary to breach one's solidarity with a given historical figure, but never with history. Christian discernment defeats the official Pharisaism of insolidarity, an irresponsible charismaticism, and the apocalyptical short circuit, and binds itself radically to history in the risk of patient obedience.

Thus, the human activity of interpreting the present moment solely within historical activity can be transformed into discernment. But which historical activity can be the vehicle of the Spirit?

The activity of the Spirit of Jesus is, as I have said, formally historical activity. Incarnation prevents the regionalization of the Spirit—the restriction of the Spirit to a determinate kind of activity. If the Spirit were not that of the incarnate Word, it would tend to become incarnate in the sacralization of a certain type of activity (with its delegates, places, and utensils). Having taken flesh (through Jesus) in humanity and all creation, the Spirit can have all history as its vehicle, but without the sacralization of that history, without its dehistoricization.[17] There is no discrimination or privilege, then. Any genuine human activity can be spiritual: work, politics, festival, human relations, religion, or what you will.

5. SPIRITUAL PRAXIS

(a) Building a Communion of Sisters and Brothers

If they are not specified by their materiality, by what are spiritual activities specified? By their fruits. What are these fruits?

Jesus is the Son of God, and therefore our elder brother. Accordingly, he reveals to human beings their human condition.[18] God created human beings that they might become the daughters and sons of God and sisters and brothers to one another. Thus, the Spirit of Jesus is that of the Son, and hence also of our brother or sister. Accordingly, the activities whose fruit is the condition of sons and daughters of God and brothers and sisters of one another are spiritual activities. But, as we have pointed out, what is last in God is first among us: Jesus is our brother in being God's Son; but we, in the historical activities by which we strike or maintain a relationship of sisters and brothers with one another, coincide with the Spirit of Jesus. That is, we become children of God. For us, then, the spiritual activity that enjoys systematic primacy is the activity that builds, in history, a humanity of brothers and sisters.[19] Without that activity there is neither discipleship, nor mission (Luke 13:25–7), nor the Lord's Supper (1 Cor. 11:20–34), nor love of God (1 John 3:17), nor filiation (1 John 3:10; 4:7). Upon this activity is founded the universality of the Christian message, since the Spirit has been breathed by Jesus upon all humanity: all creation and all times. It is this activity on the part of the Spirit that sets history in motion, and keeps it ever open in the midst of so many discriminations and absolutizations.

But no specific activity automatically creates a communion of brothers and sisters. Hence the need for discernment, and hence the fact that the act of discerning is an essential stage in any historical activity performed in order to establish this communion. In all cases, while each individual activity maintains a margin of ambiguity that is never clarified, not even "in the long run," its tendency, where present, to build a communion of brothers and sisters does constitute an element of judgment.

But it must be borne in mind that this communion proceeds not "from human lineage or the impulse of the flesh or the desire of the male, but from God" (John 1:13). Thus this communion is neither an ethical community nor an association founded on common interests. These communities are closed, by hypothesis. And yet a communion of sisters and brothers is never a direct one; it is always given through the mediation of relations, groups, and institutions, which, if they are not closed, are at least ambiguous, and have a tendency to discriminate against "outsiders." Even the church shares this tendency, and has not as yet succeeded in emerging from the Western pattern. China and India are not Christian because Western Christians rejected the possibility of a Chinese or Indian Christianity. And in Africa and Latin America Christianity entered into a crisis when its Westernizing face became obvious. Hence the need for a Christianity that springs from the people. What is in question, then, is not a confraternity of the sworn oath, or a fellowship of the elect, the set-apart, the righteous remnant, the chosen—but a communion of the children of God. It is the same Spirit who creates diversity, and who creates a dialogue amidst this diversity by maintaining it in communion without reducing it to uniformity.

(b) Liberation

While this communion is to be sought under the impulse of the Spirit of Jesus, it is nevertheless open to a certain *a priori* specification. The first specification would be that the task of building a communion of brothers and sisters cannot be performed simply "from scratch," from mere disparity, in the absence of any and all antecedent bonds. It can be constructed only from a point of departure in the chaos of discrimination, unlove, and oppression. Thus the quest for a communion of the children of God is necessarily a praxis of liberation. It is very far from being exhausted in that praxis; but it passes ineluctably through it. And the refusal to struggle against oppression betrays the inauthenticity of a pathway to a brotherly and sisterly communion. This route will not be that of the Spirit of Jesus.

Jesus' confrontation with the powers of oppression qualified his life by determining it in spite of him. Jesus defined himself as an evangelist; but in the face of the refusal of the leaders to be converted, the acceptance of the gospel included the bad news of its heralds' excommunication (John 9:22–34). Without simply whitewashing the excommunication or the excommunicators, we must nevertheless observe that it would have been a moral impossibility for the gospel to be accepted by the people of Jesus' time and place. The proclamation of the good news, then, had necessarily to include a struggle with the leaders, who had imposed upon the people a discriminatory, oppressive historical figure, sacralizing that figure as the will of God. Hence the indictment of Jesus, before the imperial power, for subverting the social order (Luke 23:2) was not without foundation. Jesus was not a subversive as were the Zealots of his time, as he sought no political power (nor did he seek to do away with all political power, in a spirit of anarchism), and consequently did not take up arms; nor did he represent any military threat. But he was a subversive in the sense that he disqualified the prevailing historical figure and its agents, proposing a society resting on other foundations (Mark 10:42–5). Hence the appropriateness of the title on the cross (Mark 15:26), an inescapable historical datum. Indisputably, the Spirit of Jesus impels its agents to the liberation of the oppressed (Luke 4:18). The liberative nature of the Spirit of Jesus sealed his fate. When Jesus became aware that to persist in his option for liberation would only carry him to a quick, violent end, he refused to change course—thereby demonstrating that, for him, in this act of discernment, life was of less worth than the struggle for liberation, even when one understands that the struggle will be unsuccessful.

To be sure, Jesus' concern with liberation was by no means restricted to the struggle for liberation from the oppression of the oppressive powers of this world alone. Jesus delivers us from sin, from the oppression of the devil. But neither sin nor the devil is a substantive entity that acts independently in the world. They are never present apart from human activity. They are human actions, although these actions secrete a mystery of evil that transcends them. The prince of this world was represented in Jesus' time and place by religious leaders, who were the economic and political managers as well, and were allied with the military power of the empire.

Even more than the engagement of building communion, the struggle for liberation is marked by ambiguity. It is not easy to determine, in a concrete case, the liberative character of an action, an institution, an economic or political proposal, a historical figure. But one thing is certain: If it is liberative, it is an action of the Spirit of Jesus.[20] The Spirit liberates in whoever liberates.

This specification of the spiritual activity of history has been rediscovered and energetically underscored in our age by the Latin American church especially. This is our greatest contribution to the church universal, and especially to the cause of the liberation of our believing, oppressed peoples. And the sign that this availability for the service of the liberation of the oppressed is an action of the Spirit resides in the fact that this project, so dolorous, so controversial (as was Jesus' journey to Jerusalem), constantly more costly, more obscure, with its ever-growing ratio of passion to action, is nevertheless lived as gospel, as good and joyful news, with increasing peace in the dark night of injustice, with the humility of those who have abandoned their messianism for obedience, and with growing lucidity and wisdom — all amidst terrors, vacillations, temptations, cowardice, contradiction, and sin, which nevertheless fail to dull or blur the evangelical tenor of our experience of liberative action.

(c) From Beneath

Another criterion specifying historical activity as that of the Spirit of Jesus is that the task of constructing a world of sisters and brothers, and of struggling against the oppressive powers which oppose this enterprise, is performed "from beneath." Jesus came as teacher, Lord, a prophet, the Messiah, the Son of God; but he lived all of these things in the form of a servant. He did not suppress these other dimensions of his; on the contrary, he developed them, consciously, bringing them precisely to their consummation. But he developed them within the historical figure of service. Service for Jesus was not a mere interior dimension, a subjective attitude, a mere style of living the figures of Messiah King or prophet or teacher. That would be how service has nearly always been preached to the great ones of this world, and how most of the mighty have been disposed to accept it, all the more so if any judgment to be passed on the quality and value of their activity is reserved to the next life. But that would not be how Jesus understood service. He said of himself (in what are generally considered his *ipsissima verba*) that he was among the disciples "as the one who serves you" (Luke 22:27) — that is, as one who serves at table (a waiter, we should say).

"But if I washed your feet — I who am Teacher and Lord" (John 13:14). Jesus' act was the occasion of a very serious dispute with Peter, who refused to have his feet washed by Jesus because he was scandalized at this historical figure of a leader. Jesus had once called Peter a "satan" (Mark 8:33) for the same reason. Now he issues him his definitive summons: "If I do not wash you, . . . you will have no share in my heritage" (John 13:8). Peter, more than the rest, should accept the fact that leadership is exercised from beneath. This had been the theme of Jesus' constant dispute with his disciples. The disagreement became sharper in the ascent to Jerusalem, when, scandalized, the disciples saw disaster looming (Mark 9:30–37). Jesus insisted to the sons of Zebedee that he had come not to lord it over others, but to bear witness unto martyrdom (Mark 10:35–40). And to the other apostles, who resented the two brothers' strivings for pre-eminence, which threatened their own aspirations, he presented his project as an alternative to the prevailing political conception, which they had all interiorized:

You know how among the Gentiles those who seek to exercise authority lord it over them; their great ones make their

importance felt. It cannot be like that with you. Anyone
among you who aspires to greatness must serve the rest;
whoever wants to rank first among you must serve the
needs of all. The Son of Man has not come to be served
but to serve—to give his life in ransom for the many [Mark
10:42–5].

This spiritual logic is in violent contradiction with what could
appear to be a law of history. Historical humankind has always
believed that only the wealthy can give, that only the wise can
teach, and that only power can be effective and change history
to suit itself. But Jesus "was born poor, and lived poor in the
midst of his people," did not attend the schools of the Pharisees
or doctors of the Law, and belonged to none of the institutions
that exercised power. And yet in this figure dwelt in all its fullness the wisdom and power of God. Indeed, he "became poor
to enrich us with his poverty" (2 Cor. 8:9).

This is not a mere paradox. But neither is it a dialectical law.
What we have here is an event, an occurrence, in which Mary
and Jesus rejoice in the Spirit (Luke 1:46–56; 10:21). But this
event has its own logic, which, while contrary to that of the
world, is charged with meaning and wisdom. Wealth, power, and
fiscal *sagesse* rest on private appropriation, which is *eo ipso*
expropriation. The wealthy as such cannot give; their logic is to
hoard, and that is their curse. Leaders have themselves been
called benefactors, beginning by regarding themselves as such;
while in reality they tyrannize, concentrating in their own person
all power of decision, and successfully preventing that power
from being called to account except in extreme cases. The wise
monopolize information, and thereby possess a power that others lack, thus gaining an advantage over all others in matters of
practical judgment. The prevailing theory is that wealth, power,
and wisdom must be concentrated, so that they will be able to
expand and grow. This is the ideology of capitalism (private and
state), of the state, and of research institutions. But as a result
the West has failed to emerge from its elitism. Despite the mas-
sification of knowledge, the democratization of power, and a
popular share in the wealth of nations, the breach between the
elite and the masses yawns wider by the day. It seems clear that

the non-people are not saving the people, nor the rich nations the poor countries.

But this coin has another side. Confronted with the exclusive clubs of the wealthy, the wise, and the powerful, who nevertheless proclaim themselves our messiahs, the activity of the Spirit in history promotes communion and liberation from beneath. Even the local and regional churches have shown themselves unable to follow Jesus' example (Matt. 4:8–10) and reject the offer of the prince of this world to place at their disposal all the necessary means for doing good and evangelizing more effectively, in exchange for entering into the established order and submitting to its logic.

The ploy by which the popular church is condemned for an alleged classism, exclusivism, and messianism only reflects the accusers' blindness to the fact that they belong to the established order, and that in a context of that discriminatory historical figure the church will never be able to correct the division between ecclesiastical institution and people, or, least of all, create a communion of brothers and sisters.

6. GAMALIEL'S CRITERION

It is impossible, then, to exercise discernment apart from historical activity. And in order to be spiritual, this activity must be directed to the creation of communion, and to liberation from the oppressions that contradict communion, and this from a point of departure among those beneath—the poor, the impoverished. The primary beneficiaries and agents of liberation must be the races victimized by discrimination, the marginalized, scorned cultures, the oppressed classes.

Thus, only such activity is compatible with spiritual discernment. It does not guarantee it, however, for the following reasons:

1. These activities comport a sinfulness of their own. It is healthy to criticize the popular church, then, and any "basism" that might be observed there. It is healthy to be on the watch when it comes to the manner in which the liberation movements develop, and especially, become institutionalized. It is healthy to analyze activities undertaken for a communion of sisters and

brothers, in order to purify them of any dross of resentment, domination, and subjugation, of fear of assuming individual responsibilities, of the spirit of compromise or the lowest common denominator, and so on.

2. These activities may lack adequate mediations. We may not have sufficient knowledge of the factors intervening in the situation and its dynamics. Thus we may be unable to appreciate the condition of the historical time in which we live, which will prevent us from recognizing the actual and possible opportunities present in this or that particular historical figure. Here is where science and wisdom come in. But these are not necessarily accompanied by the noblest dispositions or the most disinterested actions.

3. Finally, as I have repeatedly stated, history is open, and discernment of history is creative. Gamaliel's criterion, then, is absolutely indispensable (Acts 5:34–9). Yet it is perhaps the least earnestly employed. Very rarely do those "above" permit those "below" the liberty to hatch a new historical figure within the prevailing one, even when the nascent project has the spiritual energy necessary for viability. Generally speaking, the establishment prefers a struggle with God; and when the Spirit has been smothered, the law of success is cited as evidence that what has been defeated and suppressed has not been of God.

7. THE CHURCH, SUBJECT OF HISTORICAL DISCERNMENT

(a) Who Are the Church?

The Gamaliel episode poses the question of the subject or agent of discernment. Gamaliel recognizes the inadequacy of religious authority in this regard.

To resolve the question of the agent of discernment is not a simple matter. To be sure, the primary subject of discernment is the individual:

> In placing discernment at the center of Christian activity,
> St. Paul establishes the primacy of the individual and of
> what we today call individual conscience. Ultimately the

individual is the judge, and there is no appeal from his judgment. Nor is this only his right; it is his responsibility, as well. No Christian action exempts the individual from his full responsibility for the same. There is no worse subversion than an order of things that impels persons to renounce their responsibility and discharge it on others — a movement, a party, a state, a nation, or even the church.[21]

But the adequate subject of discernment *is* the church. The church is first and foremost not the ecclesiastical institution, but the congregation of the faithful. The church does not exist apart from persons. Thus, in beginning with the person and continuing with the church, we are simply invoking the personal nature of the church. The question is not *what* the church is, then, but *who* the church is. Accordingly, let us attempt to answer the question, "Who are the church as subject of discernment?" We shall base our answer on *Lumen Gentium,* numbers 13–16.

First of all, the church is the whole of humanity. Our God is the God of Abraham (Gen. 12:3), Jonah (4:10–11), Jesus (Mark 10:45), and Pentecost (Acts 2:17; 11:18). God is the creator of all, and wills the salvation of all. God wills not sinners' death, but their conversion and life (Wis. 1:13–14; 11:23–6; 1 Tim. 2:4; 2 Pet. 3:9; Rom. 11:32; Ezek. 18:23, 32; 33:11). All human beings are efficaciously called to enter into the body of Christ; in Christ all make up the family of God; upon all, the Spirit of Jesus has been poured forth. As long as we are on earth, we are all part of the people of God. God does not conform to the image maintained by the faithful, who take solace in the fact of their own fidelity for all the neglect on the part of those who ignore God. God is the Parent of all, and in Jesus has manifested an absolutely steadfast determination to be such. No other acceptation of the term *church* can cancel or relativize this primary meaning of the same. On the contrary, any other acceptation will have to meet the requirement of constituting a route to the realization of this one.

Second, the church consists of the poor of this world. Simply in virtue of their need, they are the favorite children of their divine Parent. God wills to save all, starting with the poor. Jesus is one of them, and they constitute his primordial sacrament.

Life and History

As the first acceptation of *church* is absolute, so the second reveals the absolute "whence," the absolute route to the attainment of universality.

Third, the church consists of those who form the visible body of the baptized. In the midst of a discriminatory world, they proclaim the unequivocal, unqualified universality of God's creative plan, along with the privilege of the poor along the route of its implementation. The church is the church of God to the extent that it proclaims this "situated universality" in an effective manner, and places itself unconditionally at its service. If the church is humanity, it will be the servant of humanity (Paul VI). If the church is the poor, the church will be called to take the figure of the poor. Accordingly, only as catholic (or, at any rate, en route to the realization of a genuine catholicity) and as church of the poor is the church the church of Jesus. Thus, the character of this third acceptation of *church* is entirely ministerial. But this is not merely a functional fact, but, primarily, a mystical one, since to be converted to this universality from beneath is to be transformed into a new creation. This is the meaning of witness. And among the baptized, to a greater or lesser degree, witness is always present.

Fourth, in a derived, factual way, the church consists of the concrete figures that the community of the baptized has assumed throughout the centuries—in the Latin American case, the figure of Latin American Christendom, especially as it is experienced by the people.[22] This figure is the product of a complex series of discernments, as well as the refusal to implement them. In it the inculturation of the gospel, and its acculturation, are mixed—the transformation of culture by the penetration of the gospel, and the swathing of the gospel in cultural patterns that, while not expressing it adequately, at least retain it; and on the other hand, the evisceration of the gospel by its introduction into anti-evangelical patterns.

(b) How the Church Discerns Today

In what way is the church—expressed at these four hierarchized levels—the agent of historical discernment? It would appear that the first level is all but bereft of concrete existence.

This is not the case, however, especially in our historical era, in which, as we have observed, a universal history now actually exists. Our era is a time of profound human aspirations and tendencies, which at the same time are actions of the Spirit. We Christians discern the Spirit of Jesus in these aspirations and tendencies; and even those who do not hear the Spirit speaking (Acts 19:2) nevertheless have an intuition that something sacred is occurring. One of these aspirations is the aspiration to liberation.[23] Another, doubtless, is the deep desire for true peace, with the proscription of nuclear weapons, and the groundswell for the suppression of all death-dealing violence. A third tendency, and a most important one, is the demand for the end of imperialisms, which divide the world into blocs, with a transition to international collaboration — in all respect for differences, but with the transformation of these differences into common enrichment through dialogue and cooperation. A fourth tendency is beginning to be strongly felt: a dialogue among religions from within, among religious persons of different cultures and religious traditions, in a quest not for a lowest common denominator, but for a more profound, ever more interior, dialogue, marked by cooperation and mutual correction.

In the measure that it moves toward this communion, then, humanity practices discernment, and its first fidelity is to be attentive to its discernments and to place them at the service of the communion it seeks.

The poor, too, exercise discernment. They do so whenever they refuse to abandon themselves to servile resignation, and raise their cry of agony and protest instead; whenever, from within their ethnic mystical nucleus, they resist the dominant culture, which ignores them as cultural beings; when, transcending the rationality of the system that condemns them, they demonstrate their capacity for hope, and their ability to create signs that maintain that hope; when they take advantage of some opportunity with their practicality and their sense of the appropriate moment, thereby maintaining themselves in life and winning little victories; when they bestir themselves and manage to organize, even at a rudimentary level. Especially, they exercise discernment when, being poor, they determinedly defend their dignity above all, knowing that this is their treasure, and often enough connecting it with their experience of God.[24]

It is very difficult to appreciate the discernments of the poor. If the poor are not valued as historical subjects, as agents of history, how shall they believe themselves capable of discernment? And yet the discernments of humanity are impossible without their collaboration. Neither peace, nor liberation, nor international cooperation is possible merely in the form of arrangements among the dominators of the world. All of this must transpire by way of a reconversion of the power of the mighty to the service of the poor of the wealthy nations and to the peoples of the Third World. Nor does the dialogue among religions have as its principal subjects the theologians or leaders; the agents of the interreligious dialogue must be the saints, and saints are found only among the poor or among those who have entered into solidarity with them and their cause.

That the faithful exercise a sure discernment is Catholic doctrine.[25] Lamentably, however, the *sensus fidelium,* so loudly proclaimed and so lavishly praised in theory, has no channels by which to express itself. One and one half centuries ago, Rosmini saw his church bleeding to death through five wounds, and the first wound was the separation of the clergy from the faithful in acts of worship.[26] And still today, despite all of the efforts of Vatican II, this separation seems to function practically as our primary dogma, so that teaching and learning, sanctifying and being forgiven, and all the other dimensions of Christian existence, constitute correlatives divided between the same two groups of persons: the clergy who give and the laity who receive.

This state of the institution, however, is not so inflexible that contrary figures, and discernment, are simply impossible. Indeed, the church institution in our century has shown itself capable of transcendent acts of discernment that can only be described as historic. Vatican II discerned the need for an energetic materialization of the catholicity of the church, a transformation tantamount to an operational dismantling of the identification of the church with Western culture.[27] To this purpose the church has proclaimed itself the continuation of Jesus, the good Samaritan: that is, the servant of humanity.[28] But this service would be impossible in terms of a nineteenth-century separation between clergy and faithful, and the church proclaimed its decision to make the joys and hopes, the sorrows and the anguish of the human beings of our time, especially of the poor and suffering, its own (*Gaudium et Spes,* I, 1). This act of discernment implies a complete change in the concrete figure of the church.

In order to arrive at this decision, the church had to become radical, it had to return to its source. Therefore it undertook a vigorous evangelism, and performed a historic act of *traditio* by handing over the Bible to the people. The great Constitution on the Church regards the people as the subject of the church, thereby opening the way for an awakening of the vast majority of the faithful: the laity.

In a neo-Restorationist atmosphere that threatens to smother all, it is not always easy to perceive ecclesial discernment. But the church now addresses humanity, and no longer its own clientele alone, as Pope Paul VI expressed it so beautifully and movingly in his closing discourse at Vatican II, in which he focused on the meaning of the council's religious value. This is an expression of the highest degree of ecclesial discernment in many centuries of history.

If the universal church suddenly seems so ambiguous a mediation, this is all the more the case with some of the various regional churches, especially as experienced from within. But these historical figures, themselves in such need of being subjected to a discernment, are yet capable of exercising the same: Witness the fact that the Latin American church, at Medellín and at Puebla, discerned the prophetic option of solidarity with the poor with a view to the liberation of the poor, and found in the base church communities the privileged agents of that option. The church in the United States has resolutely faced up to the problem of peace, as well as attempting a penetrating discernment of capitalism. The church of Africa is making more and more progress with the problem, so painful and so crucial by reason of the colonial character of the Christian religion, of Africanization.

Focusing on the Latin American church, we easily perceive the current moment as a "time of grace."[29] The "major fact" defining it is the awakening of a believing, oppressed people — the people's resistance and struggles, and the role of their Christian faith in that resistance and those struggles. Bound up with this phenomenon, and completely at its service, is the fact of the Fathers of the church, the prophets, the doctors, and especially, the great multitude of confessors and martyrs that God has bestowed upon that church. Latin America has a bishops' conference that, as the Holy Father has acknowledged, stands as a sign for the church universal.[30] The religious life is being reestablished in Latin America, and precisely among the people, in the image of Mary of Nazareth. And the religious creativity of the assembled faithful is beginning to bear simple, delicious fruit. This observation is scarcely triumphalistic. On the contrary, we make it in the face of our bitter experience of diffidence, helplessness, weakness, and, especially, the infinitely profound sorrow of our "dark night of injustice."

I believe it can be asserted that we are in the presence of an ever more adequate, intense, and cordial circularity among the four articulated agents of the church.

CHAPTER X

History and Eschatology

1. AN OPEN HISTORY

Let us suppose that this account of how the church interprets the present moment substantially represents the mind of the church, and that this interpretation, in its general lines, is actually an instance of spiritual discernment. If this were to be the case, we should then be guaranteed that, in committing ourselves to the activities cited, we are fulfilling the will of God, making us the witnesses of that will. And yet, this does not assure the success of these spiritual activities.

The Spirit and the Word do not impose themselves in despite of persons. They are not exterior, material, impersonal forces. These forces operate only within persons. They operate only through the moment of decision, which formally constitutes persons and history. To be sure, these decisions are made not in a vacuum, but in reality. Not just anything, therefore, can be decided at any moment. A decision can take advantage of opportunities and create capacities only if it begins with real possibilities. But this being said, we must insist that the Spirit and the Word operate only in free human acts. The Word and the Spirit liberate, yes (John 8:36; Luke 4:18; Rom. 8:2, 15; 2 Cor. 3:17; Gal. 4:6–7; 5:16). But only a free response to their liberation can constitute a spiritual activity.

Inasmuch as the Spirit and the Word act only within our freedom, we have the pseudo-power to reject the Word (Matt.

11:16–24; 17:11–12; 23:27; John 1:5) and quench the Spirit (1 Thess. 5:19). We have the freedom to frustrate God's design (Luke 7:30).

Against all arguments for foreknowledge, predestination, *scientia media,* and the like, the simple fact is that history is true for God, as well. History is not the projection of a film that has already been produced, the staging of a theatrical work whose script has already been written. The activity that defines history is human activity, human creation, from the point of view of its human author, who is its author in the strictest sense (besides being its agent and its actor); and it is divine activity, from the point of view of God, who is its author (besides being its actor). Human beings and God both make and undergo history; and God more so than human beings, although God ordinarily acts only through them (inasmuch as the operation of God transpires by means of the Spirit and the Word).

Thus, Christianity proclaims that, despite its materiality, indeed precisely because of its materiality, history is open. And the spiritual activity occurring within it, far from determining it by way of closing it, guarantees its openness.

2. "WHO SEEKS TO SAVE HIS LIFE WILL LOSE IT" (Luke 17:33)

Accordingly, we may permit ourselves to delegate the exercise of our freedom, either as individuals or as a social body, neither to the experts, who demand reverence for their plans in the name of economic laws; nor to the state and the party, which demand our submission in exchange for organizing our social life in security and stability; nor to the wise, who offer to plan our future; nor to the church institution, which guarantees us meaning and salvation in exchange for the surrender of our own judgment and will.

Our problem today is not flight, anarchism, or Promethean rebellion. Our problem today is fear of freedom. The most significant endeavors of the Western world, the Renaissance and the Enlightenment, have been attempts to cancel history through the resolution of its enigmas and contradictions and its reduction to an immanent law. Both capitalistic positivism and socialism (which is a further step in the same direction, a direction already dialecticized by Hegel) understand history (once we have arrived at the positive stage, or a socialistic society) as the development of the present, as its projection. Openness to the future is excluded.

Despite all our talk of history, we live in fear of history. We search for ways to cancel its openness, to find complete security. What contradicts freedom is not determinism, in its various forms; these are merely the absence of freedom. Even in a closed situation, there is room for witness and martyrdom. This was precisely Jesus' most exalted and decisive act, his spiritual activity par excellence, the action that consummated his whole life. What contradicts freedom is a concern for security at all costs, a life that wafts above everything in order to "preserve itself" (see Mark 8:35). No, we shall "lose it," that life; and not only because we shall die in any case, but because thus to live is to center life on itself, and to squander it in its sheer preservation.

Thus, to live historically—that is, in an open fashion and with one's feet firmly implanted in reality—is not a characteristic of Western culture as contradistinguished from traditional cultures. To live historically is not a cultural trait. It is the grace of God in the strictest sense. It is the spiritual activity par excellence, the gift of the Spirit of Jesus. After all, Jesus came in a flesh like unto ours in every way, for he came in our weakness and our vulnerability. In this weakness he was tried and tested in all things, and learned obedience through suffering, learned to remain steadfast in the trial, the *agonia*. And so, draining the cup of helplessness to the dregs, dying without receiving any response to his cry and his gift, commending himself to an utterly hidden God, he succeeded by his death in "deliver[ing] all those who for fear of death were passing their entire lives as slaves" (Heb. 2:15).

Thus, Jesus had to evangelize in poverty. Only in his material and institutional helplessness could he convincingly preach the faith that conquers fear; only thus could he preach trust in the God who delivers us from the security syndrome. The witness alone is free. Only the witness, conquering his or her anxiety, assumes the task of seeking the reign of the justice of God in this world, knowing that God will provide for all needs "besides"

(Matt. 6:33). Obviously we are not suggesting that God is indifferent to our security. An effort to render life gradually more foreseeable, and place its most elementary material needs more within reach, is but to fulfill the divine command to subdue the earth. Not to cooperate in this task is irresponsibility. What God does not wish is that we transform security into a fetish that demands the abandonment of dignity and solidarity, so that we discriminate against others and finally put them to death. "The unbelievers are always running after these things" (Matt. 6:32). Hence we qualify as a spiritual event those among our people who, without a place to lay their heads, devote themselves to living life just as it comes from the hand of God, without closing in on themselves, because they know that "today has troubles enough of its own" (Matt. 6:34).

3. "IN THIS SIGN YOU SHALL CONQUER"

The difficulty of accepting this openness resides in the fact that, if it is accepted in a consistent manner, it involves the possibility of failure, on the personal level as well as on that of a human group, a movement, a social class, an institution, a country, a whole era, or even history in its entirety.

It seemed obvious to Jesus' disciples that, if Jesus was the one anointed by the Spirit of God and come to save his people, success would accompany his every step: People would surrender to him, otherwise his conquering sword would bring them to reason. This was the reason for the ongoing altercation between Jesus and his disciples. It had begun with a confrontation with the leaders of the people (Mark 7:1–23; Luke 11:37–12:12), when Jesus had had to flee (Mark 7:24; John 7:1). Jesus had given the disciples to understand, in no uncertain terms, that things were not going well, and would go worse (Mark 8:31–8). To the very day of Jesus' ascension (Acts 1:6–8), the disciples maintained their stubborn notion of the messianic Reign, and had already begun to dispute among themselves as to which positions of authority in that Reign each of them would occupy. Jesus had rebuked Peter with unwonted sternness when the latter had attempted to win him over to the disciples' notion (Mark 8:33), and thereafter the disciples no longer spoke with him about it, simply falling silent when he sought to recall them to reality (Mark 9:30–32). But they by no means gave up their idea, as it was of capital importance to them. Long since, on a hill in Galilee, they had sought to place Jesus at the head of an insurrection, and Jesus, "realizing that they were about to carry him off to proclaim him king" (John 6:15), had had to oblige the disciples to embark for Bethsaida while he sent the people home peacefully (Mark 6:45). With Jesus' triumphal entry into Jerusalem, and the cleansing of the Temple — events much more to their taste when it came to the meaning of messiahship — they regained their courage. Hence Jesus' treatment of the subject once again at the farewell supper (Luke 22:24–30), and the disciples' haste to reassure him that they had weapons to defend him when he made the heartrending announcement that he was approaching his end (Luke 22:37–8). Even in the garden they asked, "Lord, shall we strike with the sword?" (Luke 22:49).

And hence the extremely heavy blow to their faith when God failed to answer Jesus' cry of agony, and when their great leader went down to defeat and death. "They crucified him," said the disciples on the road to Emmaus, "when we had hoped that he would be the liberator of Israel" (Luke 24:20–21).

It taxes our credulity to think that Jesus was unable to change his disciples' mind even when he appeared to them resurrected from the dead. Only when they were at last convinced that he was gone, and the Spirit had strengthened them at Pentecost, did their witness commence.

It would not be difficult to show that the mentality of ecclesiastics down through the greater part of the history of the church has remained closer to that of the disciples before their conversion than to that of Jesus. Verily they are the successors of the apostles! Indeed, the inversion has been so complete and so obtuse that, from Constantine's day to our own, the cross, that image of the most ignominious of tortures, transformed by Jesus and the first Christians into a symbol of testimony, has come to be raised as a battle standard. The sign of Jesus' victory in death has been transformed into a talisman for conquest by murder. The most sacred testimonial of the power of the Spirit, which is realized in weakness, has come to be the standard of that most unspiritual of all forces, the power of weaponry, with its brazen destruction of the deed of the Spirit, life.[1]

"In this sign you shall conquer!" To the majority of Christians (especially ecclesiastics and Christians of the dominant classes) the meaning of the motto that a certain tradition reports to have thundered down from the sky upon the ears of the Emperor Constantine has always seemed to go without saying: Jesus is risen, and the crucified one is now Lord; therefore the cross gives victory; therefore victory is proof that Jesus is with those who wear the cross as their escutcheon. Jesus' power now becomes a worldly power, at work through Christians, who thus see themselves obliged ever to triumph for the glory of that most sacred name. Hence the view of the West's conquest of the world as a demonstration of the truth of Christianity. Where is Jesus' cause? What has become of "the way"? The preaching of the Reign has undergone a complete transformation. It has become the preaching of a Western Christian civilization blessed by the church institution. The path of subjection trodden by Jesus is itself subjected to the yoke of a church institution with its obligatory guidelines. Jesus of Nazareth? A thing of the past. The only Jesus we know is King of kings and Lord of lords. It was a bitter pill, then, for the church institution when the French Revolution and then nineteenth-century liberals laicized its power. Now the church undertook a feverish quest for allies, wooing them with the naive proposition that to be on the side of the church was to secure their stability, and leaving it to God to judge the legitimacy of the powers it happened to be able to recruit, or the moral quality of their concrete deportment. The premise of this proposition, we are assured, is not opportunism, but the objective need of the church institution to flourish and be honored. After all, any honor paid to the sign of Christ is honor paid to Christ; and the world's salvation depends upon the extension of the church to all nations.

This same outlook finds its analogue on the individual level: The sign of Jesus, as a sign of honor in Christian society, is transformed into an expression of social status. The crucifix is suddenly the favorite subject of artists, in gold, silver, and pigment. The scandal of the cross (Gal. 5:11) has simply been suppressed. The stigma of the torture perpetrated on the gibbet of the first cross has been rehabilitated beyond all recognition. And what is the display of this talisman supposed to bring? Protection, security: the very contrary of the historical act effected by Jesus on his instrument of torture. But the contradiction goes unnoticed, for Jesus suffered but once, *hapax* (Heb. 9:12–28), whereas the risen one is alive forever. This cross speaks of love, then, yes; but not of the following of the historical Jesus.

In a society in which Jesus is the countersign of success and security, there is no room for the proclamation of the gospel or the testimony of the witnesses. There is no room for freedom. There is no allowance made for spiritual activity. Dostoevsky had the wisdom to see this, and portrayed it in his Legend of the Grand Inquisitor. Despite its protests, then, Western Christian society is an a-historical society. The self-styled free world rejects an open history. And the version of Christianity which continues to impregnate its every fiber contributes to the maintenance of this closure to all possibilities other than those immanent in the system.

A society enslaved to success is scarcely en route to its autonomy. And a Christianity understood as a sign of victory not only does not assist society in this task, but encourages it along its way by enslaving it to its own demons. And yet the acts of discernment that we have examined indicate that spiritual activity is still alive in the church of today. Which antithesis will prevail?

4. "THERE WAS IN HIM NO STATELY BEARING" (Isa. 53:2)

Jesus' cross prevents us from conjuring up historical figures of the Reign. On the cross, messianisms shatter and die.[2] The one who was raised is the one who was crucified; and the fact of his raising prevents the problem of the cross from being relegated to the past. The one who was raised poses the question anew to each generation, vitally, currently. The one who was raised "is not here" (Mark 16:6). "You shall be told: Look here, here he is! But do not go. Do not go running after him there" (Luke 17:23). The risen one is not a figure of this world. He was not raised "to restore the Kingdom to Israel" (Acts 1:6). "He has been taken hence, up to heaven" (Acts 1:11). He has been raised; then he is no longer buried in the past. He is not here;

then there is no Messiah here, or Reign of God. As the one who was raised is the one who was crucified, it is his historical figure that continues to be set before us: humiliation, weakness, defeat, paradox, subversion, and so on—but above all, mystery. The crucified one is risen; then history is open. The risen one is the one who was crucified; then wisdom, power, and religion are all subject to judgment. Thus, no historical figure is messianic; all that remain are sacraments, actions. But neither is any historical figure diabolical; there always remain actions, and sacraments.

In Jesus, then, we can see that history is deprived of a definitive, closed figure. What "defines" history is only, and precisely, its invincible openness. But the open is the provisional. The figures of history are provisional—not because they do not endure, but because they are not perfect: because they have not attained the dimensions of consummate humanity, the dimensions of Jesus the new human being; but also because they have not become utterly dehumanized. Still, they are under summons at the hands of both coordinates. Humanity is called by God, in absolute and irrevocable fashion, to be transformed into the historical body of Jesus, into the total Christ. But there exists the possibility that this vocation might be spurned. Yet the coordinates are not of the same scope. From the fact of Jesus' resurrection we know that there have always been and always will be persons faithful to God, persons fully human. Jesus is risen not as a private individual, but as Lord; and this title would be empty if at any time he were utterly bereft of subjects—completely without siblings of his and children of God, persons. Accordingly, the total condemnation of humanity is out of the question. But the possibility of individual condemnation remains open, and for all. The openness of history is such that it implies the possibility of absolute failure. The possibilities of failure today include the suicide of all humanity (actually a murder-suicide, in the form of the death of all humanity at the hands of its leaders), as well as eternal death, the absolute failure of the individual.

5. POSSIBILITY OF FAILURE

This historical possibility today lies buried under a conspiracy of silence. When Pope John Paul II speaks of hell, he provokes smiles of commiseration in the press and among enlightened theologians—eloquent symbols of the fear of history that paralyzes the West and enslaves it to its security to the point of necrophilia.

Who in the time of Christendom felt more threatened by the prospect of death, judgment, and hell? As in the Bible, the rich. Actually the bourgeoisie do not care for hell. They know that, if hell exists, they will be first on the list. On the other hand, if we take the viewpoint of the poor, who pass their time watching their oppressors revel with impunity, we must admit that if hell did not exist it would have to be invented. It would have to be invented for the Somozas and all the blood-soaked dictators, for the exploiters who have iniquitously murdered so many thousands of campesinos, as in El Salvador, and for all the other unpunished malefactors who triumph while their victims writhe in helplessness. The bourgeoisie wanted a religious message purified of anything like an apocalypse. And they have finally managed to get one.[3]

We do not actually wish to see Somoza, or Bush, or any other enemy of the people, in hell. On the contrary, we pray for those who persecute us (Rom. 12:14). But we think that the possibility of absolute failure, a real one for them as for us, has been completely concealed from them by religious professionals who offer them a bourgeois brand of "religion." And we think that this is the reason for their still further deprivation of the sense of reality already so lacking in their exercise of power.

History can issue in failure, then. Freedom can issue in one's own depersonalization and that of a multitude of others. History is this open.

6. CHILDREN OF THE REIGN AND "FISHES OF EVERY KIND"

This brings us to the problem of history and eschatology, the latter understood as the definitive consummation of God's plan already fulfilled in the person of Jesus: that we human beings,

with, through, and in Jesus, may come to be sisters and brothers
of one another and daughters and sons of God. The problem of
history and eschatology, then, is this: Is history open enough for
this plan to be frustrated?

As we have already indicated, God's plan is always implemented in some degree: Jesus is Lord because he is the firstborn
of a multitude of brothers and sisters (Rom. 8:29). In our concrete history, then, spiritual activity will always actually manage
to engender children of the Reign. This is guaranteed by Jesus'
resurrection. Hence history is always in some way a salvation
history, since these children of the Reign are not exceptional or
isolated individuals, but sisters and brothers; thus they compose
communions of sisters and brothers that, provisional as they are,
are visible signs of the Reign.

Now, these communions, being of the children of the Reign,
are not ethnic communities, or political or economic or religious
societies. They are, however, expressed through such communities and societies. That is, history does not admit of an eschatological configuration. As St. Augustine argued against the
Donatists, the church is a church at once of sinners and the just.
It is not a little clique of saints — as Jesus himself insisted, against
the integralist tendencies of the officialdom of his own time,
tendencies interiorized by his own disciples. This was the significance of his practice of taking his meals with tax collectors
and unbelievers, a practice that was scandalous and intolerable
in the minds of the devout of his time and place (Matt. 9:10–
13; 11:16–19). This is what he sought to inculcate in the parables
of the wheat and the weeds (Matt. 13:24–30, 36–43), and of the
net that gathered in every kind of fish (Matt. 13:47–50). Definitive judgment is not handed down in history; nor is it handed
down by human beings. As long as we are on earth, good and
evil will continue to live in inextricable composition.

7. AMBIGUITY AS PROVISIONALITY AND AS GRACE

Salvation history occurs in ambiguity. One root of this ambiguity is, as we have pointed out, the provisional character of any
figure, personal or historical. Here we must recall Jesus' words,
"Why do you call me good? Only God is good" (Mark 10:18).

Only activities are spiritual. But as long as we are in history, activity does not define us. Openness abides, and with it the possibility of tergiversation. In history we find actions, signs, spiritual trajectories, but no saved realities. Or, if you will, saved realities are such by being such, the saints are such by being such, that is, we are all still in process; even those persons who by the grace of God have never abandoned their spiritual course are but *in via;* nor is anyone more aware than they that they have not yet attained the goal (Phil. 3:12–14), and that they must continue to run the race. They can still lose (1 Cor. 9:23–7).

Thus, the Reign cannot be pared down to the dimensions of history. It is realized in history, but never in more than germinal fashion (Rom. 8:18–25; 1 Cor. 15:35–58). The Reign will contain only what will have been sown in history. Eschatology is present in history; but the historical will only be eschatological when it ceases to be historical—that is, when, at the consummation of personal reality, historical openness, historical provisionality, disappears. "We shall all be transformed" (1 Cor. 15:51). Eschatological transformation means the disappearance of our historical condition. But the disappearance of this historical openness means not our naturalization, but the consummation of a freedom now become absolutely spiritual.

Historical openness, accordingly, while it is a gift, is still provisional, inasmuch as we can still opt for our own and others' depersonalization. Hence the insuperable ambiguity of history. But history is also, and fundamentally, ambiguous by reason of the patience of God. As shown in part 1, that patience is the supreme expression of God's love; it expresses God's trust and confidence in us. It is the patience of God that "gives us time"— that "keeps history going" until it reaches its maturity. God's patience makes history a time of conversion. Hence the salvific value of historical ambiguity. To wish to resolve it by a definitive judgment, then, is an act of impiety—a sectarian, elitist action, contrary to the universal communion of brothers and sisters for which God has created us. The ambiguity of history is God's grace, and to seek to do away with it always implies the desire to exclude a part of humanity from communion by frustrating the forgiveness bestowed by Jesus on the cross.

Thus understood, an acceptance, a welcome of the ambiguity

of history in no way implies any tepidity, any lack of radicality or commitment. On the contrary, it is the flower of a love of solidarity, and the mark of Christian genuineness. It is the Christian climate.

An understanding of a history in ambiguity comports a profound liberative meaning, inasmuch as it opens the understanding subject or agent to a spirit of moderation, to the positive sense of the relative, to realism, and most of all, to reality; and hence to tolerance, to self-criticism, and to the genuine use of democracy. It opens us to the practice of freedom.

CHAPTER XI

Call and Benediction: History and Life

According to the Bible, life is the object of God's blessing, and history opens with God's call. The blessing asks service of the human being; and the call asks discipleship. What is the relationship between blessing and call, service and following, life and history?

1. AN UNRESOLVED TENSION

(a) Salvation History, or Hope against Hope?

In God's plan, in the experience of men and women of God, and in theological elaboration, there is a synthesis of the two, surely, or in any case an open road in that direction. But in the experience pointed up by so many biblical events, the experience to which so many of the psalmists' prayers, the prophets' oracles, and the maxims of the Wisdom authors refer, we observe rather a lively, unresolved tension. Religion centered on life tends to absolutize and sacralize life (wealth, fertility, success, power), exchanging obedience to the transcendent God for service (without ethical commitment) to the state and the Temple (condensations of the ethnic group's will to power). Indeed, is it possible to institutionalize a religion based on discipleship and following? For large numbers of people over long periods of time, does not the attitude of openness and transcendent obedience postulated by discipleship become insupportable?

Thus, in the Bible the drama appears to oscillate between, on the one hand, those shining hours in which the people get under way, more or less grumbling, accepting God's leadership through the mediation of some exceptional human being, and so manage to overcome straitened situations of slavery and oppression; and on the other hand, the rest of the time—the greater part—in which this impulse gives way, and the nation is structured on the basis of the artificial powers to which worship is rendered (wealth, power, sex, political and military might), despite the intent to historicize worship and prophetic judgments. In this latter situation, the normal one, the religion of following is seen as an alienating fanaticism, foolishness, missed opportunities, pure lost time and energy.

To be sure, the Bible recounts and celebrates deeds of salvation. But were not most of these accounts written in times of suffering and humiliation, to reawaken a glorious memory and motivate hope through a faith in things unseen? Surely the sacred authors, like the personages of whom they tell, loved life with a passion, and threw themselves into living it with exceptional intensity; but abundant, happy life, despite them, is not the situation that prevails throughout the greater part of their narratives and reflections.

Rather than being the history of certain tribes, and a nation, the Bible resembles a testimony that runs against the grain of the prevailing situation. In terms of the God whose summons is to discipleship, the Bible is a judgment rendered upon disobedience and unremitting rebellion. In terms of the God who blesses, it is a petition for life on behalf of the plundered, miserable faithful.

(b) From Fulfillment in David (and Jesus) to Apocalyptic Expectancy

The Lord's call to discipleship comports the promise of a blessing. And in the foundational era, culminating in David and Solomon, the blessing is indeed bestowed. But the very writings that celebrate the blessing present the sin of David and the apostasy of Solomon, deeds that culminate in violence, division, and finally, ruin. This is the subject of the rest of the material in the books of Kings, the work of the chronicler, and the books of the prophets. Second Isaiah issues the call for a new exodus, a call bursting with abundant, fertile promises. How could we help being discouraged at the meager fruits of the divine blessing in the Persian era? How understandable, here, the transition from discipleship to the service performed by a religion of law. Now discipleship is transcendentalized and dehistoricized, and blessing is spiritualized, while at the same time the thesis is maintained, in principle, of a correspondence between obser-vance and felicity. But in the face of the evident insufficiency of this solution, was it not inevitable that discipleship should be radicalized by way of its dehistoricization? And so it is converted into a death-defying testimony laden with the hope of the abso-lute blessing of the victory of the saints and a prolongation of their life. With the loss of hope in a historical route, then, apo-calypticism transforms following into a martyr's impatience for the definitive struggle that will bring salvation to the faithful.

It is significant that, despite Jesus' resurrection having in prin-ciple resolved the tension between following and blessing, the Gospels should have sought to recall to the Christian commu-nities the inability of Jesus of Nazareth either to convert the leaders of Israel to discipleship (impotence of the absolutized Law and Temple), or sway his own disciples from a Davidic, immediatistic understanding of the Reign which was to become present with him. The leaders rejected discipleship and the promise of the banquet because they were already enjoying the "blessings" — altogether earthly ones, to be sure — of the Law and the Temple. The disciples continued to live in the hope of the "blessing" inherent in the restoration of Israel's sovereignty. At all events, with the coming of the Spirit, witness is inaugu-rated; yet the imminent coming of Jesus does not materialize; and the New Testament, like the Old, ends with an apocalypse.

2. THE CULTURALISTIC SOLUTION: FOLLOWING/NOMADISM, BLESSING/SEDENTARISM

(a) Reading of the Old Testament in This Perspective

One way of explaining this tension and of resolving it in prin-ciple consists in assimilating the basic religious forms, the call to following and the blessing of service, to two respective cultures. The people who had experienced liberation from the power of Egypt and undertaken the journey through the desert constitute a nomadic group. The very existence of the followers depends entirely on their leaders.[1] Everything depends on the maintenance by the followers of their union with the one at their head. To abandon him is sin. Faith means a decision for following; apostasy is abandoning the journey. Obedience and following are equivalent terms. The experiences of the journey provide the ongoing structure of one's relationship with God; there is no other, antecedent law. Along the road, one experiences the marvels of salvation and preservation; and thus occur the revelation of God, which works as the constitution of the people, and simultaneously the revelation the people have of their own weaknesses and of the fact that, upon these weaknesses, healing them and forgiving them, God never ceases to build, out of pure mercy.

But with the conquest of the land of promise, the existential form of discipleship comes to an end. Once established, the people are born to a new manner of existing, and their sedentary life gradually yields up a new way of relating to God. They learn to see God acting in a continuous, silent way, throughout their own beginnings, increase, and prosperity. The basic biblical word for this experience is blessing: blessing of the land, blessing of the body, increase and prosperity of persons, animals, and plants; and health and salvation, in all their forms, especially the health and salvation of the community—the blessing of peace.

The price of Israel's success in wresting from the deities of the country (the baals, divinities of fertility) their activity of blessing, in opposing their cults, and in recognizing as Lord of the country and dispenser of blessings the God who had delivered them from Egypt and had led them through the desert, was a tremendous struggle. They succeeded, however. They established an identity between the Lord who had led the people and the one who now blessed them. Indeed, the blessing was but the fulfillment of the promise for which God had called them to discipleship and following.

The correspondence seemed to be perfect. Still, to assert the material identity of the savior of the past and the one who blessed the present was altogether insufficient unless the two functions were to be internally related and mutually interpretative. If the activity of liberation was confined to a past proclaimed by creeds and recalled in worship, current blessing would inevitably be configured according to Canaanite religious sentiment and ritual expression. This would mean the Baalization of Yahweh. Under the cloak of Yahwist orthodoxy, an effective conversion to the religion of the land would have been wrought.

This process would undoubtedly have been stimulated by contact with the agricultural Canaanite peoples; but on a deeper level, it would be a function of the transformation of the Israelite tribes themselves into sedentary peoples. The mystery that filled their daily lives was that of the fertility of land and livestock, whose obvious symbol was sexual generation. Dependence on rains and seasons would suggest the mythic marriage of the divinities of sky and earth, whose political transposition was at hand in the relationship between the king and the scions of the land. These conceptualizations, joined to an economic activity and a societal model, created a favorable atmosphere for religious practices of the Canaanite type. The temptation was to embrace the same practices in honor of Yahweh. And in large measure this is what occurred.

The extreme case of the perception of the bond between a sedentary life and the baalization of Yahwism was that of the recalcitrants who for this religious reason refused to be transformed into farmers and continued to dwell in tents and make their living from their herds.

(b) Meaning of Yahwism (and Christianity) in a Sedentary World

A genetic relationship between Yahwism and nomadism is beyond dispute. Now, if this relationship were to become structural as well, Yahwism in a sedentary world could only be understood as a proposition for exceptional beings (prophets, apocalyptics), or else as an ideal value system now detached from a way of life, from a historical existence — that is, as a religious ideology.

This double interpretation is a phenomenon of Christianity, as well. When Jesus left his family home, he became a nomad, to pursue the existence of an eschatological prophet.[2] And he proposed this manner of existence to his disciples.[3] His proposition radicalized the first discipleship of Israel's foundation, inasmuch as the following of Jesus was no longer a discipleship within a culture, but a breach with and abandonment of cultural bonds and the embracing of an eschatological lifestyle. Jesus makes no attempt to establish a new ethnic people as the people of God; on the contrary, he calls persons to leave their flesh and blood, to live as persons born of God, of the Spirit, to live as sisters and brothers in one family of the daughters and sons of God.

If this is Christianity, then Christianity must either be understood as a leaven in the paste of humanity, or be reinterpreted as a mere internal attitude, an ideal, with its historical realization reserved to a handful of the elect (with the consequent temptation of the church institution to identify itself with the elect and thereby to justify its ascendancy over and domination of the Christian people). Ought this interpretation of Yahwism and Christianity to be maintained?

3. COEXISTENCE OF CALL AND BLESSING THROUGHOUT THE BIBLE

It is impossible to reduce Old Testament theology to lines of a salvation history restricted to liberation and judgment, election and covenant, sin and pardon. Other themes, too, must be taken into account, likewise pertaining to events occurring between God and the people of God: themes in which the maelstrom of life—of generation, birth, and death, blessing, growth, and decline, prosperity and attainment, peace and maturation—is the only consideration.

The definitive coincidence of salvation and benediction comes to manifestation in, for example, the structure of the Pentateuch. While its central part (Exodus and Numbers) is totally determined by the guiding and saving activity of God, in both Genesis and Deuteronomy the capital theological concept is blessing. The people's salvation history is enclosed within, on the one side, a pre-history in which the birth and growth of Israel is recounted, beginning with the patriarchal family, and on the other side, Deuteronomy, whose gaze is directed to a lasting dwelling place in a land which promises the people all blessings, provided they maintain their fidelity to the God who delivered them.

The same holds true for the structure of worship. The most specific element in worship is the fact of its determination by history. Worship is the celebration of the wondrous works of God in the face of the terrors and threats of the present. But worship is a quest for blessing, and finds its fulfillment there; after all, it is only by the blessing of God that the people can continue to subsist in the land of conquest. The Psalms, intimately bound to worship, likewise embrace both vectors. And even the prophets, those heralds of God's judgment, conclude their prophecies with oracles of benediction.

In the New Testament, the capital theological line is utterly determined by God's single, definitive salvific act in Jesus Christ, through his passion, death, and resurrection. Historical event, then, is the focus of all. But Easter is told in the Gospels only after the presentation of a Jesus who was born and grew to adulthood sharing our life and then promoted this life of ours, blessing it, healing it, defending it, and guiding it. Within this context of God's activity of benediction figures a whole series of accounts—healing, the blessing of children, meals taken in community, and, along with the blessing of nourishment, many words entrusted for preservation and observance. But it is Jesus' parables, especially, that give us to understand that gradual growth and maturation, an obscure life of silent becoming, form part of the coming of the Reign of God inaugurated by the event that is Jesus. This same bond is to be observed in the missionary discourse (Matt. 10:5–13), in which the disciples are not only sent to preach the irruption of the Reign and conversion, but are vessels of benediction. The letters of Paul, as well, which treat of the revelation of the Christian mystery in the Jesus event, begin and end with blessings.

4. CORRESPONDENCE BETWEEN CALL AND BLESSING

This summary review has already suggested the relations and correspondences we seek. Let us make them explicit.

(a) Discipleship and Life

Historically, Israel springs into being as a people with a call from God to discipleship and following, that they may emerge from non-life (the house of oppression). They are encouraged in this project by the promise of full life (a land flowing with milk and honey). But between rescue from non-life and the possession of full life come struggle and wilderness—two variations on the theme of a physical life accounted as of little worth in comparison with genuine, real life, which is still to be won: the life that is freedom. Here, to prefer freedom to life is discipleship, following, obedience to the voice of the Lord, which arouses a longing for deliverance. Freedom, then, is the fruit of obedience. Deliverance is following, not Promethean or Satanic excess. The sources are quite clear on this point, emphasizing the people's fear, and their incessant temptation to turn back. And so the passage to fullness of life by way of the event of liberation is obedience to the call of the Lord—being taken in tow by the voice of the Lord. Thus, obedience is the form (the event) whose matter (content) is life.

The experience of life in the desert is the experience of living by the word of God, as the desert is the place where there is no life. Faith is the attitude of the one who believes that, while there is no life for the people now, there will be; hence one seeks and creates life rather than returning to the security of the marginal life of slavery.

Once the land is attained and possessed, faith yields to vision. The revelation, the unveiling of God, is followed by thanksgiving. Blessing received is linked to discipleship, to the keeping of the covenant. But gradually the relationship becomes less transparent. Gradually blessing seems to come from the land itself, from the heaven that stretches across this land, and from a socio-political organization eventually felt as representing these powers.

The prophets re-establish the connection between blessing and discipleship. For them, a failure in discipleship (injustice, idolatry) will bring down a curse on the heads of the remiss. Ruin is understood as the consequence of unfaithfulness. In the sedentary life, then, the relationship with God, when it is in order, is certainly manifested as blessing; but blessing presupposes fidelity to a path, a pilgrimage—for there are attractions even in the sedentary life that tempt a person to abandon the following of the Lord.

The temptation to abandon the call is presented so forcefully because the relationship between call and benediction, between following and well-being, prosperity and peace, is now no longer so very palpable. Yes, the Lord delivered the people from the hand of Pharaoh, and when they were in the desert food and water were not lacking. Yes, God raised up judges who saved the people in moments of prostration and danger, and in David God gave them independence and greatness. But all of this is little by little receding into the past. The judgment pronounced by Elijah on Mount Carmel as to which God—the Lord or Baal—held the keys to reign was handed down but once. And yet Hezekiah has not managed to rescue Judah from enthrallment to Assyria, and the devout, vigorous Josiah has gone down in defeat. Granted, the oracles of Amos and Hosea concerning the destruction of Israel have come true, like those of Jeremiah a century and a half later. But even then contrary interpretations have not been lacking: "Then we had enough food to eat and we were well off; we suffered no misfortune. But since we stopped burning incense to the queen of heaven and pouring out libations to her, we are in need of everything and are being destroyed by the sword and by hunger" (Jer. 44:17–18).

(b) Faith: Affirmation of Life and Plumbing of Its Content

It is not always actually possible, of course, to demonstrate a relationship between following and blessing. But this is precisely why there is a Bible constructed on faith in that relationship. With this faith the history of Abraham opens, and all the rest of the Bible is only a development of it: "The Lord said to Abram: 'Go forth from the land of your kinsfolk and from your father's house. . . . I will make of you a great nation. . . . All the communities of the earth shall find blessing in you.' Abram went as the Lord directed him" (Gen. 12:1–4). The father of all believers heard the call and set forth, trusting in the promised blessing, which, when all is said and done, still awaits fulfillment.

This, with all its harmonics, will be the keynote of the whole Old Testament. How was this tension maintained throughout so many centuries? By way of historical sacraments. But these deeds, small or great, nourished faith because there was faith; and because, besides having their own substance, they were perceived as the food of faith. In sum, through this history of calls and blessings, God was being revealed as a trustworthy God, and faithful people put their trust in God. Here was a God present in prodigies of salvation and the blessings of life, but ever more and more transcendent in them; and people fulfilled by the gifts of God, but more and more interested in the gift of the human self.

The closing era of the Old Testament is electric with expectancy—not only because of a national prostration, and the misery and oppression of the people, but because a frustrated faith aimed even higher each time it had to be renewed. If all begins with the creator's blessing, not only upon human beings but upon everything alive, endowing all with vital strength (whose effectiveness has always been maintained, and will be maintained until the end of the world), then the lesson of adversity is that "your faithfulness is worth more than life" (Ps. 3:4). "For though my spirit and my flesh rot away, God is the rock of my spirit, and my heritage everlasting" (Ps. 73:26). "For in you is the living spring, and in your light shall we see light" (Ps. 36:10). Indeed, persecution generates the paradox of a preference for fidelity over life, and a view of this destiny as a blessing: "The Lord in his holy knowledge knows full well that, although I could have escaped death, I am not only enduring terrible pain in my body from this scourging, but also suffering it with joy in my soul because of my devotion to him" (2 Mac. 6:30). This blind confidence finds a route for self-expression in a life that overcomes death.

That this hope does not abandon today's struggles, or those engaged in those struggles, is evinced not only in the fact of martyrdom in our midst, where it is expressed explicitly, but in its counterpart, the activity of the persecutor, where it is implicit: "Only wait, and you will see how his great power will torment you and your descendants" (2 Mac. 7:17). Discipleship, then, consummated in the extreme case of martyrdom, leads at one and the same time to an apocalyptical conviction of the retribution of God and the triumph of the saints, and to hope in the life that this same God will raise up from the midst of death.

Like Second Isaiah, Jesus assumes the figure of an evangelist. He preaches the imminence of the Reign, but without either the paradisiac expressions of a second exodus in the spirit of Second Isaiah, or the militaristic messianism and ethnocentrism of the apocalyptical writers. Jesus is an evangelist because he preaches the imminence of the Reign as grace—as God's blessing, as the fruit of an utterly gratuitous love. The font of discipleship is blessing. Discipleship, following, is not a condition for the receiving of blessing, and still less a cause of salvation. It is the fruit of blessing. It is certainly free, and fully human; but it springs from the Spirit through whom Jesus, God's Word, issues the divine call to discipleship. Thus, Jesus' call to follow him communicates the Spirit of Life, who becomes the fountain, deep within us, that wells up to eternal life (John 4:14).

(c) Life and Eternal Life: Not Dichotomy, but Dialectic

The Old Testament, then, delves into the content of blessing. For the patriarchs it is fertility (of the people, the earth, the livestock), long life, and peace. Gradually it comes to light that God is not only the bestower of life for us, but Life itself. Finally, a hope dawns that God will rescue the faithful from the clutches of a death suffered out of faithfulness. Jesus will take a further step in the same direction: One must give one's life in order to keep it. Life is not booty to be clung to, but a gift to give; only by giving it away does one retain life—that is, only in bestowing one's life does one move from a state of existence as an ensouled being to that of a spirit and wellspring of life (1 Cor. 14:45).

This state of the question implies a dialectization of the concept of life. This is one of the structural themes of the Gospel of John: There is a life proper to this world, which we must surrender in order to fulfill ourselves in a new quality of life. This consists in the new identity of children of God: The self-surrender of gratuitous love makes us like our divine Parent. This is the life that corresponds to those who are spirit.

On this key point John and the Synoptics completely agree:

"Who seeks to save his life will lose it; but who loses his life for me will find it" (Matt. 16:25; Mark 8:35; Luke 9:24). Our life must be risked in discipleship if we are to attain to the possession of life indestructible. But discipleship is the reply, rendered possible by the Spirit (and *therefore* most personal and personalizing), to Jesus' call, which is a creative call, a blessing, a communication of the Spirit. It is not the merely normative and imperative word of law, but "the words of eternal life" (John 6:68).

Jesus initiates a history of discipleship by communicating a life. And suddenly a history and a life are born that contrast with the history and life of all times past. We must change direction, then, and be born anew. But this dialectization of the concept of life does not mean the establishment of a dualism. It means saving what has been lost (Luke 19:10); it means being "filled with life" (John 10:10). The fullness toward which human life is directed is the life of the daughters and sons of God. This life materializes when we are moved by the Spirit and begin to live as sisters and brothers. But neither flesh and blood nor sin can produce this universal family. Hence the necessity of subordinating natural ties, and of dying to the sin of the world (which also dwells within us to the extent that we are an active part of the present order, to the extent that we contribute to its shaping and maintenance).

(d) The Paradox of the Historical Realization of This Dialectic

This is the mystery revealed in Jesus. The historical manner of its occurrence contributes to its unveiling; new life is born whenever life is given as a gift to those deprived of it. This is illustrated in the parable of the good Samaritan, composed by Jesus precisely as a response to the question of what to do in order to inherit eternal life (Luke 10:25). This is also the message of the scene of the last judgment in Matthew (25:31–46). Those who give food and drink, those who give shelter and clothing, those who pay visits "to these my least brothers and sisters" are called just, and will "go to eternal life." New life, then, is realized in the rescuing, healing, and fortifying of life, beginning with the primary, material aspects of life. Those who act in this way are declared "blessed of my Father."

And who are those who act in this way? Who are these blessed? There are no signs by which they can be known *a priori,* for "of these very stones God can raise up children to Abraham" (Luke 3:8). By their fruits shall they be known (Matt. 7:16). Blessed, then, happy, fortunate, are the merciful (Matt. 5:7), those who hunger and thirst for the coming of the Reign of God and the divine justice (5:6), those who toil for peace (5:9).

And the poor, those who suffer from hunger, those who weep (Luke 6:20–21), those who suffer, the subjugated, those persecuted for justice (Matt. 5:4, 5, 10)—why are they blessed? For the same reason as the others. By the pure good pleasure of their God, who offers them a Reign "where there will be neither death nor mourning, weeping or pain" (Rev. 21:4), where there will be neither hunger nor oppression.

These beatitudes express the tension between salvation and blessing. They promise blessing, in all its eschatological splendor; but they promise it precisely to those cursed by their fellow human beings. Now, unless all of this merely shows the divine taste for paradox, might we possibly be able to discern some sense and meaning in this irrenounceable Christian proclamation? Is there perhaps some intrinsic relationship between the blessing on the merciful and the blessing on the poor? The answer is "yes." The tendential identity of the two subjects is revealed in Jesus: Jesus the good Samaritan was poor. He was born poor, and he lived in poverty in the midst of his people. In Jesus we are reminded that it is ordinarily the poor who are merciful. The merciful are the poor in spirit (Matt. 5:3).[4] Hence it is primarily those who are deprived of life who, in giving away the little they have in order to live (Mark 12:41–4), attain to imperishable life. The reason they are so generous, as their Father is generous (Luke 6:36), is that they have received God's blessing. This paradoxical route was the path of Jesus, who, being rich, made himself poor in order to enrich us with his poverty. Could he not have enriched us with his wealth? What the way of Jesus tells us is that full life is not achieved through the crumbs that fall from the tables of the plump and sated onto the heads of the emaciated and starving. On the contrary, it will be the mutual gift of those deprived of life that will bring full life to themselves and to all who wish to receive it. This is history's route to prolonged life. "Who has believed our message? To whom has the Lord shown his arm?" (Isa. 53:1).

CHAPTER XII

Holiness of God and Human Sacrality

1. THE CHRISTIAN EXPERIENCE OF THE HOLY GOD

The Latin American people do regard God as the Holy. That is, they regard God as the one having decisive weight and importance, the one who has the last word, the source of life and existence, and the one who, while at the mercy of none, nevertheless undertakes a self-communication to all, in a self-bestowal on all who seek to attain such a holy God. God is the one who has glory and power for ages of ages, neither changing, nor tiring, nor withdrawing. This experience of God produces an aura of reverence (without anything of the servile about it) that is the source of wisdom and freedom, since all is now viewed from a suitable perspective, that of God, and all is measured by the appropriate criterion, the one applied by God and not the one that happens to prevail at a given moment. And a great peace comes over us, because, when all is said and done, we are in the hands of God and not in those of oppressors or the elements or weakness.

But the people know that the holiness of the transcendent, gracious God engages us, as well. We are asked to endorse the divine plan. That plan will finally triumph. God will not be trifled with. God will not be suborned, and therefore does not compromise with the mighty but requires them to do justice to the

217

poor. Indeed, God is the avenger and the savior of the poor.
But by this very fact, neither will God be resigned to any discouragement or loss of dignity on the part of the people that
would incline them to wreak vengeance on their oppressors. This
holy God is entirely good, and therefore loves unconditionally.
But, being entirely good, God is not content with a lukewarm
gift of self. God seeks us as private property, private and exclusive—and hence free from all slavery. This would be the meaning of God's "jealousy" as part and parcel of the divine holiness.
For Christians, "Be holy as I am holy" (Lev. 19:2) means far
more than living at a distance from evil and practicing ritual
purity. To be holy as God is holy means "be perfect as your
Father is perfect" (Matt. 5:48). That is, be as Jesus, full of grace
and truth. Be filled with the love and faithfulness that Jesus
brought us from our divine Parent. Ultimately, to be holy as
God is holy means: Be generous as your Parent is generous
(Luke 6:36). God does not ask us to create anything that will
never emerge from our clay. God asks us to activate the capacities placed within us by the divine creation.

2. ABSOLUTE AND RELATIVE DIMENSIONS OF OUR SACRED CONDITION

We are all sacred because we are all "of" the one Holy, the
one Lord. But we are "of" that Holy, that Lord, not in the sense
of ownership, as if we had been marked with God's number like
a beast, or in token of slavery, but in the sense that God has
given us to share in the divine glory. The measure of our importance and our splendor is the measure of the gift of God. In
virtue of our condition as sacred, we are inviolable (belonging
only to God) and of value (we share in God; there is deity within
us). Anchored to the sphere of the Holy, we have absolute worth
and inviolability, and we can never lose them. Nothing can
deprive us of our immunity and our value, because we belong
to the orbit of God, which is beyond the reach of creatures, and
because God, who alone could revoke that immunity and value,
is faithful and will never repent this decision.

Accordingly, to spill someone's blood, to violate a person's
dignity, to prefer things to a person, to seek to possess a person

as property—for example, as part of a work force which I may regard as a mercantile commodity—and so on, are sacrileges. To assign a person the same kind of value I assign things—solely in view of their utility, solely in function of the profit I can extract from them, and so on—is to ignore the value of the divine.

But if we are all sacred, then we are all called to become holy. To this end, each and every one of us, beginning with Adam, has been given the Holy Spirit, whose sacrament is baptism (thus the one baptized will be transformed into a witness, firstfruits, and servant, of the presence of the Spirit in the world). To come to be holy is to choose the life in which we are to participate, and receiving it, to share it with others. In this manner, in creating a communion of siblingship, we fall in with the person and activity of the Spirit of the Son, and come to be the sons and daughters of God in that Son. But in a world of such autarchy and oppression, the receiving of the divine life calls for a desolidarization with the established order, and a struggle for the liberation of persons, including oppressors. We come to be holy when we follow the path of Jesus and follow it in his manner, since the Holy Spirit is the Spirit of Jesus.

Thus, while the value of the person, as sacred, is absolute, it is also greater or less. It is greater or less in the degree that, through acceptance of the gift of God, it continues to grow, as Jesus grew (Luke 2:40–52), to the point of the maturity intended for it in the fullness of Christ (Eph. 4:13). This dynamic, relative meaning of holiness (a secondary meaning, but an essential one) includes as well, correlatively, the possibility of the refusal to receive the gift of God—the possibility of sin. But both possibilities ultimately fall under the judgment of God, and therefore do not diminish the inviolability which I am emphasizing.

Only the prophetic judgment, whose subject, strictly speaking, is God alone, is legitimate vis-à-vis the relative holiness of each individual. Human beings can judge only the impersonal dimension of persons. This judgment is not only possible, but necessary.

CHAPTER XIII

What Are the Traits of the Image of God?

1. PROBLEMS OF A *LOCUS THEOLOGICUS*

That God created human beings in the divine image and likeness is a classic *locus theologicus* in the theology of creation. According to the Priestly source, this is the central assertion concerning creation, and the theological definition of the human creature. In the New Testament, Paul insists that Jesus is the image of God, and that our calling consists in becoming the image of Jesus. The theme is basic for patristics, and is still the object of a lively theological controversy. Nowadays it serves as the basis of a Christian focus on the theme of the dignity of the person.

(a) Is the Concept of Image Accessible?

(i) Anthropological premises. The concept of image implies an anthropology in which a key role is played by the notion of exemplarity, or exemplar cause. Our creation in the image of God means that God is our Model. To come to be as God is not originally and basically a diabolical pretension. It is originally and basically a calling. Even more than this, however, it is the expression of our original constitution. It means that we have our ultimate foundation not in ourselves but in God. We have

our definition in terms of God. We are defined in terms of God not in the sense of the structure of the categories, as if God were our genus, from which we emerge as specific differences; nor in the sense of coinciding with God in categorical determinations (understanding, will), since these are predicated differently of God and us; still less, surely, in the sense of being of God's lineage, being God's blood relatives; but in the sense that God has been posited as our end—we have received a capacity for the divine, and this is the orientation that marks our entire being, preventing it from being defined in terms of anything categorical and mundane. God created us to the divine image, in such wise that we can comprehend and possess ourselves only in terms of God, face to face with our Model, living before that Model, in all responsibility, with the rest of created beings. In these terms, human realization consists in transcending oneself, by hearing, by obeying, by activating one's Model so as to be able to show it forth as a true, trustworthy image.

If human beings have been created in the image of God, then they are referred to another. They are re-linked, they are symbolic. They are not abstract beings having to determine themselves, but beings born already designed, already situated against a horizon. They are concrete beings, then. This being the case, however, "concrete" is not equivalent to "defined," inasmuch as it is precisely their primordial reference to God that impedes their definition and delimitation. In virtue of this original re-linking, the person, being of earth and of human lineage, is not imprisoned by these coordinates, but transcends them from within. In measuring themselves by the divine paradigm, persons overflow any possible cultural model. Hence the provisional and inadequate nature of any kind of humanism, indispensable as humanism may be.

The concept of image, as described here, is inscribed in a determinate anthropology. Is it comprehensible? Does it have validity today? Can it be received as good news?

(ii) In traditional cultures. In traditional cultures, human beings are conceptualized by reference to models, and are fulfilled to the extent that those models invest them. In these cultures, the biblical message of the human being created to the image of God is an established principle, then. There may be a

problem here, in view of the fact that persons are defined by their cultural coordinates, which include re-linkage. Human beings constitute the central element of a culture, surely; still, from start to finish, they are an element of the whole, and reduced to that element. Were this the total picture, we should find ourselves caught in the Feuerbachian dialectic: Human beings create God to their own image, and this god, in turn, creates the human being to his image. Ultimately, then, human beings create themselves, by way of the detour of God, which permits them to exteriorize their authentic essence, thereupon to reappropriate it when they finally recognize it as such. Traditional cultures have not reached this last step; thus they remain within their cultural contexts, and their remarkable localism betrays their nature as expressions of culture. Obviously this is what all religions are, inevitably, and indeed ought to aspire to be; but this they are, and ought to be, from within their own substantivity and transcendence, of which the manifestation includes their discernment of culture, their judgment, and salvation in a subsequent transformation.

In traditional cultures such as we know them today in Latin America, there is still space for a genuine transcendence. But the fluidity with which the concept of image adapts to this cultural logic should also place us on our guard against a culturalistic reductionism — or rather, move us to maintain a constant purification of this reductionism, since it will never be possible to uproot it altogether.

(iii) In modern Western culture. Modern Western culture is built on the rejection of any paradigms in the human constitution. Reacting against the asphyxiating rigidity and discriminatory sacralizations of the models of traditional society, it does so with such radicality that it not only disqualifies these unjust, paralyzing applications of the concept of paradigm, but demolishes the concept as such. Thus the citizen will be an abstract entity, the product of a convention; rights and duties will be only those determined by convention. Under the protection of this fictitious, abstract identity, each individual must project his or her own model (each will have to be the author of his or her own argument), and execute it insofar as each finds possible. The model includes no guidelines. The modern human being is

a composite being.[1] He or she forms a structure on the base of free-floating components, each selected by each person in conformity with "personal" opportunity, advantage, and aspiration. Culture appears not as a system of paradigms, but after the fashion of a kind of supermarket, displaying and hawking every sort of opportunity for every kind of preference—however incompatible mutually, provided they fall within the social contract that shapes the general framework.

This culture publicizes successful projects (businessman, academic, politician, film star, and so on). These projects are advertised as models for realization. But they are models neither in the ontic sense of traditional society, nor in the transcendent sense of the theology of creation. They are proposals for a wager, and their substance rests exclusively on their social force and effect—on the success and happiness they gain for the one adopting them. True, part of their public character and self-justification is the transcendent service they offer society; but even in cases in which the vocation to service is the deciding motivation, the model is never more than a project that opens a future, that is, something rushing recklessly to the fore to stake out a field to be progressively occupied and constructed through one's own originating activity and option. Utterly absent from the concept of model is any reality antecedent to myself, to whose image I have already been shaped. Is it not precisely this absence of an antecedent reference that makes it possible to adopt a model in the form of a wager? Is it not the absence of any reverse link and antecedent mission that makes it necessary to contrive a totally new project?

This is indeed the case, in view of the salvific compulsion with which these projects are so frequently embraced. They are not mere historical projects. They pretend to be out-and-out self-creation (and thereby salvation), beginning with a creation of the elements, so often comprehended as chaotic. We observe this compulsion not only in individual projects, but in collective ones, as well—projects sprung from atheism, in an enormous effort to palliate its sense of void by assuming the functions that, in a theistic conception, had been the prerogative of the divine.

This is not always the case, however, nor need it be. The concept of model examined is also compatible with a project, provided the model be maintained at its transcendent level and the project within it remain purely intrahistorical. To be sure, not every project will be suitable for the attainment of the model. Still, in virtue of their condition as image of God, modern human beings are not only permitted, but required to mount a project, and undertake a creation.

It might be argued that if the historical model is Jesus of Nazareth, then there is no room for projects. And this would indeed be the case had that Jesus not gone "to prepare a place for us" and sent his Spirit to us to "teach us all things." But without Jesus among us, we must act; and as we possess his very Spirit, we must go beyond imitation and take up a creative discipleship. There is room, then, in our culture, to conceptualize ourselves, and to live, as images of God—but not without a profound transformation of many of the elements of that culture.

(b) Image of What God?

The reason Jesus' contemporaries refused to admit that he rendered God present among them was that they failed to see in him the glory of God. And so they sentenced him for blasphemy. The God who had become present through Jesus was not the all-powerful, irresistible God, the God of gods and Lord of lords, who exalted his official representatives and humiliated his enemies to the very dust. The God made present through Jesus was not the national god of the Law and the Temple. The God made present through Jesus was not the one the leaders of the people had been expecting. Therefore, instead of being converted to Jesus' proposal, they thrust him from their midst, accusing him of charlatanry and incitement of the people, whom they regarded as ignorant in matters of religion. From his own point of view, Jesus, too, grasped the paradox. The revelation of the face of God had remained opaque to the wise and the theological experts, and yet simple folk had grasped it. The mystery consisted in this, that God is our Father. This was good news for the poor, and for sinners, but bad news for the establishment. From the standpoint of their respective notions of God, then, Jesus was either a blasphemer or a revealer of God for his contemporaries. There are conceptions of God, then, that prevent a person from seeing the true image of God.

If we define God in terms of power, the divine image will be materialized in those who dominate peoples. The representatives of God will be the authorities (from the patriarchal to the political to the technological). If God is infinitely happy in heaven, who will reflect God better than those who triumph — those on whom life smiles, and for whom things turn out well? If God is infinite and eternal, will not God's mirror be nature (ever identical with itself in its variations, and immeasurable), grandiose, age-old institutions, and imposing, majestic monuments? If God is characterized as immeasurable wisdom, who will be God's image but the intelligent, the enlightened, and the wise? In terms of suchlike characterizations of God, how will it be possible to recognize the image of God in the dominated, the suffering, the little, the ignorant?

Thus the question is unavoidable: Of what God are human beings the image? After all, there are many gods and many lords — or rather, many who receive these names — but one alone who is the living, true God (1 Cor. 8:5-6). If we know God through the divine image, however, our notion of God will be closely tied to our human experience. Are we caught in a vicious circle? By no means, if the Spirit of God who is poured forth in our hearts is the Principle who exercises discernment in history from within persons, transcending them in immanence. When all is said and done, it is the works of the Son of God and of his sisters and brothers that reveal the face of God, as well as constituting human beings in the divine image. Spiritual praxis (which constitutes genuinely human praxis) is thus the hermeneut, the interpreter, of God. Our cultural configuration secretes a darkness that prevents persons from grasping either their actual situation (they believe that they see, whereas they are blind) or God's glory. But in this situation, Jesus, the adequate image of God, shines forth, revealing to us God's mystery and our own.[2] He reveals it to those who follow him in spiritual praxis.

The question, "Of what God are we the image?" cannot, then, be solved apart from the human experience of living as images of God.

(c) Various Images of God

Many classes of persons hold themselves out as, and are held by others to be, the representatives of God — as the images of God on earth. I refer to those invested with power, wisdom, felicity, and grandeur. Then we should have to add the saints, since we define them as those who most resemble God by their virtues, those who through their nearness to God participate in the sphere of the divine power. And above all, the image of God is Jesus, who is the only adequate image. Amidst this plethora of images and representatives, will not the assertion that human beings, simply as such, are the image of God, while true, be irrelevant in the presence of these other, far more specific, figures? Do not these other images of God irremediably devalue the elementary assertion that every human being is the image of God? In this world of qualifications and hierarchies, will not one who vaunts no other title than that of simple image of God by human condition, instead of being protected and attended to, be ignored and neglected? In short, there are those who are viewed as being more proximate, more proper images of God, and there are those who are the image of God only in virtue of being creatures. Do the latter have any right to the privilege accorded to the former?

By way of an answer, let us consider the obvious example. The pope, as vicar of Christ, is called His Holiness. He is venerated. We kiss his hand. We kneel before him. He is listened to as an oracle of God. The great and the small surround him with protection, reverence, admiration, and affection. We treat the pope in this way because he is the pope. Hence we do not treat in this way one who is not the pope. In our consideration and practice, in the presence of the title of pope, does not that of image of God pale to insignificance? What would we say were someone to tell us that it is impossible to find anyone more deserving of honor than the lowliest human being, by virtue of his or her condition as image of God? But this is precisely the praxis of the saints, who therefore paid special honor to the poor, since it is in the poor that this single condition of honor shines more simply.

2. A CHRISTIAN REFLECTION ON GENESIS 1:26–30

(a) The Meaning of Image

According to the exegetes, in the Priestly account of creation the concept of the first woman and man as image of God seems to refer to participation in the power of God, as creator, over creation.[3] This explanation, we are told, is suggested by the mission assigned by the creator to the image: to subdue the animals. But surely this specific mission ought to be understood as a consequence, rather than the substance, of the condition of image shown forth by human beings.[4] The image as such would consist in a similarity, with the connotation of a representation. Similarity indicates the human being's proportion, affinity, and reference to God; representation connotes the field of God's relations with the divine creation. At bottom, however, with similarity as with representation, the notion of image would refer to the origin of the human being, inasmuch as, in context, the expression "image of God" replaces "according to their kind," used in the account of the creation of the plants and animals.[5] From this standpoint, the expression underscores the difference between human beings and the rest of living creatures, placing humanity in the orbit of God. This origin provides the measure of the grandeur, the glory, and the dignity of the human creature.

Still, the human being is not God's equal. Hence the expression, "Let us make . . ." is understood by many exegetes not as a majestic or deliberative plural, but as a figure of speech in which God blends into the heavenly court, the heavenly world, in the image of which ("of his angels," the Septuagint says) humanity is created.[6] According to others, this same function would fall to the expression "likeness," which would attenuate the significate, too brutal for Yahwist ears, of the concrete, graphic expression, "image."[7]

In any case the expression is difficult to exonerate of anthropomorphism, and there is no need to exercise our lucubrations upon whether Yahweh was at some time represented by statues or paintings in human form; we have merely to note the numerous biblical descriptions of Yahweh not only with a human shape, but with typically human feelings and reactions. Hence in attempting to specify the similarity we need not point to qualities like immortality (which would reside in the soul [see Wis. 2:23; 9:15]); we need only think of the concrete person, beginning with an erect body and a noble bearing. Neither, however, need we focus on the body; the text refers to the human person as a whole. It is the whole person that belongs to the world of God; and it would be in this sense that we should have to interpret the anthropomorphisms, which in no way mean that God is similar to human beings (the text expressly insists on the opposite), but that God strikes a relation with human beings, and that as image of God, we are called to a particular relationship with God.[8] Hence it does not seem arbitrary to infer from this text that God created human beings "in such wise that something could occur between this creature and its creator—that the creature could hear its creator and make a response."[9]

At the same time, the concept of image indicates that, antecedent to any relationship struck by human beings with God, an irrevocable relationship is already bestowed by God on them. Hence the inviolability of this image, not only for the animals and for human beings themselves, but for God.[10] This would be the meaning of the Yahwist's plastic expression of the curse pronounced by the Lord: "Who kills Cain, will pay sevenfold" (Gen. 4:15), and the mark placed upon Cain. Cain, the first murderer, lives still, under the protection of the Lord, who becomes none other than his avenger in blood. More abstractly, in the blessings of the covenant with Noah, the Priestly code forbids the shedding of human blood with this express argumentation: "Because God has made man to his image" (Gen. 9:6). The reason for this prohibition will not be the sanctity of human life considered in itself. Protected here in concrete fashion will be "the life bestowed on the human being by Yahweh."[11] Thus, whatever be their particular moral condition or personal situation, human beings bear the mark of God, belong to God alone, and are inviolable for all that is not divine. And even God wills not the death of sinners, but rather that they be converted and live.

(b) Mission of the Image

It is with these profound roots as our point of departure that we must understand the sense of the mission to have dominion over the earth and subdue it—expressions of a despotic rule. The emphasis, then, is on what the Yahwist indicates more humanistically in the observation that, among all the animals, human beings have found none sufficiently like to themselves as to be able to function as their companions and work partners (Gen. 2:20). In assigning human beings a function with regard to animals, God separates them from the natural whole. If human beings belong to the sphere of God, and have a mission with regard to the beings of nature, then they must not be beings of nature. If their charge is to have dominion, they must not allow themselves to be dominated by animals, as if the latter were divine. Nature is for human beings, and not the other way around. But at all events, if nature is consistently us, then our dominion must consist not in depredation, but in symbiosis and solidarity. Indeed, if we are to exercise dominion as does God, then our dominion must be entirely at the service of life and creativity. It will be a dominion of guardianship, preservation, and consummation of God's creation. What is called for is neither a naturalistic ecologism, since creation is for the sake of human beings, nor a despotic rule devoid of solidarity, seeing that the purport of the divine charge is to lead creation to God.[12]

The exegetes emphasize our responsibility before God in the execution of this mission. This demand is intrinsic to the concept of representation. And it constitutes a fundamental part of the relationship between God and us. In its relations with nature, humankind responds to God. It responds objectively, and ought also to respond subjectively, steeping itself in this reality in order thus to be able to discern it, in order not to deviate in its management, and in order to experience it with gratitude.

(c) Subject of the Image

If we ask who is the subject of the image, we shall receive a variety of responses. Some will stress that it is Adam—that is, the human being as a couple, whose sexual condition (male and female) the sacred writer specifies in reaction to discrimination against woman (which we still find in a Pauline text based not on Genesis but on rabbinical texts of whose weakness Paul himself is aware [1 Cor. 11:7–16]). The explanatory clause, "Male and female he created them," then would mean that women, too, are images of God. Karl Barth, on the other hand, maintains that, in view of the parallelism between "male and female" and "image of God," the latter expression must mean male and female. One might be tempted to tax Barth with reductionism and oversimplification, but the tenor of the text makes it difficult to disqualify his explanation. Obviously it would be meaningless to claim that God is a sexual couple and that therefore human beings, in order to be in the image of God, must be a sexual couple. It would be equally meaningless to cite the fecundity with which human sexuality is endowed, which (like dominion over nature) is the object of God's special blessing. Still, if we are to be consistent, we shall have to say, here as well, that the multiplication of the human species is a consequence of the condition of image shown forth by humanity.

In what sense does the human couple bear a similarity to God? In its relationship of fertile love. In terms of the rigorously monotheistic Old Testament, it seems difficult to maintain that the image of God is a human community rather than an individual, although the text does lend some weight to such an interpretation. I refer to the conceptualization in which "Male and female he created them" would mean that the image of God is adequately expressed only in a community whose model and prototype is constituted by male and female.

A Christian might argue, against such an interpretation, that Jesus, the perfect and proper image of God, was celibate. And yet even St. Paul applies to Jesus the symbolism of marriage, which he terms a "mystery" because it represents and realizes a far more profound union, that between Christ and the church, which is in turn a symbol of humanity. Thus Jesus of Nazareth is the universal brother; and the total Christ is a community, the whole human community, the finished image of God, whose embryonic symbol is the community of male and female.

3. ABSOLUTE AND RELATIVE DIMENSIONS OF OUR CONDITION AS IMAGES OF GOD

As with our sacred condition, our constitution as image of God, as well, comprises two dimensions. First and foremost comes a genuine, primordial condition; but this unconditional, immovable constitution embraces a dramatic, inexhaustible dynamism.

(a) An Imperishable Dignity

First of all, our condition as image of God is a point of departure never to be neglected, for it is this that constitutes each of us a person, bestowing on each of us our proper name and peculiar constitution. It is the very creator who made man and woman heterogeneous vis-à-vis the lower animals (within their earthly condition, however) and similar to the creator—that is, pertaining to the sphere of the divine, sensitive to the divine voice, and capable of responding to it. Then this dimension (in which the act and content of human creation consist), in virtue of its strictly transcendent character, will be accessible to human beings only in the form of response. That is to say, we human beings can neither establish it nor efface it. It is given to us only to activate it or not—activate it either with the very Spirit of the creator, or with the spirit of slaves (rebellious or servile). But whatever our response, the imperishable, inviolable point of departure is our dignity as images of God.

Such a response calls for both self-respect and respect for others. Self-respect must have no part with vainglory, as our dignity is not based on our own works, or on flesh and blood. It is gratuitous, and antecedent to any human determination. Acknowledgment of this dignity is the immovable, sure foundation of self-esteem.[13] And if we are utterly realistic, this self-esteem must always be greater than the suffering and humiliation that spring from a consciousness of our own sin. This sense of personal dignity is the most precious treasure the poor possess. And to be poor in spirit consists precisely in living by this dignity and defending it as an inexhaustible treasure.

It might be thought that the highly developed sense of personal dignity exhibited in the West is due to its Christian heritage. And indeed, the latter may certainly be one source. But the powerful hierarchization of this dignity, and the consequent practical refusal to attribute it to other peoples, to one's own poor, or to scorned minorities, raises serious doubts as to the authenticity of its Christian quality. Society has exalted the dignity of governmental leaders, the wealthy, and the successful. The church has emphasized the dignity of the members of the ecclesiastical establishment, whether in the hierarchy, priestly orders, or the religious life. A society founded on dichotomy and privilege is incapable, both in theory and in practice, of acknowledging the dignity of the poor as images of God. And yet, without the recognition of the dignity of others, there will be no opportunity for a Christian acknowledgment of one's own dignity. Now, self-acknowledgment and self-esteem are based on one's own works, on merits acquired, on belonging to a dominant people or privileged social class, on the discharge of an exalted task, and so on. For the evangelist John, this is to prefer the dignity given by human beings to the dignity bestowed by God (John 12:43). Such an elitist, misled sense of dignity culminates in a contempt for the dignity of Jesus, and his murder—the fate of one who refused to engage in a contest for privileges (religious and social) based on a contempt for the dignity of the people and the judgment of God.

The established order in Latin America is founded on a disregard in practice of the dignity of the people. Hence it is in the order of sin. Under these conditions it is scarcely easy for the people to maintain a sense of dignity and reduce it to action. The despised will despise. The neglected will neglect. Paradoxically, however, it is first and foremost amidst a believing, oppressed people that a Christian sense of dignity is maintained and renewed in Latin America. Here, among a people caught up in a struggle to the death with self-contempt and the compulsion to play the animal or savage beast, we see respect, delicacy, and courtesy—not expressed, obviously, in courtly refinement, but demonstrated in an attitude of sensitivity to the dignity that God has placed within us and entrusted to us that we may live in harmony with the divine creator as images of God. This primordial, underlying sensitivity is the tender nerve that throbs in the base church communities. It is this that resounds when the word of God is proclaimed, and which progressively manages to impregnate the relationships of family, neighborhood, group, organization, and community.

(b) Dynamism and Paradoxes

Thus, when we acquire a consciousness of the dignity inherent to the condition of image of God, this sense is transformed into a mighty dynamism, which tends to shape everything in accordance with its own demands. These demands are basically the two expressed in the text of Genesis upon which I have commented: to have dominion over the earth with a view to a full life, and to transform human society into a genuine community. Recent times, however, have brought us into confrontation with a paradox. Is it not the oppressors who have dominion over the earth, and is it not they who have achieved a more civilized, urbane community life? Is it not precisely the masses of the people who have never managed to emancipate themselves from the tyranny of the cycles of nature? Are not the barrios zones of insecurity in which a neighborly life and peaceful coexistence itself are all but impossible?

(i) To subdue the earth. In the matter of the dialectic between ourselves and nature, the Spirit is anything but absent from the many technological innovations that make life easier and fuller. Our people are the first to admit this, and to be grateful for it. Still, we cannot conceal the necrophilic bias that has predominated in this technological race, and the serious threat it poses to human life, as well as to a great part of the life of our planet. This manner of subduing the earth does not correspond to our creator's plans. Humankind does not exercise its condition as image of God along this route. The fear of a nuclear holocaust and the exhaustion of our vital resources are not the right course to adopt. Decision-making is always postponed "for the time being," so that when decisions are finally made they are maintained in the current (elitist and discriminatory) scheme of

things. Conversion may require some rude jolts; otherwise we may never see the reality of the case. But there will be no conversion in the absence of biophilic developmental alternatives — nor, especially, without the sense of dignity that is the basis and motive force of such alternatives.

In a Latin American perspective, the coinciding of the hour of the peoples with their historical awakening to their dignity is providential. To the extent that their assimilation of modernity is carried out in the spirit of their awakening, the possibility of a salutary dialogue with the current builders of this society grows more realistic. However, this historical transaction will attain its objective only if it manages to transcend the bounds of the merely political and become a genuine conversion. For now, it is not given to us to foresee the actual manner of this encounter, or indeed its very feasibility. If we manage to move in a more biophilic direction in our subduing of the earth, a great part of what we shall have attained will be profitable, and we may discover that even sin will have served the building of the Reign, since even in sin the divine sower has sown good seed. But will this change of course ever occur?

(ii) To people the earth in a humane way. When we move from the dialectic between us and nature to the interhuman dialectic, the panorama is still more shattering. We have surely multiplied and filled the earth; but not as images of God, since the relations that predominate among us do not follow the paradigm of the divine relation that founds us. They are not responsible relationships. To the creator's question to Cain, "Where is your brother?" we have frequently given Cain's answer: "Am I my brother's keeper?" (Gen. 4:9). We discharge our responsibility in a bureaucracy that is not only impersonal itself, but often enough actively depersonalizing, and thus we believe ourselves dispensed from the primordial solidarity inherent in our condition as images of God under the formality of human community.

We have come to a universal history, and we have constituted various organisms to express this on an ideal level. But our century has been one of constant war; and even where there is no war, political and economic guidelines have been prescribed through confrontation. God has granted us true prophets — witnesses and martyrs of a community life of peace with justice, to be shared by a single human race in its irreducible variety. This constitutes a sign of the times. But shall we endorse or quench the Spirit?

To be sure, respect, understood negatively—as the art of living without disturbing others or being disturbed ourselves, each performing her or his social role in a style in which good manners prevail—is an achievement of the developed world, in which there is no more public ridicule, insult, contempt, physical abuse, or any of so many other habits inveterate in other societies. But all of this is achieved at the price of frigidity in communication, and solitude instead of constitutive human relations. To many Christians, this price does not seem too high. They have decided that such social anonymity is a necessary condition for the expenditure of one's limited energies of love within the little community of the elect.[14] Does not the acceptance of a dichotomy between the areas of the personalized private and the impersonal public, however, reduce the latter to that of the merely useful, devaluating it to a level on which everything will be determined by managers and planners? Does not a goodly portion of what is most meaningful and most decisive for humanity occur precisely on this level?

Still, we cannot leave out of consideration as signs of the times the zeal of so many persons for the improvement of the quality of life, translated not into a search for comfort, but into the establishment of more symbiotic relations with nature, and even more so, into the constitution of more humanizing and participatory environments of social life. The movement is not without its ambiguity, as it is sometimes elitist, and we focus on "us" and turn our backs on the people and their many problems. But at other times it is conducted with more openness to others, and the modesty of its accomplishments is the result not of a breach in solidarity, but of a concrete apprenticeship in socialization, a constantly renewed effort toward a global society of the future.

This movement embraces the base church communities. They will receive considerable help from it in the long term, and will contribute to it their own radicality—their humble, serious attempt to found a community and a people of sisters and brothers from a starting point in their rediscovered dignity as images of God in a milieu in which the sin of the world is materialized and objectified. Because this dynamism is a responsible one, it seeks to transcend all messianic voluntarism, and proceeds at the rate of the maturation of this divine seed—that is, it advances in step with the interior growth of persons and the development of new social opportunities. In not a few places in Latin America, not only in the church, but in society at large, the embryo of this new socialization is already making its appearance.

(iii) To call God by name. However, the intrinsic dynamism of the image of God, which is the image of female and male, does not reach its culmination in a life-giving dominion over the earth, nor in the reconciliation of universal history with its subject. The condition of the image of God reaches its climax when this humanity not only responds to God by taking this communitary, biophilic direction (that is, when it carries out the mission that the Lord has entrusted to it), but when it responds to God, who calls it by its name, by pronouncing in its own turn the holy name of the Lord—when it at last appreciates the tenderness of a Ruler who sovereignly pronounces its new name, and in reply, in the midst of its mission, pronounces, with this same tenderness, that Ruler's gift, the intimate divine name. This is the most exalted way in which the living image can reflect the source of light that has created it.

God has pronounced the name of every person on the face of the earth, every member of humankind. Accordingly, this response to God ought to transport the entire world into the heart of the cosmic democracy, and all humanity into a differentiated whole united by love. Hence the impossibility of effectuating this supreme realization of the person as image of God in an a-cosmic or solipsistic way.[15] And so the definitive constitution of this community with God takes on an eschatological character, although this process has never been, nor ever will be, absent from history. Indeed, it is this process that unlocks history.

4. PROHIBITION OF FASHIONING IMAGES OF GOD

The prohibition against worshiping anything or anyone other than the Lord is based on the objective fact that God is the sole

Lord—that is, the one who alone has wrought the deliverance of the people and hence who reserves all the glory thereof—the meaning of God's "jealousy" (Exod. 20:1–6).[16] But the prohibition against fashioning images of the *true* God (related to, but not identical with, the other) is a consequence of the creator's autonomous decision to be imaged in living human beings alone. The reason for this prohibition is not that the transcendence of the one true God prevents any representation of that God; it is that the only representation authorized by that God is the one to be found in human persons. In them (even in their bodies) the transcendence of God shines forth—not as a work of human operation, however (their personalities), but as a primordial gift that the creator has been pleased to bestow on each human being (his or her imperishable condition of person).

If human beings fashion images of God, these will inevitably be images of themselves, as well, seeing that they have only the visible world on which to model them (the elements and powers of the universe, and its diverse beings) with their fantasy and their artistry. Human beings must not worship the work of their hands, which as such can only be inferior to themselves, their authors. Nor must they adore personalities (leaders, magnates, geniuses), personality being the subjective deed of persons just as surely as images and institutions are their objective deeds. On the contrary, they must respect other persons (and themselves into the bargain), images of God that they are, as sacred.

This stubborn refusal on the part of the Old Testament to countenance any objectification of the Lord is based, then, not on any importance attributed to the invisible incorporeal as one of the poles of a matter-spirit dichotomy, but to the importance of the human subject as the living icon of God.[17]

This reasoning retains its validity in the Catholic Church. Images of Jesus, Mary, and the saints are images of these living images. Hence (as they are also inevitably images as well of those who create them) one must be constantly on the watch to observe which images wrought by human hands authentically render the spirit of the model, and which introduce a different, even contrary spirit, leading, under the disguise of the model, to other models being venerated, different from, and even contrary to, the historical person whose name the image bears.

5. JESUS OF NAZARETH, IMAGE OF GOD

(a) Sectarian Exclusivism?

For Paul, the image of the creator is Jesus (Col. 3:10). It is Jesus who is the image of the invisible God (Col. 1:15). As Jesus is the image of God, his face reflects God's glory (2 Cor. 4:4–6). He is the radiance of the glory of God and the imprint of God's being (Heb. 1:3). He possesses the form of God (Phil. 2:6). In him dwells all the fullness of the divinity corporeally (Col. 2:9).

In Jesus, then, for Paul, the image of God is, on the one hand, radicalized and completed (as it is no longer a mere resemblance, or even a pertinency to and personal relation with the divine, but a perfect adequation and total compenetration); and on the other, concentrated (as it is Jesus alone who realizes this absolute conformity with God). The consequences of the mystery revealed to Paul are drastic: there is no other religious way, no other path, but Jesus. The proud Pharisee has to perceive his flawless observance as offal, to be cast on to the refuse heap if he is to gain Christ and be incorporated into him (Phil. 3:8). That is, in order to attain to the status of image of God (in which human realization and fullness consists) one must become an image of Jesus. If Jesus is the irreplaceable mediator, the one high priest, then what of all that I have said of the imperishable character with which the image of God invests every person? Thunderstruck at the revelation of Jesus, which has rocked through his life like an earthquake, filling it to overflowing, does Paul not deny all human sacredness—indeed, does he not demonize it—that thus the glory of Jesus may gleam in solitary radiance upon the ruins of all that is human? "All men have sinned and are deprived of the glory of God. All men are now undeservedly justified by the gift of God, through the redemption wrought in Christ Jesus" (Rom. 3:23–4).

The Christian communities had experienced this change. They had seen their lives divided into a "before" and an "after," and the line of demarcation was Jesus' irruption into those lives. Paul does not hesitate to qualify the point of rupture as a death and a new birth. Until now, Christians have lived as slaves both to the powers that lorded it over their natural and cultural world (Col. 2:8–23), and to their passions. It has been a carnal, a fleshly existence, and naturally it has led to death and corruption. Now these same Christians are living a life of freedom from those powers, whether ambient or internal. Their way of life is new, superior, spiritual, heavenly. It is a life that leads to eternal life. How do they conceptualize this change? "Just as we resemble the man from earth, so shall we bear the likeness of the man from heaven" (1 Cor. 15:49).

> After all, you have died! Your life is hidden now with Christ in God. . . . Put to death whatever in your nature is rooted in earth. . . . Stop lying to one another. What you have done is put aside your old self with its past deeds and put on a new man, one who grows in knowledge as he is formed anew in the image of his creator [Col. 3:3, 5, 9–10].

And so he can say to these reborn: "All of us, gazing on the Lord's glory with unveiled faces, are being transformed from glory to glory into his very image by the Lord who is the Spirit" (2 Cor. 3:18). And to the Galatians, who have not reserved this place to Jesus exclusively and completely, and still cling to the Law, he writes: "You are my children, and you put me back in labor pains until Christ is formed in you" (Gal. 4:19). To his beloved Philippians he makes a prediction: "He will give a new form to this lowly body of ours and remake it according to the pattern of his glorified body" (Phil. 3:21). To the Christians of Rome, whom he has never seen but loves and longs to meet: "Those whom he foreknew he predestined to share the image of his Son" (Rom. 8:29).

(b) Experience of Initiation

This experience of initiation into a new life (not only a change of action, but a distinct existence, conceptualized as an investiture in the image of Jesus) is the great contribution of Christianity. Christianity mainly represented not a new philosophy or religion, or superior social organization, but a new heart—the very attitude of Jesus (1 Cor. 2:16), occasioning new interpersonal and social relations. Christians experienced this not only as a transformation into the image of Jesus, but also, and even more radically, as an incorporation into Jesus himself. Embodiment in Jesus meant joining the community of his followers, for this community cherished the claim to be the community of Jesus in the precise sense that it was Jesus himself who was both its shape and its soul—Jesus who "formed" and "animated" it, then, in the strictest meaning of these expressions. This was the content of the experience that Paul underwent on the road to Damascus: Jesus was the Christians (Acts 9:5).

This is precisely what we Christians continue to proclaim, and it is this alone that justifies (and judges) the church institution. To the extent that this newness of life grows opaque, and the church takes on the transitory shape of this world (1 Cor. 7:31), the salt loses its taste, and is no longer good for anything but to be trampled on by those who hold it in contempt. Thus the saints (who bear about in their bodies the figure of the death of Jesus, that his resurrection, too, may be manifested in them [Phil. 3:10–11]) are those who literally "verify" Christianity, maintaining it as the light of the nations and the sacrament of Jesus. And we today, sinners that we are, continue to belong to the church of Jesus, inasmuch as, despite all our cowardice and faithlessness, still we beg, ever and again, to be clothed in the image of Jesus of Nazareth, and strive to have that image shine forth in our existence. We too experience the dolorous, saving transitus, unfinished though it be, from the shape of this world to the image of Jesus, the new humanity.

Thus the life of the church begins with a salvific event, an experience of initiation: its death to the passing shape of the world and to the image of the worldly human being, and its birth to a humanity in the image of Jesus and to a social body that is the body of Jesus in history. This experience can be conceptualized in terms of a dichotomy, with emphasis on the event. This is psychologically appropriate and therefore valid. But it is not an adequate conceptualization.

(c) *Universality of Jesus*

In Jesus we have the decisive event, surely; but this event is only the revelation of the mystery hidden since the foundation of the world (Rom. 16:25; Eph. 3:9; Col. 1:26). God "administers everything according to his will and counsel" (Eph. 1:11). The content of this divine project is to bring history to its fullness (Eph. 1:10). Even before creating the world, then, God willed and intended "to bring all things in the heavens and on earth into one under Christ's headship" (Eph. 1:10). It is a matter of a plan for unification, then; and Jesus is precisely the artisan of that unification. Its radicality is expressed in the hymn of the Letter to the Colossians. The reconciler of the world, the head of the church, the one who holds the primacy in all, is: "The image of the invisible God, the firstborn of all creatures. In him everything in heaven and on earth was created. . . . All were created through him, and for him. He is before all else that is. In him everything continues in being" (Col. 1:15–17).

Christ is the very model of the universe. And if the unique Jesus event affects all persons and all times, then, even before occurring, this Jesus, this event, was already active as the basic structure of creation (model, end, artisan, and ground of existence). From all eternity, Jesus is the uncreated and created image in whom we have been constituted images of God.

Indeed, the opportunity enjoyed by male and female human beings to be the image of God is founded precisely on the intradivine "face to face." Thus, despite all the strictness of its monotheism, the Old Testament nevertheless moves toward a gradual hypostatization of the divine Wisdom.[18] In the New Testament, it is the Logos that is thus hypostatized.

Far from depreciating the content of the image of God that constitutes the human person, then, the full revelation of the mystery of God in the Jesus event enhances, bases, discerns, and culminates it. It thereby constitutes the "ultimate foundation of the dignity" of the person (Puebla, 333). This is what constitutes the indissoluble unity between the irreducible particularity of the Jesus event and its universal meaning: irruption in continuity (Puebla, 331). But the union of what is revealed in Jesus with what we have said up to this point is even more specific.

(d) Figures of Glory

The evangelists all testify to the glory of Jesus as the adequate image of God. For Mark this glory is manifested in Jesus' power—a power that causes admiration not only because it is seen to be irresistibly superior to all worldly powers, but because it is exercised in a hidden manner. It approaches human beings in all weakness, and seeks not to force them, but to persuade and to serve them. Still, the voice heard at Jesus' baptism, the transfiguration, the tremendous cry on Calvary, and the words of the angels to the women at the tomb, lift this veil, however partially, and lead the seeker from inquiry to profession.

For Matthew, Jesus' glory is manifested in his fulfillment of the Law, and not only its prophetic oracles, ethical prescriptions, and practical wisdom, but also, and especially, precisely its Old Testament dynamism, to the point of the absolute consummation and transcendence of the same. Thus Jesus recapitulates the old era, drawing from its heart the new era of all that is definitive.

Luke contemplates Jesus' glory in counterpoint with the Old Testament, as manifested especially in mercy. Mercy reveals a generous Parent. But mercy is the most demanding, free, and incorruptible of dispositions—hence Luke's social radicalism and proclamation of liberation. At the end, Jesus' glory culminates in forgiveness and abandonment into the hands of the Father.

For John, Jesus' glory gleams in the testimony of John the Baptist and the prophets, and, even more so, in the testimony of the Father. But its guarantee is found in his works, his portents, those signs of life calculated to complete the original creation, to renew and fulfill life. The definitive proof of Jesus' biophilic attitude, and accordingly, of his full constitution as revealer of God, is his gift of his life. Thus for John the glory of Jesus shines forth especially on the cross. Jesus reigns from the tree indeed, in the surrender of his spirit.

(e) The Glory of One among So Many

But what makes this mystery so "mysterious" even in the colloquial sense is that we human beings conjure up an "image of God" according to the guidelines for human greatness. We "imagine," precisely, an image of God endowed with wealth, power, and seduction. By contrast, Jesus lived the greater part of his life hidden in anonymity (Phil. 2:7)—so much so that none even noticed his glory or suspected that it dwelt in him. Of him one could indeed say:

> To whom has the arm of the Lord been revealed?
> He grew up like a sapling before him,
>   like a shoot from the parched earth;
> There was in him no stately bearing to make us
>   look at him,
>   nor appearance that would attract us to him.
>   [Isa. 53:1–2]

Of course, at the same time, Jesus alone is perfectly described by the words of the psalmist (which in their literal sense of homage to an earthly ruler have only the hollow ring of flattery): "You are the most beautiful of men; from your lips flows grace" (Ps. 45:3). But this only means that God and human beings have different criteria of greatness and glory. In order not to have to draw such a conclusion, one so painful for us, we imagine the history of Jesus to have been simply that of the classic fairy tale in which a king goes disguised as a beggar. Pious as this supposition may appear, it is pure ideologization. It conceals the truth. The Son of God lived as he judged he should live. He lived his only life, and he lived it to the hilt. He was not acting out a charade. He was not the familiar god of mythology who disguises himself as a mendicant in order to test those who worship him. If we see no glory in Jesus' life, it is not because this glory lies buried beneath a mantle of sackcloth, but because we do not have eyes to see it. It is because our taste is spoiled, and appearances seduce us. The sign wrought by Jesus that we may see it and believe in him is himself, his life (John 6:30, 35). To the scandalized, who objected, "This is no way to talk! This is awful! We know his folks!" (John 6:60, 42), Jesus replied: "No one can come to me unless the Father draw him" (John 6:65). That is, only our divine Parent can open our eyes to an understanding that flashy ostentation is really shame, and true glory consists in giving life to the world.

To be sure, the priests killed Jesus for meddling with the Temple treasury, which was their god, and not a few Pharisees and doctors of the Law condemned him because his leadership undermined the establishment. But some of the Pharisees and theologians had authentic difficulties of conscience in accepting Jesus. They were genuinely scandalized at him. Jesus was not the Messiah they awaited. Jesus did not do justice to the scriptures. In him the glory of Yahweh Sabaoth did not appear. He was not like a refiner's fire. He did not scatter his enemies in the might of his arm. Where was the vengeance of "our God," and his terrible power? How was Jesus in any way like the hero of Psalm 72? How was he anything like the presence of God in Psalm 50 (vv. 1–6)? How was he like the Shepherd of Israel promised by Ezekiel (Ezek. 34:20–30)? How was he like the Restorer in Jeremiah (Jer. 30), or the Deliverer prophesied in Isaiah (Isa. 9:1–6; 33:17–24)? And so on and so on. Was this not blasphemy, Jesus' pretension that, in himself, the Lord had burst upon history, and in eschatological wise to boot?

(f) Glory of the Cross

The mystery becomes still more opaque if we consider not only the imperceptible manner in which the image of God par excellence lived among us and with us for the greater part of his life, but the even more disconcerting fact that his dominion was scarcely irresistible. Indeed, he fell into the hands of his enemies, who tortured him so hideously that "we thought of him as stricken, as one smitten by God and afflicted" (Isa. 53:4), "spurned and avoided by men, a man of suffering, accustomed to infirmity" (Isa. 53:3), "a worm, not a man; the scorn of men, despised by the people" (Ps. 22:7).

When the religious authorities had sentenced him to death for blasphemy, they saw in the fact that God had not hastened to deliver him from their hands proof positive that he had been a misguided visionary, a mere fanatic. The destruction on the cross of this supposed image of God was for them God's judgment pronounced on his inauthenticity. The abandonment Jesus felt was interpreted by them as proof that God had never been with him in the first place. Jesus was not the consummate image of God, God's eschatological revealer. They could rest assured. The image of God that they represented and defended had been endorsed. God could go on being Lord of lords, the one who governed with equity and without appeal, but with the same external force, when all was said and done, with the same violence, as was exercised by those who styled themselves lords and benefactors of the gentiles. The only difference was God's absolute superiority and justice; ultimately, the divine power and glory resided, as with everyone else, in the power to strike down recalcitrant enemies.

And yet, what Jesus' resurrection reveals is that, precisely in the life and death of Jesus of Nazareth, the glory of God was definitively manifested. Jesus was God's image commensurately: He was not merely similar to God, he was God's absolutely adequate image and hence exhaustive revelation. For those who seek mighty portents, Jesus seems stupidity and folly. For those who seek knowledge in terms of the established order, Jesus is a fool. He is out of his mind. The one who according to the eternal plan of God was to be our glory went unrecognized by any of the leaders of his history, since if they had discovered the Lord of glory they would not have crucified him (1 Cor. 2:7–8). This is the crisis of discernment that Jesus introduces into the world (John 9:39–41; Luke 2:34), and it is a crisis of the church institution itself when its representatives hold themselves out as leaders of our present history.

(g) Glory of the Crucified

Only when it has eyes to see the dignity of the poor as images of God, then, will the established order be able to profess the glory of God in Jesus. And only when it perceives the glory of God in the concrete life and death of Jesus of Nazareth, rather than in the Christs invented by the sublimated projection of its cultural paradigms, will it be able to recognize in practice that this Jesus has his favorite brothers and sisters in the poor. Hence the fact that Jesus (he alone in himself, and others in him) is the image of God is the firmest foundation for a recognition of the dignity of the poor, and for entry into solidarity with them, in order that they may precisely cease to be poor, and that thus all of us, they and we together, may achieve our fulfillment in poverty of spirit.

This is what the Latin American church has been given to understand through the mediation of prophets and witnesses. Puebla solemnly proclaims: "Every attack on human dignity is simultaneously an attack on God himself, whose image the human being is" (Puebla, 306). And hence the concretization of this same proclamation to the poor:

> For this reason alone, the poor merit preferential attention, whatever may be the moral or personal situation in which they find themselves. Made in the image and likeness of God (Gen. 1:26–28) to be his children, this image is dimmed and even defiled. That is why God takes on their defense and loves them [1142].

But let us focus on the concrete discovery of the identity between Jesus and the poor of Latin America — the discovery of the true image of God in the real, actual faces that constitute our challenge to action. We might well begin by referring to Puebla's celebrated listing of the faces of the oppressed (31–9). This text, which joins an analytical precision to a prophetic challenge and a mystical insight (besides summarizing our theme), is the expression of an adequate comprehension of the praxis of not a few Latin American Christians. And it may well serve as a rallying standard for both the rest of the Latin American church, as well as for any churches whose prosperity is based on the irresponsibility of a practical neglect of the revelation made to Paul for his salvation: "I am Jesus whom you persecute" (Acts 9:5).

6. CONCLUSION: CHILDREN OF GOD AND SIBLINGS OF CHRIST

The leaders of present history lack eyes to perceive the glory of the image of God shining in Jesus of Nazareth. But unless we are merely to rest content with the paradox, we must ask: In what does Jesus' glory consist?

John, one who accepted him, and who thus contemplated his glory, describes it to us as "the glory of an only Son coming from the Father, filled with enduring love" (John 1:14). Thus, if to be a person consists in being an image of God, and to be an image of God consists in following Jesus until we are transformed into him, then to be a person means being a son or daughter of God in the "only Son" of God. This is what we proclaim in the Profession of Faith: "We believe in one God, the Father, the Almighty, maker of heaven and earth. ... " The creator is the Father of Jesus, who is the firstborn of humanity. In him, we, as God's creatures, are God's children, as well.

This is what is revealed in Jesus' baptism, the paradigm of what his mission is to be: Jesus the innocent one enters into solidarity with a sinful people and receives the baptism of repentance. Here is the actualization, now ritual no longer, but historical, of the authentic scapegoat: Jesus is the lamb of God who takes up, to discharge it from our midst, the sin of the world. In this solidarity, Jesus is revealed as our brother. It is as if, in receiving baptism, he expressed himself in the plural: "Forgive us, Father: have mercy on your people." And lo, as Jesus thus expresses his condition as our brother, the heavens open and God speaks: "This is my Son" (Matt. 3:17). That is, being my child consists in the solidarity just expressed. My favorite person is the person of solidarity. What is revealed in Jesus' baptism is no timeless abstraction, but the occurrence of a relation that is called to make history: the relation of filiation-and-siblingship. The activity of Jesus and the activity of God are but two sides of the same coin. Through his solidarity with us, Jesus reveals God as grace. Jesus comes not as a judge, but as a brother, in solidarity with us; God is not a judge, then, but a justifier. God is Lord only as our Parent. To be person, then, consists in entering into a particular siblingship (to which purpose Jesus has bestowed his Spirit). In coinciding with and falling in with the Spirit of Jesus in spiritual activity, we are constituted daughters and sons of God (in the Spirit of Jesus). Thus, the image of God which Jesus consummated on the cross consists in being person as Son of God, and accordingly, sibling of human beings. We are constituted persons when, striking a siblingship with other human beings, we come to be children of God. This is no deed of ours; it is an activity, in the Spirit, of the condition of images of God, which, from all eternity, we have received in Jesus, who is thus the firstborn of so many siblings.

Accordingly, when we understand ourselves as creatures, it is then that we receive the revelation in Jesus that our most personal name is that of Child and Brother, Child and Sister. These are eschatological relationships; all others pass away with the shadow of this world. Those who live in the activation of these relationships are those who have worth; those who activate them more are of greater worth; and "as often as you neglected to do it to one of these least ones, you neglected to do it to me" (Matt. 25:45). In all cases, however, God is faithful, and Jesus is God's irrevocable "yes": Each of us continues to be God's child and Jesus' sibling, however little we may wish to behave as such. The love of God, which has shaped us, and which knows us from within, is inexhaustibly patient.

Notes

PART ONE: CREATION IN HISTORY

I. Experience and Faith

1. J. Sobrino, "La esperanza de los pobres en América Latina," *Diakonía* 25 (March 1983), p. 6. Eng. trans. in *Spirituality of Liberation* (Maryknoll, N.Y.: 1988).

2. Ibid.

3. X. Zubiri, *El hombre y Dios* (Madrid: Alianza Editorial—Sociedad de Estudios y Publicaciones, 1985), pp. 118–23; E. Gilson, *El tomismo* (Pamplona, Spain: EUNSA, 1978), pp. 93–138; I. Kant, *Crítica de la razón pura* (Madrid: Alfaguara, 1978), pp. 506–30.

4. J. Auer, *El mundo, creación de Dios* (Barcelona: Herder, 1979), p. 113.

5. Sobrino, "Esperanza de los pobres," pp. 10–11; idem, "El resucitado es el crucificado," *Diakonía* 21 (April 1982), pp. 25–40. Eng. trans. in *Jesus in Latin America* (Maryknoll, N.Y.: 1987).

6. J. L. Segundo, "Derechos humanos, evangelización e ideología," *Christus* (Mexico City) 516 (November 1978), pp. 33–5.

7. Various authors, "Dimensión histórica de la filosofía latinoamericana," *Anthropos* 9 (1984/2), pp. 12–16.

8. "The expression, 'Holy One of Israel,' means first of all that Yahweh is close to Israel, and cannot abandon it without negating himself" (E. Jacob, *Teología del Antiguo Testamento* [Madrid: Marova, 1969], p. 89).

9. "When it is said that the events of the exodus, or Yahweh's other salvific actions, are so many miracles, the marvelous element is not precisely in the deed wrought by Yahweh in nature, which is always wonderful, but rather in his will to save. This is the supreme marvel—at once mystery and miracle—of faith and Israelite history. All phenomena of nature and the events of history are integrated into Yahweh's salvific will" (*Comentario Bíblico San Jerónimo* [Madrid: Cris-

tiandad, 1972], 5:633). Eng trans.: Englewood Cliffs, N.J.: Prentice Hall, 1968).

10. J. L. Segundo offers a perceptive analysis of the desperate cycle of subversion and repression that has swept into Latin America, all but irreparably damaging the social ecology. See his *Faith and Ideologies* (Maryknoll, N.Y.: Orbis, 1984).

11. Sobrino, "Esperanza de los pobres," pp. 3–23.

12. P. Trigo, "Pastoral liberadora y experiencia espiritual," *Servicio de Intelectuales Cristianos* 462 (February 1984), pp. 74–8.

13. See *Centro América* (1979–85), dispatch 55–6 (January-February 1986).

14. G. Gutiérrez, *We Drink from Our Own Wells* (Maryknoll, N.Y.: Orbis, 1984).

15. A. Neher, *La esencia del profetismo* (Salamanca: Sígueme, 1975), p. 213.

16. Ibid.

17. Sobrino, "Esperanza de los pobres," p. 10.

18. This view, in secularized form, is maintained by Hegel and historical materialism.

19. I. Ellacuría, "Historicidad de la salvación cristiana," *Revista Latinoamericana de Teología* 1 (January-April 1984), pp. 5–45.

20. "Although Genesis 1 presents creation as a beginning, faith in creation is not a mere protology. The creative action is a present act, and remains faithful to itself till the hour of eschatological salvation" (*Sacramentum Mundi,* ed. K. Rahner, et al. (New York: Herder & Herder; London: Burns & Oates, 1968-1970), vol. 2, p. 24.

"Neither of the two presentations [Gen. 1 and 2] actually asserts that God created the first human being (or the first human beings). . . . It is asserted that humanity, and accordingly, every human being, owes his existence to God, no more and no less." This is "history that can be experienced" (E. Jenni and C. Westermann, *Diccionario teológico manual del Antiguo Testamento* [Madrid: Cristiandad, 1978], 1:97). It would be protology in Rahner's sense. For Rahner, protology "is the teaching of the current (but with a determinate origin) created condition of the world as the context of the human being and as the premise that makes salvation history possible" (K. Rahner, in *Mysterium Salutis* [Madrid: Cristiandad, 1969], 2/1:468), inasmuch as it is a matter of a "permanent determination of the human being" (ibid., p. 466).

21. "In order to strike a relationship with his origin, the human being need not transcend his history and accede to a mystical dimension; he can find his origin in his own history. . . . His history is only the prolongation of his beginnings. Such is the deepest meaning of

creation in the biblical economy. Creation is history, not myth. Accordingly, it cannot bring any pressure to bear on biblical religious thought, for example by obliging it to manage an escape, to seek refuge either in rites or in a doctrine of the eternal return. It does not saddle human beings with an obsession they must bear. On the contrary, it invites them to proceed with their history, by giving them to know that the source of their liberation is in that history" (Neher, *Esencia del profetismo,* pp. 120–21).

22. D. Bonhoeffer, letter of July 19, 1944. Obviously Bonhoeffer is not confining himself to this level.

23. A. Pronzato, *Un cristiano comienza a leer el evangelio de Marcos* (Salamanca: Sígueme, 1983), 2:248–62.

24. *Sacramentum Mundi,* 2:28.

25. Sobrino, "Esperanza de los pobres," p. 16.

26. E. Schillebeeckx, *Jesús, la historia de un viviente* (Madrid: Cristiandad, 1981), pp. 591–92 (Eng. trans.: *Jesus: An Experiment in Christology* [London and New York, 1979]); Zubiri, *El hombre y Dios,* pp. 148–50, 158–64, 174–8; St. Augustine, *Confessions,* book 3, chap. 6; Thomas Aquinas, *Summa Theologiae,* I, q. 13, a. 11, c.

27. *Sacramentum Mundi,* 2:28; Auer, *El mundo, creación de Dios,* p. 75; S. Croatto, *Historia de la salvación* (Buenos Aires: Paulinas, 1970–72); E. Brunner, *La verdad como encuentro* (Barcelona: Estela, 1967), pp. 120–31; Gilson, *El tomismo,* pp. 196–97.

28. For the following material, see P. Trigo, *Salmos del Dios enteramente bueno* (Caracas: Centro Gumilla, 1983), pp. 11–25.

29. For "cosmic democracy" see L. Boff, *San Francisco de Asís: Ternura y vigor* (Santander, Spain: Sal Terrae, 1982), pp. 58–60. Eng trans.: *Saint Francis: A Model for Human Liberation* (New York: Crossroad, 1984).

30. *Brasil, ¿milagro o engaño?* (Lima: CEP, 1973), p. 111.

II. Israel: From Liberation to (Re)creation

1. G. von Rad, *Teología del Antiguo Testamento* (Salamanca: Sígueme, 1972), 1:184ff.; E. Jenni and C. Westermann, *Diccionario teológico manual del Antiguo Testamento* (Madrid: Cristiandad, 1978), 1:489; G. Auzou, *En un principio Dios creó el mundo* (Estella, Spain: Verbo Divino, 1982), pp. 115, 121, 124–25; *Sacramentum Mundi,* ed. K. Rahner, et al. (New York: Herder & Herder; London: Burns & Oates, 1967), 2:23, 2:5; *Comentario Bíblico San Jerónimo* (Madrid: Cristiandad, 1972), 5:629.

2. Von Rad, *Teología del Antiguo Testamento,* 1:185; W. Zimmerli,

Manual de teología del Antiguo Testamento (Madrid: Cristiandad, 1980),
p. 32; L. Scheffczyk, *Creación y providencia* (Madrid: BAC, 1974), pp.
2–3; P. Schoonenberg, *El mundo de Dios en evolución* (Buenos Aires:
Carlos Lohlé, 1966), p. 64; *Comentario Bíblico San Jerónimo*, 5:1c; *Mysterium Salutis* (Madrid: Cristiandad, 1969), 2/1:520–21, 491ff., 2/2; R.
Latourelle, *Teología de la revelación* (Salamanca: Sígueme, 1967), pp.
419–22.

3. Auzou, *En un principio Dios*, pp. 113–48; von Rad, *Teología del Antiguo Testamento*, 1:167–75; A. Neher, *La esencia del profetismo* (Salamanca: Sígueme, 1975), pp. 192–213; *Sacramentum Mundi*, 2:4–5; Scheffczyk, *Creación y providencia*, pp. 2–3.

4. Von Rad, *Teología del Antiguo Testamento*, 1:175.

5. Ibid.

6. I follow Neher, *Esencia del profetismo*, pp. 194–208, almost verbatim in this section.

7. Jenni and Westermann, *Diccionario teológico*, 1:490; "A new, unforeseen, and decisive truth-event" (Auzou, *En un principio Dios creó el mundo*, p. 124); "a marvelous act of God that produces something surprisingly new" (W. Eichrodt, *Teología del Antiguo Testamento* [Madrid: Cristiandad, 1975], 1:112); "an act by which God produces a new or prodigious thing" (P. van Imschoot, *Théologie de l'Ancien Testament* [Tournai: Desclée, 1954], p. 139).

8. Von Rad, *Teología del Antiguo Testamento*, 2:302–3, 310–11, 313, 323, 1:185–86; Auzou, *En un principio Dios*, pp. 138–48; Zimmerli, *Manual de teología del Antiguo Testamento*, 38–40; *Mysterium Salutis*, 2/1:498–99; S. Croatto, *Historia de la salvación* (Buenos Aires: Paulinas, 1970–72), pp. 254–9; L. Alonso Schökel and J. Sicre, *Las Profetas* (Madrid: Cristiandad, 1980), 1:266–71; Neher, *La esencia del profetismo*, pp. 211–12; Xabier Pikaza, *La Biblia y la teología de la historia* (Madrid: Fax, 1972), pp. 173–78; Scheffczyk, *Creación y providencia*, p. 7.

9. Jenni and Westermann, *Diccionario teológico*, 1:486–91; Auzou, *En un principio Dios*, pp. 123–24, 132–38, 140–48; E. Jacob, *Teología del Antiguo Testamento* (Madrid: Marova, 1969), pp. 136, 138–39; Zimmerli, *Manual de teología del Antiguo Testamento*, pp. 35–36; Eichrodt, *Teología del Antiguo Testamento*, pp. 110–12; van Imschoot, *Théologie de l'Ancien Testament*, pp. 135–36, 139; von Rad, *Teología del Antiguo Testamento*, 1:191–92; *Sacramentum Mundi*, 2:23–5; *Mysterium Salutis*, 2/1:477–8, 499–500; Neher, *La esencia del profetismo*, p. 114; Schoonenberg, *El mundo de Dios en evolución*, pp. 66–67.

10. *Comentario Bíblico San Jerónimo*, 2:91–107.

11. Von Rad, *Teología del Antiguo Testamento*, 2:302.

12. C. Mesters, *Paraíso terrestre, ¿nostalgía o esperanza?* (Buenos Aires: Bonum, 1972), pp. 35–41, 67–71, 94–7.

13. Idem, *Misión del pueblo que sufre.* Perspectiva-CLAR, no. 14 (Bogotá: Perspectiva-CLAR, 1983).

14. For a broader presentation of this characterization, see *Vocabulario bíblico* (Madrid: Marova, 1968), p. 66.

PART TWO: FROM CHAOS AND COSMOS TO FAITH IN CREATION

III. From Ambivalent Experience to Faith in Goodness

1. G. Gutiérrez, *We Drink from Our Own Wells* (Maryknoll, N.Y.: Orbis, 1984).

2. F. Hinkelammert, *Ideologías del desarrollo y dialéctica de la historia* (Santiago, Chile: Ediciones Nueva Universidad, 1970).

3. Various authors, *La lucha de los dioses* (San José, Costa Rica: DEI, 1980). Eng. trans.: *The Idols of Death and the God of Life* (Maryknoll, N.Y.: Orbis Books, 1983).

4. Various authors, *La Iglesia que nace en el pueblo* (Bogotá: Indo-American Press Service, 1979), p. 27.

5. W. Pannenberg, *La fe de los apóstoles* (Salamanca: Sígueme, 1975), p. 51.

IV. Israel: Faith in Creation as Victory

1. L. Boff, *San Francisco de Asís: Ternura y vigor* (Santander, Spain: Sal Terrae, 1982), pp. 58–60. Eng. trans.: *Saint Francis: A Model for Human Liberation* (New York: Crossroad, 1984).

2. M. Noth, *Historia de Israel* (Barcelona: Garriga, 1966), pp. 275–308.

3. G. von Rad, *El libro del Génesis* (Salamanca: Sígueme, 1977), pp. 53–80; idem, *Teología del Antiguo Testamento* (Salamanca: Sígueme, 1972), 1:189–200; H. Gross, in *Mysterium Salutis* (Madrid: Cristiandad, 1969), 2/1:469–80, 495–6; J. McKenzie, *Espíritu y mundo del Antiguo Testamento* (Estella, Spain: Verbo Divino, 1968), pp. 111–34; W. Eichrodt, *Teología del Antiguo Testamento* (Madrid: Cristiandad, 1975), 1:110–23; W. Zimmerli, *Manual de teología del Antiguo Testamento* (Madrid: Cristiandad, 1980), pp. 33–8; P. van Imschoot, *Théologie de l'Ancien Testament* (Tournai: Desclée, 1954), pp. 139–46; A. Neher, *La esencia del profetismo* (Salamanca: Sígueme, 1975), pp. 113–21; G. Auzou, *En un principio Dios creó el mundo* (Estella, Spain: Verbo

Divino, 1982), pp. 187–304; S. Croatto, *El hombre en el mundo, 1* (Buenos Aires: La Aurora, 1974).

4. P. Seux, et al, *La creación del mundo y del hombre en los textos del próximo oriente antiguo* (Estella, Spain: Verbo Divino, 1982); Auzou, *En un principio,* pp. 43–81, 95–9; Croatto, *El hombre en el mundo, 1,* pp. 68–95; P. Ricoeur, *Finitud y culpabilidad* (Madrid: Taurus, 1969), pp. 465–506; van Imschoot, *Théologie de l'Ancien Testament,* p. 146.

5. Van Imschoot, *Théologie de l'Ancien Testament,* pp. 131–5.

6. In this and the next section, I follow P. Ricoeur, *Finitud y culpabilidad,* pp. 465–74.

7. Still, Josiah's reform, as we see in Deuteronomy, while abandoned by his successors, will triumph in the post-exilic restoration, to mark Judaism for good and all.

8. Neher, *La esencia del profetismo,* p. 115.

9. Ibid., p. 116.

10. McKenzie, *Espíritu y mundo del Antiguo Testamento,* p. 119.

11. G. von Rad, *El libro del Génesis,* p. 61.

12. *Mysterium Salutis,* 2/1:478.

13. K. Jaspers, *Origen y meta de la historia* (Madrid: Revista de Occidente, 1968).

14. *Mysterium Salutis,* 2/1:496–97.

15. Von Rad, *El libro del Génesis,* p. 58.

16. E. Schillebeeckx, *Jesús, la historia de un viviente* (Madrid: Cristiandad, 1981), p. 129. Eng. trans.: New York, Crossroad, 1979).

17. Neher, *La esencia del profetismo,* p. 116.

18. This would be the pretentious error of Flew's parable, which Robinson adopts, after a fashion: to claim to be able to call God to account by taking a superior position. See P. Trigo, *El éxodo* (Caracas: Centro Gumilla, 1978); K. Rahner and W. Weger, *¿Que debemos creer todavía?* (Santander, Spain: Sal Terrae, 1980), pp. 63–81.

19. "The last word of creation is uttered in the God-man; but that the creator was so interested and involved in his creation will probably never be deduced by metaphysics" (*Sacramentum Mundi,* ed. K. Rahner, et al. [New York: Herder & Herder; London: Burns & Oates, 1968-70], 2:27). "I share Duns Scotus' thinking, that creation is a truth of faith, but not of reason" (X. Zubiri, *El hombre y Dios* [Madrid: Alianza Editorial—Sociedad de Estudios y Publicaciones, 1985], p. 153).

20. R. Latourelle, *Teología de la revelación* (Salamanca: Sígueme, 1967), pp. 419–32.

21. Von Rad, *El libro del Génesis,* p. 77.

22. Exegetes have even attempted to expunge what they regard as

interpolated material and reconstruct a hypothetical original version. See N. Lohfink, *Exégesis bíblica y teología* (Salamanca: Sígueme, 1969), pp. 104–6.

23. E. Jenni and C. Westermann, *Diccionario teológico manual del Antiguo Testamento* (Madrid: Cristiandad), 1:489. Creation is "something we cannot actually define, so foreign is it to the conditions of human existence" (E. Gilson, *El tomismo* [Pamplona, Spain: EUNSA, 1978], p. 203). It is presented to us as a "kind of reception of existence, without any attempt to represent it to us" (ibid.).

24. E. Jacob, *Teología del Antiguo Testamento* (Madrid: Marova, 1969), p. 136; Neher, *La esencia del profetismo*, pp. 116–19.

25. *Sacramentum Mundi*, 2:27.

26. Eichrodt, *Teología del Antiguo Testamento*, p. 119.

27. *Mysterium Salutis*, 2/1:568.

28. J. Auer, *El mundo, creación de Dios* (Barcelona: Herder, 1979), p. 149.

29. Eichrodt, *Teología del Antiguo Testamento*, pp. 118–19.

30. Auer, *El mundo, creación de Dios*, p. 167.

31. Ibid., p. 96.

32. Croatto, *El hombre en el mundo, 1*, pp. 43–7, 95–6; von Rad, *El libro del Génesis*, pp. 57–60; Auzou, *En un principio Dios creó el mundo*, pp. 217–25; McKenzie, *Espíritu y mundo del Antiguo Testamento*, pp. 122–8; H. Renckens, *Creación, paraíso y pecado original* (Madrid: Guadarrama, 1969), pp. 57–60, 86–8; Eichrodt, *Teología del Antiguo Testamento*, pp. 109–13; van Imschoot, *Théologie de l'Ancien Testament*, pp. 137–41; Jacob, *Teología del Antiguo Testamento*, pp. 136–7; Zimmerli, *Manual de teología del Antiguo Testamento*, pp. 33–34; *Mysterium Salutis*, 2/1:563; von Rad, *Teología del Antiguo Testamento* (Salamanca: Sígueme, 1972), 1:201.

33. Von Rad, *El libro del Génesis*, p. 59.

34. Ibid., p. 60.

35. This supposes the interpretation of the "spirit of God" as a chaotic element. Other authors understand it, on the contrary, as a creative element.

36. L. Scheffczyk, *Creación y providencia* (Madrid: BAC, 1974), p. 3; Eichrodt, *Teología del Antiguo Testamento*, p. 110.

37. Von Rad, *El libro del Génesis*, p. 60.

38. Croatto, *El hombre en el mundo, 1*, pp. 36, 147–59, 32–33; von Rad, *El libro del Génesis*, pp. 65–6; Auzou, *En un principio Dios creó el mundo,*, pp. 244–51.

39. *Comentario Bíblico San Jerónimo* (Madrid: Cristiandad, 1972), 1:68.

40. A Christian attempt to do justice to any actual validity there may be in astrology: G. Voss, *Astrología y cristianismo* (Barcelona: Herder, 1985). For a biblical approach, see A. Romaña, "La astrología," *Servicio de Intelectuales Cristianos* 404 (April 1978), pp. 185–92.

41. Eichrodt, *Teología del Antiguo Testamento*, pp. 119–20; Jacob, *Teología del Antiguo Testamento*, pp. 142–44; *Mysterium Salutis*, 2/1:476.

42. Von Rad, *Teología del Antiguo Testamento*, 1:91.

43. Eichrodt, *Teología del Antiguo Testamento*, p. 119.

44. Franciscan Leonardo Boff, in the authentic spirit of his founder, has explained that the renunciation of despotic dominion, and accordingly, of ownership—*jus utendi et abutendi*—is the necessary condition for taking a position in reality, perceiving its articulations and connections, and devoting oneself to the consummation of its possibilities (L. Boff, *San Francisco de Asís: Ternura y vigor*, pp. 60–67).

45. Jacob, *Teología del Antiguo Testamento*, p. 144.

46. Auzou, *En un principio Dios creó el mundo,*, pp. 179–87; Croatto, *El hombre en el mundo, 1,* pp. 117–19, 200–201; von Rad, *El libro del Génesis*, pp. 62, 72–3; Eichrodt, *Teología del Antiguo Testamento*, pp. 115–16; Lohfink, *Exégesis bíblica y teología*, pp. 88–9.

47. McKenzie, *Espíritu y mundo del Antiguo Testamento*, pp. 119–20.

48. And the theology of liberation is a theology of reconciliation.

PART THREE: EVIL IN CREATION

V. State of the Question

1. J. L. Ruiz de la Peña, *Teología de la creación* (Santander, Spain: Sal Terrae, 1986), pp. 159–66; J. Moltmann, *Trinidad y Reino de Dios* (Salamanca: Sígueme, 1983), pp. 62–67 (Eng. trans.: New York, Harper & Row, 1981); H. Renckens, *Creación, paraíso y pecado original* (Madrid: Guadarrama, 1969), pp. 154–6; *Sacramentum Mundi*, ed. K. Rahner, et al. 4:328-34; Thomas Aquinas, *Summa Theologiae*, I, q. 2, a. 3.

2. The discussion of the problem of evil in Teilhard is instructive: X. Léon-Dufour, *Teilhard de Chardin y el problema del porvenir del hombre* (Madrid: Taurus, 1969), pp. 84–88; L. Domenach, *Teilhard de Chardin y el personalismo* (Barcelona: Nova Terra, 1969), pp. 30–34, 99–112; H. de Lubac, *El pensamiento religioso de Teilhard de Chardin* (Madrid: Taurus, 1967), pp. 191–99.

3. A nihilistic thinking appearing after World War II has perpetuated itself among the elite in the form of an anomia.

4. H. Assmann, *Teología desde la praxis de la liberación* (Salamanca:

Sígueme, 1973), p. 40. Eng. trans.: *A Practical Theology of Liberation* (Condon: Search Press, 1975).

5. Thomas Aquinas, *Summa Theologiae*, I, q. 2, a. 3, obj. 1 and ad 1.

6. Moltmann, *Trinidad y Reino de Dios*, pp. 124–8.

7. Medellín, 2, 14.

8. G. Gutiérrez, *On Job: God-talk and the Suffering of the Innocent* (Maryknoll, N.Y.: Orbis, 1987).

9. C. Duquoc, *Cristología* (Salamanca: Sígueme, 1974), pp. 486–504, 563–71.

VI. Inculpable Evil

1. J. L. Segundo, "Derechos humanos, evangelización e ideología," *Christus* (Mexico City) 516 (November 1978), pp. 333–4.

2. St. Augustine, *The City of God*, book 14, chap. 28.

3. P. Ricoeur, *Finitud y culpabilidad* (Madrid: Taurus, 1969), pp. 513–41.

4. "The Spinozan proposition, 'Conatus sese conservandi primum et unicum virtutis est fundamentum' (*Ethica*, part 4, proposition 22, corollary), is the authentic maxim of all Western civilization. . . . But the more the process of self-conservation is realized through the bourgeois division of labor, the more the said process requires the self-alienation of individuals" (M. Horkheimer and T. W. Adorno, *Dialéctica del iluminismo* [Buenos Aires: Sur, 1971], p. 45).

5. Gutiérrez, *On Job*.

6. Ricoeur, *Finitud y culpabilidad*, pp. 227–9.

7. G. Auzou, *De la servidumbre al servicio* (Madrid: Fax, 1966), pp. 215–30; G. von Rad, *Teología del Antiguo Testamento* (Salamanca: Sígueme, 1972), 1:31–38, 352–61; M. Herrmann, *Historia de Israel* (Salamanca: Sígueme, 1969), pp. 89–118; R. de Vaux, *Historia antigua de Israel* (Madrid: Cristiandad, 1975), 1:406–7, 2:61–70, 75, 85–101; J. Bright, *Historia de Israel* (Bilbao: Desclée de Brouwer, 1966), pp. 127–35.

8. *Mysterium Salutis* (Madrid: Cristiandad, 1969), 2/1:481, 485; von Rad, *Teología del Antiguo Testamento*, pp. 93–6, 113–14; H. Renckens, *Creación, paraíso y pecado original* (Madrid: Guadarrama, 1969), pp. 189–97, 277–81; John Paul II, *Laborem Exercens*, nos. 4, 9, 27.

9. Paul VI, *Populorum Progressio*, nos. 34, 43–50, 86; J. Comblin, *Tiempo de acción* (Lima: CEP, 1986), pp. 456–66.

10. Paul VI, *Populorum Progressio*, nos. 20–21; Medellín, intro., 6.

11. G. von Rad, *El libro del Génesis* (Salamanca: Sígueme, 1977), pp. 172–86.

12. John Paul II, *Laborem Exercens*, no. 25.

13. Ibid., no. 9 (emphasis added); cf. Paul VI, *Populorum Progressio*, no. 27.

VII. Evil as Sin

1. J. L. Ruiz de la Peña, *Teología de la creación* (Santander, Spain: Sal Terrae, 1986), pp. 95–101; *Mysterium Salutis* (Madrid: Cristiandad, 1969), 2/1:556–9; *Sacramentum Mundi*, ed. K. Rahner, et al., 2:279-83; L. Scheffczyk, *Creación y providencia* (Madrid: BAC, 1974), pp. 38–48, 60–62; J. Auer, *El mundo, creación de Dios* (Barcelona: Herder, 1979), p. 96.

2. For the devil or Satan, see: *Mysterium Salutis*, (Madrid: Cristiandad, 1969), 2/2:1097–1119; *Sacramentum Mundi*, 2:70-5, 112-15; "Adversario," in E. Jenni and C. Westermann, *Diccionario teológico manual del Antiguo Testamento* (Madrid: Cristiandad, 1985), 2:1032–35; W. Zimmerli, *Manual de teología del Antiguo Testamento* (Madrid: Cristiandad, 1980), pp. 195–96; various authors, "Satán, los demonios y el satanismo," *Concilium* 103 (March 1975), pp. 331–400, 436–50; "La Seducción y el seductor," *Concilium* 56 (June 1970).

3. Antiochus Epiphanes (Dan. 7:1–8), the Roman Empire (Rev. 13:1–8; 17:3, 7).

4. J.-P. Jossua, "Fue precipitada la antigua serpiente," *Concilium* 103 (March 1975), pp. 437–41.

5. P. Ricoeur, *Finitud y culpabilidad* (Madrid: Taurus, 1969), pp. 558–82.

6. For the notion of a situation of sin, and sinful structures, see Puebla, 28, 281, 328, 437, 452, 1032, 1269; Medellín, 2, 1; *Libertatis Conscientiae*, 74; J. González Faus, "Pecado estructural: Pecado del mundo," *Revista Latinoamericana de Teología* 7 (January-April 1986), pp. 83–110.

7. *Sacramentum Mundi*, 4:328-34.

8. According to Mark 15:11 and John 19:6, the chief priests incited their servants and followers. The Galilean pilgrims who entered Jerusalem so tumultuously on Palm Sunday were not present.

9. G. Gutiérrez, *On Job: God-talk and the Suffering of the Innocent* (Maryknoll, N.Y.: Orbis, 1987).

10. See Fyodor Dostoyevsky, "The Grand Inquisitor," in *The Brothers Karamazov*, part 2, book 5, chap. 5.

11. *Mysterium Salutis*, 2/1:505–13; Ruiz de la Peña, *Teología de la creación*, pp. 63–87; A. Ganoczy, *Doctrina de la creación* (Barcelona: Herder, 1986), pp. 70–103.

12. John Paul II, *Dominum et Vivificantem,* nos. 55–60.
13. Ibid., parts 2, 3.

PART FOUR: LIFE AND HISTORY

VIII. Reading the Signs of the Times

1. I. Ellacuría, *Filosofía de la realidad histórica* (San Salvador, El Salvador: UCA, 1984), p. 396. The remaining quotations in this section are from pp. 398, 399, and 396.
2. Ibid., p. 486.
3. Ibid., pp. 399–411.
4. For a catalogue of historical and other forces intervening in history, see ibid., pp. 493–505.
5. To a large extent they coincide, although the number of those without a place in the labor and consumer markets increases daily.
6. *Teología desde el reverso de la historia* is the title of a work by G. Gutiérrez (1977). In English: "Theology from the Underside of History," in idem, *The Power of the Poor in History* (Maryknoll, N.Y.: Orbis, 1983), pp. 169–221. See also idem, *La verdad los hará libres* (Lima: CEP, 1986), pp. 18–24, 38–39, 157–64. In English: *The Truth Shall Make You Free: Confrontations* (Maryknoll, N.Y.: Orbis, 1990).
7. J. Comblin, *Antropología cristiana* (Madrid: Ediciones Paulinas, 1986), pp. 213–21. In English: *Retrieving the Human: A Christian Anthropology* (Maryknoll, N.Y.: Orbis Books, and London: Burns & Oates, 1990).
8. Ibid., pp. 43, 49–57, 221.
9. Ellacuría, "Filosofía de la realidad histórica," p. 518.
10. An individual life, of course, is not cyclical (hence the indifference to the individual that we feel on the part of nature); nor is the life of the collectivity as a totality. See ibid., p. 357.

IX. Discerning History

1. And not only to theology, but also, and more so, to the proclamation of the gospel. On the other hand, not all theologians will have reason to exercise propheticism, but only those who feel called to do so, and with the strictures I have indicated.
2. G. von Rad, "Los comienzos de la historiografía en el antiguo Israel," in *Estudios sobre el Antiguo Testamento* (Salamanca: Sígueme, 1976), pp. 141–76. The quotations in this section are from pp. 149, 173, 174, 175.

3. J. Comblin, *Tiempo de acción* (Lima: CEP, 1986), pp. 28–31.

4. G. von Rad, *Teología del Antiguo Testamento* (Salamanca: Sígueme, 1972), 1:445–59.

5. This and the following quote are from ibid., pp. 457–9.

6. J. M. Arguedas, *Todas las sangres* (Buenos Aires: Losada, 1970), 2:228.

7. I. Ellacuría, *Filosofía de la realidad histórica* (San Salvador, El Salvador: UCA, 1984), pp. 369–77.

8. J. Jeremias, *Teología del Nuevo Testamento* (Salamanca: Sígueme, 1977), pp. 59–66.

9. Comblin, *Tiempo de acción*, p. 499.

10. L. Espinal, *El grito de un pueblo* (Lima: CEP, 1981).

11. "Gloria Dei, vivens pauper" — Archbishop Romero's expression.

12. As early as 1839, in his extensive essay on Europe and America, the Venezuelan thinker Fermín Toro not only formed this idea, but on its basis concluded the need to create an economic science which would invoke it as a premise.

13. G. Gutiérrez, "Liberation and the Poor: The Puebla Perspective," in idem, *The Power of the Poor in History* (Maryknoll, N.Y.: Orbis, 1983), pp. 237–302.

14. Puebla, 437–38, 452; *Libertatis Nuntius,* parts 1–3; *Libertatis Conscientiae,* no. 17b.

15. José de Acosta (*De Procuranda Indorum Salute*) would be the frantic witness and pathetic theoretician of this impossible reformism. His disincarnate analyses of the military entries, tributes, work in the mines, personal services, and consequent Christian judgments are smashed to smithereens by the colonial constitution, whose acceptance made a travesty of the proposed reforms. This monstrous book sheds light on the particular Christendom of Latin America, which still holds the church institution in its clutches.

16. Medellín, 2, 14.

17. M.-D. Chenu, "Los laicos y la 'consecratio mundi,' " in *La Iglesia del Vaticano II,* ed. G. Baraúna (Barcelona: Juan Flors Editor, 1966), 2:999–1015.

18. *Gaudium et Spes,* no. 22.

19. In the personal history of each of us, God has the sovereign power to burst into our lives directly, through religious activity, and Jesus can appear in our path and send us tumbling just as he did Paul. Our reference is to a systematic primacy, not a temporal one.

20. J. L. Segundo, *Liberación de la teología* (Buenos Aires: Carlos Lohlé, 1975), p. 92 (Eng. trans.: *The Liberation of Theology* [Maryknoll, N.Y.: Orbis Books, 1976]); idem, *Faith and Ideologies* (Maryknoll, N.Y.: Orbis, 1984).

21. Comblin, *Tiempo de acción,* p. 502.

22. Puebla, 447, 437, 450, 452, 1147.

23. *Libertatis Nuntius,* 1:1; Puebla, 452.

24. John Paul II in Recife (July 7, 1980), no. 5, and in São Paulo (July 3, 1980), no. 5.

25. *Lumen Gentium,* nos. 12, 35; *Mysterium Salutis,* (Madrid: Cristiandad, 1969), 2/1:627–36; L. Boff, *Iglesia: Carisma y poder* (Santander, Spain: Sal Terrae, 1982), pp. 219–26. Eng. trans.: *Church: Charism and Power* (New York: Crossroad; London: SCM Press, 1985); Yves M.-J. Congar, *Ministerios y comunión eclesial* (Madrid: Fax, 1973), pp. 145–49.

26. A. Rosmini, *Las cinco llagas de la santa Iglesia* (Barcelona: Península, 1968), pp. 43–59.

27. For the council's emphasis on an authentic catholicity, see K. Rahner, "Una interpretación teológica a fondo del concilio Vaticano II," *Razon y Fe* 980–81 (September-October 1979), pp. 983–95.

28. Paul VI, *El valor religioso del Concilio* (December 7, 1965), no. 13; see P. Trigo, "Una Iglesia para servir," *Servicio de Intelectuales Cristianos* 445 (May, 1982), pp. 196–99.

29. G. Gutiérrez, *We Drink from Our Own Wells* (Maryknoll, N.Y.: Orbis, 1984).

30. Message of the pope to the bishops of Brazil (April 9, 1986), in *Servicio de Intelectuales Cristianos* 485 (May, 1986), pp. 234–38.

X. History and Eschatology

1. F. J. Hinkelammert, *Las armas ideológicas de la muerte* (Salamanca: Sígueme, 1978), pp. 242, 268. Eng. trans.: *The Ideological Weapons of Death* (Maryknoll, N.Y.: Orbis Books, 1986).

2. C. Duquoc, *Vida y reflexión* (Lima: CEP, 1983), pp. 101–20.

3. J. Comblin, *Tiempo de acción* (Lima: CEP, 1986), pp. 345–6.

XI. Call and Benediction: History and Life

1. In these sections I follow, at times verbatim, C. Westermann, *El Antiguo Testamento y Jesucristo* (Madrid: Fax, 1972), pp. 107–17.

2. M. Hengel, *Seguimiento y carisma* (Santander, Spain: Sal Terrae, 1981), pp. 93–105.

3. Ibid., pp. 105–29; G. Theissen, *Sociología del movimento de Jesús* (Santander, Spain: Sal Terrae, 1979), pp. 25–31, 104. Eng. edition: *Sociology of Early Palestinian Christianity* (Philadelphia: Fortress, 1978). Idem, *Estudios de sociología del cristianismo primitivo* (Salamanca: Sígueme, 1985), pp. 13–47.

4. S. Galilea, *Espiritualidad de la liberación* (Bogotá: CLAR, 1979), pp. 16–32, 39–48.

XIII. What Are the Traits of the Image of God?

1. Peter Berger, B. Berger, and J. Kellner, *Un mundo sin hogar* (Santander, Spain: Sal Terrae, 1979), pp. 30–39. Eng. edition: *Homeless Mind: Modernization & Consciousness* (New York: Random House, 1974).

2. *Gaudium et Spes,* no. 22.

3. E. Jenni and C. Westermann, *Diccionario teológico manual del Antiguo Testamento* (Madrid: Cristiandad, 1978), 2:705–07; *Comentario Bíblico San Jerónimo* (Madrid: Cristiandad, 1971), 1:69; G. von Rad, *El libro del Génesis* (Salamanca: Sígueme, 1977), pp. 69–71; *Mysterium Salutis* (Madrid: Cristiandad, 1969), 2/2:903, 2/1:479–80; G. Auzou, *En un principio Dios creó el mundo* (Estella, Spain: Verbo Divino, 1982), pp. 266–67; J. McKenzie, *Espíritu y mundo del Antiguo Testamento* (Estella, Spain: Verbo Divino, 1968), p. 138; E. Jacob, *Teología del Antiguo Testamento* (Madrid: Marova, 1969), p. 163; W. Zimmerli, *Manual de teología del Antiguo Testamento* (Madrid: Cristiandad, 1980), p. 37.

4. Thus von Rad (*El libro del Génesis*) and Jacob (*Teología del Antiguo Testamento*); McKenzie (*Espíritu y mundo del Antiguo Testamento*) disagrees.

5. *Mysterium Salutis,* 2/1:479–80.

6. *Mysterium Salutis,* 2/2:903; Jenni and Westermann, *Diccionario teológico,* 1:704–5; von Rad, *El libro del Génesis,* pp. 69–70.

7. *Mysterium Salutis,* 2/2:902–3. Contrast Jenni and Westermann, *Diccionario teológico,* 1:704.

8. E. Brunner, *La verdad como encuentro* (Barcelona: Estela, 1967), pp. 192–93.

9. Westermann, in Jenni and Westermann, *Diccionario teológico,* 1:98; *Mysterium Salutis,* 2/1:526.

10. That is, against Luther, this image is not effaced by sin.

11. W. Zimmerli, *Manual de teología del Antiguo Testamento,* p. 152; von Rad, *El libro del Génesis,* p. 159.

12. Von Rad *El libro del Génesis,* p. 71.

13. "All human beings in Latin America should feel loved and chosen eternally by God (1 John 3:1), however much they may be vilified or however low may be their self-esteem" (Puebla, 335).

14. For the possible (limited) validity of this proposition, see H. Cox, *The Secular City* (New York: Macmillan, 1965). Puebla defends the Christian relevancy of the political (Puebla, 515–16), which, as we saw

in the foregoing chapter, is the ambit of the "impersonal," that is, the individual, which, in the face of the nonpersonal and depersonalized, is one of the inalienable dimensions of personhood.

15. "The divine mystery of communion was to be reflected in human beings and their fraternal life together through their active transformation of the world" (Puebla, 184).

16. Jenni and Westermann, *Diccionario teológico,* 2:817–19.

17. L. Vives, *La justicia que brota de la fe* (Santander, Spain: Sal Terrae, 1982), pp. 63–127.

18. G. von Rad, *La sabiduría en Israel* (Madrid: Cristiandad, 1985), pp. 183–221.

Index